The
Paper Trail

The
Paper Trail

Systems and Forms for a Well-Run Remodeling Company

SECOND EDITION

William Asdal and Wendy A. Jordan

BuilderBooks.com®
BOOKS THAT BUILD YOUR BUSINESS

A Service of
NAHB®
NATIONAL ASSOCIATION
OF HOME BUILDERS

The Paper Trail: Systems and Forms for a Well-Run Remodeling Company, Second Edition

BuilderBooks, a Service of the National Association of Home Builders

Courtenay S. Brown	Director, Book Publishing & Copy Editor
Natalie C. Holmes	Book Editor
Torrie L. Singletary	Production Editor
Circle Graphics	Cover Design
Circle Graphics	Composition
The P.A. Hutchison Company	Printing

Gerald M. Howard	NAHB Executive Vice President and CEO
Mark Pursell	NAHB Senior Vice President, Marketing & Sales Group
Lakisha Campbell	NAHB Vice President, Publishing & Affinity Programs

Disclaimer

This publication provides accurate information on the subject matter covered. The publisher is selling it with the understanding that the publisher is not providing legal, accounting, or other professional service. If you need legal advice or other expert assistance, obtain the services of a qualified professional experienced in the subject matter involved. Reference herein to any specific commercial products, process, or service by trade name, trademark, manufacturer, or otherwise does not necessarily constitute or imply its endorsement, recommendation, or favored status by the National Association of Home Builders. The views and opinions of the authors expressed in this publication do not necessarily state or reflect those of the National Association of Home Builders, and they shall not be used to advertise or endorse a product.

Printed in the United States of America

13 12 11 10   1 2 3 4 5

ISBN -10: 0-86718-649-6
ISBN-13: 978-0-86718-649-9

Cataloging-in-Publication Information

Library of Congress Cataloging-in-Publication Data

Asdal, William.
 The paper trail : systems and forms for a well-run remodeling company /
William Asdal and Wendy A. Jordan. — 2nd ed.
   p. cm.
 Includes index.
 ISBN 978-0-86718-649-9
 1. Construction industry—Management. 2. Dwellings—Remodeling. I. Jordan,
Wendy Adler, 1946- II. Title.

HD9715.A2A83 2009
651.7'4—dc22

For further information, please contact:

National Association of Home Builders
1201 15th Street, NW
Washington, DC 20005-2800
800-223-2665
Visit us online at www.BuilderBooks.com.

Contents

List of Forms

Chapter 1

Chapter 2

Chapter 3

Chapter 4

Chapter 5

Chapter 6

Chapter 7

Foreword

Systems are the information highways in your business. Forms are the 18-wheelers and pickup trucks that ferry the information back and forth among you and your prospects, clients, employees, trade contractors, suppliers, and service providers. By using this transportation system to get information to the right people at the right times, you can ensure

- customer satisfaction
- profits
- a sustainable business

Forms drive systems: A big rig (for example, a design-build agreement for a whole-house remodel) hauls loads of information needed to keep your systems humming. A pickup truck (a time card, for example) carries a lighter load, but also is a crucial information link in your system.

The Paper Trail: Systems and Forms for a Well-Run Remodeling Company provides an overview of each of the six systems that are crucial to a successful remodeling company. To support these systems the book brings together 160 forms from some of the best remodeling companies in the country. In other words, this book gives you a wide range of proven remodeling business documents that you can adapt for your company's use.

Beginning remodelers will find the book and CD a treasure trove of ideas for maintaining their businesses on a profitable track. Remodelers who already have fairly well-functioning systems and forms will find new ideas for streamlining their operations with new or improved documents. You might even find a way to reduce your paperwork by simplifying your systems. Keep this book and CD close at hand. When a challenge arises, turn to the book to see how another remodeler's form might address your problem and prevent it from occurring again.

The members of the NAHB Remodelers frequently share hard-earned information in seminars, Remodeler 20 Clubs, and other venues. *The Paper Trail: Systems and Forms for a Well-Run Remodeling Company* is another product of their efforts to share secrets of success to help fellow remodelers and benefit the industry as a whole.

William Owens, CGR, CAPS, CGP
Past Chair, NAHB Remodelers

Preface

Since the first edition of *The Paper Trail: Systems and Forms for a Well-Run Remodeling Company* was published in 2002, the remodeling landscape has changed significantly. The housing industry, remodeling included, has seen historic highs and lows:

- The first of the enormous baby boom generation has transitioned from middle age to social security eligibility, heightening interest in aging-in-place remodeling.
- Green construction and energy-saving products and construction techniques have moved from the progressive fringe of remodeling to the mainstream.
- The range of products available for kitchens, baths, and home improvement in general has continued to expand and diversify.

Yet one thing has remained constant: remodelers' need for a goal-oriented, well-structured, and systematic approach in running their businesses. The goals you set for your company will define and direct it. Solid systems for organizing every aspect of the business will maximize its efficiency and ensure a firm foundation for continued success. The crux of this book is the included forms, which are provided on a companion CD so you can customize them as necessary. These documents comprise the systems that impose discipline, maintain standards, and eliminate weak spots in your operation. The book is a tool kit for running a smart remodeling company.

Naturally, some tools require sharpening or replacement from time to time, and new and better tools need to be added. This second edition of *The Paper Trail* offers both new and revised remodeling tools to help you run each remodeling job, and your company as a whole, smoothly. By incorporating the tools in this new and expanded edition, you will build an operation that integrates sound day-to-day practices and strategic controls to stay on a profitable course in today's demanding business world.

Acknowledgments

Our thanks go to the following people for their generous contribution of forms, feedback, insights, and ideas: Kerry Bramon and Tami Humphreys, Kerry Bramon Remodeling & Design, Columbia, Mo.; Vince Butler, CGR, GMB, CAPS, Butler Brothers, Clifton, Va.; Michael K. Carden, CGR, MUI Corporation, Birmingham, Ala.; Skeeter Coleman, Coleman Construction, Franklin, Tenn.; Robert Criner, CGR, Criner Construction, Yorktown, Va.; Darlene and Chris Gayler of Gayler Construction, Danville, Calif.; Joseph Gilday and Susan Wimsatt, Gilday Renovations, Silver Spring, Md.; Alan Hanbury, Jr., CGR, CAPS, CGP, House of Hanbury Builders, Newington, Conn.; Stephen Hann, CGR, Stephen K. Hann Custom Builders, Houston, Tex.; Jeff Hunt, CGR, GMB, CAPS, CGP, Brothers Strong, Houston, Tex.; Allison Iantosca, F.H. Perry Builder, Inc., Hopkinton, Mass.; David S. Jaffe, Vice President of Legal Affairs, National Association of Home Builders, Washington, DC; Tom Kelly, Certified Remodeler (CR), Neil Kelly Designers/ Remodelers, Portland, Ore.; Jim Kuhn, Consolidated Construction Group, St. Louis, Mo.; Steve Maltzman, SMA Consulting, Redlands, Calif.; Sandra McAdams, CGR, Sandy's Design and Remodeling, Kirkland, Wash.; Scott McClurg and Chris Cummings, McClurg Remodeling & Construction Services, Marcellus, N.Y.; Bill S. Medina, CGR, Medina Construction, Salina, Kans.; Diane Menke, Myers Constructs, Philadelphia, Pa.; Michael A. Menn, A.I.A., CGR, CAPS, Design Construction Concepts Ltd., Northbrook, Ill.; Jud Motsenbocker, CGR, JUD Construction, Muncie, Ind.; William Owens, CGR, CAPS, CGP, Owens Construction Contracting, Powell, Ohio; Larry Parrish,

CGR, CR, Parrish Construction, Boulder, Colo.; Matt Plaskoff, Plaskoff Construction, Tarzana, Calif.; Bob Peterson, CGR, CAPS, CGP, ABD Design/Build, Fort Collins, Colo.; Claiborne Porter, CGR, NCP Construction, Anchorage, Alaska; Mark Richardson, CR, Case Design/Remodeling, Bethesda, Md.; Donna Bade Shirey, CGR, CAPS, CGP, Shirey Contracting, Issaquah, Wash.; Jim Strite, CGR, CR, Strite Design + Remodeling, Boise, Idaho; Michael Strong, CGR, GMB, CAPS, Brothers Strong, Houston, Tex.; Thomas Swartz, CGR, J.J. Swartz Co., Decatur, Ill.; Tom Turnage, The Turnage Company, Jacksonville, Fla.; Matthew Weiss, MWC Carpentry, LLC, Union, N.J.; Jan Williams, CGR, and Harry Williams, CGR, Williams-Builder, Robbinsville, N.J.; Paul Winans, CR, and Nina Winans, CR, Winans Construction, Oakland, Calif.

The NAHB Remodelers provided forms they have collected. Checklists from the NAHB workbook for the Certified Aging in Place Specialist (CAPS) designation also appear here with permission.

All of these contributions supplemented the forms and enriched the systems co-author Bill Asdal, CGR, culled from his company with the able assistance of Joan Brookes.

We also thank two business consultants for generously sharing their knowledge: John L. Lombardi, a construction industry executive whose Brooklyn, Conn., company, the Orchard Group, LLC, provides management assistance to contractors; and Stanley F. Erhlich, a longtime remodeler who now runs S.F. Ehrlich Associates, a financial planning company in Westfield, N.J.

NAHB's BuilderBooks skillfully guided this book to publication. We appreciate the assistance and hard work of Director of Book Publishing Courtenay S. Brown and Book Editor Natalie C. Holmes.

BuilderBooks thanks the following people who reviewed the outline and/or part or all of the manuscript for *The Paper Trail*: James L. Anderson, Anderson Construction Services, Summerville, S.C.; Dan Diemer, DGR, Diemer Building and Remodeling, Inc., Las Cruces, N.M.; David Ellis, Executive Vice President, Greater Atlanta Home Builders' Association; Cindy Knutson-Lycholat, CGR, East Troy, Wis.; Robert Matuga, NAHB assistant vice president, Labor, Safety, and Health; Larry Schaffert, CGR, Schaffert Constructions, Inc., Myersville, Md.; Finley Perry, F.H. Perry, Builder, Hopkinton, Mass.; Paul Sullivan, CGR, The Sullivan Company, Newton Highlands, Mass.; Janet W. Williams, CGR, Williams—Builder, Robbinsville, N.J.

About the Authors

William Asdal, CGR, owner of Asdal Builders, LLC, of Chester, New Jersey, (www.asdalbuilders.com), is a remodeler and diversified builder. A former chairman of the NAHB Remodelers, he has won many awards, including the 2009 National Green Building Award for Townhouse Project of the Year, National Green Remodeler of the Year (2006), National Remodeler of the Year (2000), and induction into the Remodeling Hall of Fame (2007). A frequent speaker on remodeling issues, he is active in various industry leadership roles and serves as chairman of the Industry Committee for the Partnership for Advancing Technologies in Housing (www.pathnet.org).

Wendy A. Jordan, CAPS, is author of numerous books on remodeling management and design. A former vice president of Hanley-Wood and founding editor of *Remodeling* magazine, Jordan runs her own editorial business in Washington, D.C., and serves as a senior contributing editor of *Professional Remodeler* magazine. Her remodeling journalism has garnered many awards, including four Jesse H. Neal Editorial Achievement Awards, two Neal Award Certificates, and a special Editorial Excellence award from the Chairman of the NAHB Remodelers.

Introduction

It was late summer—vacation time for most Americans, but peak business season for many remodelers, including the design-build remodeler we'll call Dan. On this August morning, Dan was not at work. He was heading to the airport for the first leg of a two-week tour of Europe. Dan knew his business would run smoothly without him because of the systems he'd put in place. Thanks to these systems, every aspect of each remodeling project would be handled according to company standards in a well constructed process, even while Dan was away enjoying a vacation.

Dan had learned the hard way the importance of company systems. In the remodeling company he launched prior to his current business, he was responsible for every task, every decision, and every piece of information—a typical scenario for a small remodeler. As the company grew and he added staff, Dan knew he needed to delegate responsibility and decision-making authority. Unfortunately, he couldn't because he had no systems, no standard procedures, and no written company policies. Methods, procedures, and decision-making criteria were all locked in Dan's head.

Drawing on what he learned from these typical start-up business mistakes, when Dan launched a new design-build company, he decided to operate differently. Before opening his doors for business, Dan enlisted staff to help him carefully design the company's process architecture. Together, this team drafted company objectives, policies, and procedures. They charted the flow of work for a job from start to finish. They wrote job descriptions, accounted for every task, and detailed the hand-offs from person to person. They developed checklists to assure that nothing would be forgotten and that no task would be overlooked. They devised forms to collect and transfer information and to help monitor job progress and profitability.

That was eight years ago. With solid systems in place, Dan's business has flourished. With a foundation of good systems, making minor adjustments has been easy. Dan's experience demonstrates that sound systems are integral to the well-run remodeling company. They are the difference between chaos and control, waste and efficiency, error and accuracy, loss and profit.

Company systems positively impact businesses by standardizing processes and procedures, creating a useful roadmap from point A to point B. They assure consistency—that tasks are handled in a uniform, predictable manner. They also assure that people, materials, and work adhere to prescribed standards, minimizing errors and omissions. With systems in place, everybody who works for the company knows what to do, how to do it, when to do it, and why they are doing it.

Forms animate systems. They are communication tools that trace and monitor information flow within live systems in action. Well-chosen, well-designed forms prompt the use of planned company procedures and make information accessible to everyone in the company who needs it. They also help identify weak spots in the operation so these vulnerabilities can be fixed. The company's systems—its methods, policies, and procedures—are built around this framework. Although most companies have this framework, few document it. Documentation is essential, for with documentation in place a manager can monitor the company and work to improve its processes.

The Paper Trail: Systems and Forms for a Well-Run Remodeling Company, Second Edition, is designed to help remodelers develop and implement strong business systems for their companies. The forms and documents in _The Paper Trail_ were carefully selected to cover the most important tasks and concerns of remodeling companies. Use them to help you draw a blueprint for building comprehensive business systems. Then select the specific forms needed to animate your systems. Each form appears at the end of the chapter in which it is referenced. In addition, forms are indexed by subject matter and form type at the end of the book to help you locate specific forms.

Certainly, no two remodeling companies are exactly alike. Therefore, each one will format its forms differently and with varying levels of detail. To assist you in customizing the forms, the book includes a companion CD with all of the documents referenced and shown in the text. (Although the content of the forms on the CD is the same as what's in the book, the forms' appearance may be different because the forms on disk are, for the most part, Word and Excel files.) You can modify the forms as necessary to suit your company's particular needs.

By using a "search and replace" command, you can insert your name in place of "Company Name" on the forms. (For forms with headers/footers that appear to be "grayed out," just click header or footer on the Insert menu in Word 2007 or View header/footer in earlier versions of Word.) Your company's operating style, goals, and procedures will dictate the forms that will become part of your paper trail.

The Paper Trail focuses on six key systems that will help you run a successful business:

1. Sales and marketing
2. Communication
3. Estimating
4. Production
5. Business management
6. Financial management

The Paper Trail also includes a list of Resources at the back of the book to help you improve your business practices and increase your knowledge of construction management.

Keep in mind that systems continually evolve with their companies. Therefore, don't hesitate to modify forms more than once or abandon those that have outlived their usefulness. Systems change as a business dictates and as remodelers learn new best practices on the job. The ultimate goal of forms is to standardize processes and practices and reinforce continuous improvement, both of which will help good remodeling companies become outstanding ones.

Setting and Reaching Your Goals

The old saying, "If you don't know where you are going, any route will take you there," is all too true in the remodeling business. That is why the first step in developing a system to enhance your company's success is to define what success means to you. Once you have done that, you can establish specific goals and develop strategies to reach them. Some remodelers equate success with sales volume, or the dollar volume of projects sold. Other remodelers equate success with the revenue realized for a specific time period. When remodeling company owners see that their crews are busy producing beautiful projects and a backlog of eager clients waits in the wings, many believe their businesses are successful. But success in the remodeling business is not defined simply by how busy you are.

Truly successful remodelers are the ones whose profits meet or exceed their financial goals. If you equate success with busyness, slow periods may tempt you to lower prices to attract clients. However, keeping busy without protecting profits can drive a company into the ground. Sage industry veteran Stan Ehrlich says, "There is good work and there is no work." If the job cannot be produced at a profit, you should not take it. Every job must contribute to meeting company profit goals.

In fact, many small-volume remodeling companies are as profitable as those that have more volume. Sales are the means to an end. Therefore, rather than merely having a sales quota, specify a financial result—a desired annual net profit for your efforts.

Even profit may not embody all of your aspirations, however, because the ultimate purpose of business ownership is the achievement of your personal goals. Therefore, identifying company goals is a two-step process. You must first define your personal goals as the business owner. After that, you can create a business plan that will yield a healthy, profitable company and enable you to achieve those personal goals.

Personal Goals

For anyone, personal goals include both lifestyle and income objectives. How many hours a week do you want to work? Do you want to work evenings or weekends? Does your spouse want to work? Do you want to take big vacations? Do you have expensive hobbies, interests, or property? Do you need to support a vacation home? Maintain a boat? Pay for your kids' college education? Do you have expensive taste, or are you happy with a simpler, more conservative lifestyle? What do you want your personal financial portfolio to look like this year, next year, 5 or 10 years from now, and when you retire? By answering questions such as these, you can establish a lifestyle plan and corresponding personal income goal to make that lifestyle a reality.

A Lifestyle Budget (1.1) provides a starting point for company financial planning. An owner needs to know how much he has to make in business. "All I can" is not a reasoned financial goal. Determine what it costs to live the life you choose and, from there, build a company that generates income that will exceed your needs. The excess goes to savings, risk reduction, or perhaps enhanced goals. Understanding your own personal spending and saving habits injects a dose of reality into the business planning process.

Chances are you have a general dollar figure in mind. However, as a rule, financial goals will have a longer shelf life if they are expressed in percentages compared with your personal expenses, or ratios rather than dollars and cents. That's because with inflation, market shifts, and other financial fluctuation, expenses and returns are a moving target. Strive to hit your income target by earning 125% of your lifestyle budget so that you have savings, a cushion, some growth potential, and a safety net to cope with business volatility.

The company must generate enough money to support your personal needs. If you want a $200,000-a-year lifestyle, for instance, a business that generates $300,000 in gross sales will not be adequate if you follow the rule of thumb that projects owner's compensation in a small business at approximately 20% of gross sales. You can adjust either the personal spending expectation downward or the business revenue goal upward to make the numbers work. That's the beauty of planning. Perhaps the company niche should be changed. Alternatively, you could scale back personal lifestyle goals. Take a moment to fill in the lifestyle budget before determining your company financial goals. Be sure to collaborate with your life partner so you are on the same track, and get buy in from anyone else who will have authority to spend money.

Some years ago, a successful remodeler started chatting with the man sitting next to him at an industry seminar. The man shook his head and said, "If I had a dime for every . . . [referral, or happy client, or whatever]." The second half of the sentence did not matter to the remodeler because it got him thinking about the first half. He suddenly realized how much money he was allowing to evaporate by not having a savings plan. That very week he started placing 2% of every check his company received into a savings account. The set-aside had a minimal impact on his company's day-to-day operations. "Two percent doesn't vaporize the net profit," the remodeler explained. But over time that savings account compounded and grew significantly. It bolstered the company's standing with the bank, gave it more borrowing power, and helped the business qualify for bonding on large commercial jobs. As the company owner, the remodeler saw his equity rise to an impressive level. "You are not in business just to draw a paycheck," he says. "Your plan needs to incorporate various means of accumulating equity and wealth outside the company."

Creating a Business Plan

With your personal goals as the foundation, you can create a business plan that not only guides your business but also supports you personally. The business must perform well enough to generate your personal income. The company's gross sales figure also must cover all current and anticipated operating expenses; materials and labor for jobs; expenses for company employees; and, if this is part of your plan, adequate seed money for company growth. To communicate your business plan to others, you must write it down. The list of resources at the back of this book includes Web sites where you can obtain business planning templates.

Collecting Leads, Sales, and Completed Jobs

Chapters 2 and 7 include tools for collecting data on leads, conversions, and the dollar amount and gross margin of jobs sold. Using that information, calculate the number of leads, sales, and completed jobs your company needs to reach its year-end profit goal for the coming year. Then calculate what your company will need to meet its profit goals three to five years in the future and beyond.

These calculations should bring you to a fork in the road. Owners of companies without reliable systems usually cross their fingers at this point and head off on an unmarked, meandering path, hoping they will end up where they want to be financially. Owners of companies with strategic, goal-oriented systems, however, confidently march down a direct route to financial success. This road will have frequent progress markers, checkpoints, and opportunities to correct and change course, if necessary. Your benchmarks can be year-over-year comparisons of your own financial history or comparisons of your business's performance to industry standards.

You are in business to earn enough net income to help you achieve your personal goals. Therefore, net profits, not gross sales, are the most important numbers to watch. Moreover, as your business matures, you will begin to look beyond net income to net worth. This is the ultimate prize of owning a business—that your work and investment returns will provide sufficient funds to pay living expenses and still grow each year. Only a well-thought-out plan, not just hard work or luck, will increase your net worth.

A lifestyle budget is the foundation of a financial plan. Do you have a lifestyle budget which charts your expenses throughout the year? If not, use last year's expenses as a starting point and write down all of the costs of the life you have chosen. Now you have to build a company to support that lifestyle.

Involving Others

Developing a sound operating plan for your company takes time and hard work, but is well worth the effort. If you have employees, enlist their help. They will be able to contribute knowledge, insights, and ideas. They also will appreciate being asked, and will buy into the system they help create.

You should revisit your plan regularly to evaluate what is working and what needs refinement. The company managers might do this quarterly. At your annual meeting, go over the plan again, soliciting comments and suggestions from all staff members who attend. When everyone participates, everyone wins. You benefit from workers' practical feedback and new ideas. Your employees learn that you value their contributions as members of the company team.

Mobilizing Resources

The most successful companies reach their goals efficiently—with the least amount of waste and with few or no errors. They do this by analyzing their operations and systematically applying repeatable processes to complete the work. These companies control resources—financial and otherwise. Physical resources—plant and equipment—either help or hinder a company's capacity to achieve its goals. Personnel—staff and trade contractors—are another company resource. Their time, expertise, and skill affect how a company plan moves forward. Suppliers, manufacturers, code and compliance officials, architects, past customers, professional service providers, others with whom your company works, your company's reputation, and referrals you cultivate are also resources. Do you have successful businesspeople in your network? Tap their insights and ask for advice; they too can be a resource to your company. Put all these resources to work as you strive for optimal company performance and achievement of your financial goals.

Creating a Paper Trail

You have a goal-oriented plan. You have developed systems to implement it. The systems address every procedure or process your managers, workers, and contractors must repeat for the business to run, and every task, procedure, and resource employed along the way. Your plan is task oriented, rather than personality oriented. In other words, it is so well defined that the company can run smoothly even if one or another key staff person is absent. Now you need forms to activate your system. You need a paper trail to follow. Business forms guide the plan by

- prescribing how to implement every task
- gathering essential data
- communicating the data to everyone who needs it
- pinpointing omissions in information or procedure
- highlighting flaws in the system
- building a record

On a larger scale, business forms are tools for tracking company progress toward meeting goals, assessing progress, and making changes along the way to keep the company on course.

The forms in each of the following chapters organize and monitor various parts of a remodeling company operation. In a well-run remodeling company, no area is completely separate from the others. All systems interconnect seamlessly, charting every project from the first contact with clients to job completion and beyond. With tightly woven systems and well-crafted forms, each staff member, trade contractor, and client has the information they need when they need it. The company works well, works smart, and works steadily toward achieving your business and personal goals.

Chapter 1 Forms

1.1   Lifestyle Budget

		Annualized
Monthly Gross Income:	$0	$0
Child Support:		$0
Federal Taxes Withheld:	$0	$0
Social Security Taxes Withheld:		
State Taxes Withheld:		
Local Taxes Withheld:		
Medical Insurance Withheld:		
Dental Insurance Withheld:		
Life Insurance Withheld:		
Disability Insurance Withheld:		
401K (Retirement) Withheld:		
Savings Account Withheld:		
Other Withholdings:		
Net Take Home Pay:	$0	$0

Category 1—Current Needs

Household		Annualized	Food		Annualized
Electricity	$ -	$0	Groceries	$ -	$0
Improvements	$ -	$0	Lunches	$ -	$0
Insurance	$ -	$0		$ -	$0
Maintenance	$ -	$0			
Gas/Oil/Wood	$ -	$0	**Transportation**		
Office Supplies	$ -	$0	Gas/Oil	$ -	$0
Mortgage/Rent	$ -	$0	Insurance	$ -	$0
Postage	$ -	$0	License/Tags	$ -	$0
Real Estate Taxes	$ -	$0	Maintenance	$ -	$0
Pers. Prop. Taxes	$ -	$0	Payments/Lease	$ -	$0
Tax Preparation	$ -	$0	Other Trans.	$ -	$0
Telephone	$ -	$0		$ -	$0
Water/Sanitation	$ -	$0			
Yard Care	$ -	$0			
Other Household	$ -	$0			
	$ -	$0			

1.1   Lifestyle Budget (continued)

Category 1—Current Needs

Clothing		Annualized		Insurance		Annualized	
Purchase	$ -	$ -		Medical/Dental	$ -	$ -	
Clean/Laundry	$ -	$ -		Disability	$ -	$ -	
	$ -	$ -		Life	$ -	$ -	
					$ -	$ -	

Non Covered Medical

Dental	$ -	$ -		**Misc. Household**			
Doctors	$ -	$ -		Furnishings	$ -	$ -	
Eye Care	$ -	$ -		Appliances	$ -	$ -	
Hospital	$ -	$ -		Other Misc.	$ -	$ -	
Minerals/Vitamins	$ -	$ -			$ -	$ -	
Prescriptions	$ -	$ -					
Other Medical	$ -	$ -					
	$ -	$ -					

Category 2—Future Needs & Wants

Savings

(Items NOT taken out of paycheck)

I R A	$ -	$0
Tax Deferred	$ -	$0
Money Market	$ -	$0
Mutual Funds	$ -	$0
Stocks	$ -	$0
Bonds	$ -	$0
CD's	$ -	$0
Savings	$ -	$0
Other Savings	$ -	$0
	$ -	$0

Category 4—Misc.

Misc. $0

Allowances	$ -	$0
Barber/Beauty	$ -	$0
Child Care	$ -	$0
Cosmetics	$ -	$0
Education	$ -	$0
Pet Care	$ -	$0
Other Misc.	$ -	$0
	$ -	$0

Category 3—Contributions

Sharing

Church	$ -	$0
Sponsored Child	$ -	$0
United Fund	$ -	$0
Other Contributions	$ -	$0
	$ -	$0

1.1 Lifestyle Budget (continued)

Category 5—Wants
(Preferably No Debt Here)

Fun Stuff		Annualized	
Art	$ -	$ -
Boat	$ -	$ -
Cell Phone	$ -	$ -
Club Dues	$ -	$ -
Computer Stuff	$ -	$ -
Decorative Furniture	$ -	$ -
Dining Out	$ -	$ -
Entertaining Others	$ -	$ -
Entertainment	$ -	$ -
Sports, Fishing . . .	$ -	$ -
Gifts	$ -	$ -
Internet Service	$ -	$ -
Jewelry	$ -	$ -
Memberships	$ -	$ -
Knickknacks	$ -	$ -
Photography	$ -	$ -
Stereo & Music	$ -	$ -
Mag. Subscriptions	$ -	$ -
TV/Cable/Movies	$ -	$ -
Vacation/Trips	$ -	$ -
Other Fun Stuff	$ -	$ -
	$ -	$ -

monthly net income	$ -	annual net income	$ -
monthly expenses	$ -	annual expenses	$ -
debit/credit/mo.	$ -	debit/credit/yr.	$ -

2

Maximizing Sales and Marketing

Sales and marketing is both an art and a science. It is a process for controlling the type of customers you attract, your brand, and the clients you qualify to be your customers. The sales process begins a relationship with the client that you cultivate with an efficient hand-off to estimating and then through production. It comes to a successful close when you receive references from your customer and referrals of future clients.

Your sales process should collect all the information needed to accurately price and professionally produce problem-free jobs. Doing so will yield happy customers and more jobs from repeat business and referrals. The forms in this chapter will help you achieve your strategic marketing and sales goals. Create your system, and then use the forms to carry out the system's various functions professionally and keep everyone up-to-date on projects.

Your goal is not simply to generate leads, but to generate leads that fit your market niche. You don't want to just sell jobs; you want to sell the most profitable jobs for your company. The Sales History and Projection Report (2.1) shows you the trend line in sales and leads, which helps you to project realistically and adjust your efforts and resources to meet sales goals.

Strategically target your marketing. Maintain a professional, consistent, and ubiquitous company image on your letterhead, fax cover sheets, signs, advertisements, business cards, other client communication forms, trucks, employee uniforms, and Web site. Market your company steadily during both upward and downward business trends so your leads don't dry up. In the most difficult markets, keeping your image fresh and in front of potential clients can be a lifesaver.

Marketing Strategically

A Remodeler's Marketing Plan (2.2) must generate enough leads to produce the sales needed to achieve the company's profit goal. The plan defines the target market, which will help you refine your company's image, communicate your brand promise, and determine how to allocate marketing expenditures to best target your market. The Marketing Budget (2.3) flows from the plan.

You want to produce the best return, in quality leads and sales numbers, for every marketing dollar spent. Use the Company Introduction (2.4) and Working in the Neighborhood (2.5) letters to introduce your company and invite business from home owners in areas where you already have clients. Send form 2.4 at any time to widen your market. Send form 2.5 prior to beginning a job, alerting neighbors about the project and providing contact information in case the neighbors have a complaint or question.

You can also foster recognition of your company name and reputation by using the Press Release Template (2.6) format to announce news about your company, such as awards, new hires, company participation in community events, and completion of unusual or otherwise newsworthy projects. Distribute these releases to local print, broadcast, and Internet media. In addition, send releases regarding accomplishments of national interest to trade and business publications.

When a prospect contacts your company because of a client referral, immediately send the Referral Thank You Letter (2.7), and perhaps even a gift such as flowers, candy, or a gift certificate to a restaurant or movie theater. By expressing your gratitude, you encourage them to refer your company to someone else and you further reinforce your company's brand. They may provide references or allow you to show their project to prospects. Nurturing their goodwill encourages them to mention your company in their networking with friends and associates.

After project completion, the Sales Associate Job Closeout (2.8) is attached to the summary of job costs (chapter 7). It records the bonuses due to project participants and the gift sent to the person who referred the clients to your company.

Tracking Leads

Use the Lead & Job Tracking Form (2.9) and Lead & Job Tracking Database Report (2.10) to monitor the investment and return on your lead generation efforts. These forms track leads from the date you receive them all the way through estimating, construction, project completion, and final billing. They enable you to keep each project moving and monitor its progress. Analyze the report at least twice a year to help you allocate your marketing budget to yield the greatest possible return. It consolidates job tracking information for all leads, allowing you to see how long it takes your company to process leads—that is, how efficient your process is. It also maps the flow of all active projects from estimate to construction, helping you to plan which crews to assign to projects.

You also can employ Web-based and off-the-shelf software to keep track of leads and analyze results. These programs will save you time. They consolidate lead receipt, data entry, qualification, and lead conversion within one application that office, sales staff, managers, and company owner can access.

Qualifying Leads

Beginning with the first telephone conversation with a prospect, you or your sales professionals can use the Telephone Qualifier Sheet (2.11) to gather information to qualify a customer and increase the likelihood of making a sale. Train employees to use the Telephone Message Procedures (2.12) and to record phone calls on the Telephone Log (2.13) to ensure that all incoming phone calls are recorded, routed to the person best qualified to respond, and addressed promptly.

Although you can tailor the specifics for conducting an initial phone call, questions and checkpoints should follow logically to help determine as soon as possible if callers are tire-kickers or serious prospects; if their job and/or budget fits your niche; and whether they seem predisposed to have your company handle their remodeling project. Use the Lead Sheet (2.14) to gather general information about the lead and the type of remodeling project they are considering. The Client Screener (2.15) integrates a scoring system for rating the strength of the lead and a checklist with prompts to record the lead in your database and issue a thank-you note or gift to clients who made referrals.

Incorporate information learned from telephone conversations into your marketing planning to help you retool and refine your plan. For example, recording how the callers heard about your company can help you evaluate the effectiveness of your marketing campaigns.

To plan the appropriate time for follow-up calls, ask whether you may call prospects at work. You may also glean conversation points a salesperson can use later. Do the callers work at the same company as one of your satisfied customers? Do they have concerns that can be addressed earlier rather than later? Relationships are the heart of remodeling companies and you surely need solid relationships with your clients. These relationships are built one transaction at a time. A value-generating transaction could be as simple as a phone call, a good day's work, or sharing your professional knowledge during a sales call. Every interaction should be directed toward building solid relationships that lead to more work for your company.

Preparing for Sales Appointments

It pays to standardize your sales appointment procedures so that you are sure to cover all the information you want to convey about your company, and collect all the information you need about the proposed project. Once an initial sales appointment has been scheduled, send a Confirmation Letter (2.16) to the prospective client. Before heading out for an appointment, the salesperson should gather tools such as a digital camera, tape measure, presentation book, and Preconstruction Site Checklist (2.17). Assuming the lead still looks strong at the appointment, you will need the information gathered using the checklist to prepare an estimate. It has space to detail site access considerations, structural issues, and key dimensions.

You can use the following tools to help home owners think through their remodeling needs before design and estimating begin:

- Bathroom Remodeling (2.18)
- Bathroom Selections (2.19)
- Kitchen Design Questionnaire (2.20)
- Kitchen Final Selections (2.21)
- Kitchen Remodeling Project Guide (2.22)
- Aging in Place Audit (2.23)
- Remodeling Project Checklist (2.24)

The salesperson can complete these forms as they discuss the project with the client at a first meeting, leave the forms with the client to complete before a subsequent meeting, or send the forms with the aforementioned appointment confirmation letter for the client to complete.

The Salesperson's Project Checklist (2.25) and New Job Setup Information (2.26) are used to set up a new project. These forms list everything that needs to be done to prepare for a job before construction begins. The salesperson uses the list to make sure jobsite records, trade contractor estimates, and client contracts are completed prior to handing off a project to production.

Follow-Up

An important part of sales and marketing is ensuring client satisfaction. Sending post-project survey cards, letters, or questionnaires demonstrates that you appreciate your clients' business and offers an opportunity to collect feedback to help improve client satisfaction in the future. Shortly after a project has been completed, while the experience is still fresh in the minds of your clients, ask them to evaluate your company's performance and the trade contractors you assigned to their project, using any of the following tools:

- Client Feedback Postcard (2.27)
- Client Evaluation of Company Questionnaire 1 (2.28)
- Client Evaluation of Company Questionnaire 2 (2.29)
- Client Evaluation of Trade Contractor (2.30)
- Performance Evaluation (2.31)

When you e-mail or mail your surveys, be sure to include the Survey Cover Letter (2.32). Choose the surveys you think your clients are most likely to complete and adjust the questions as needed. Use the positive feedback to commend your personnel and contractors, and the negative feedback to guide improvements.

Another approach is to send clients the Request for Letter of Referral (2.33) after project completion. This letter also asks for feedback on performance.

By instituting a formal evaluation process, you will gain valuable information to improve your business and, hopefully, customer endorsements you can use in your marketing materials. Many remodelers obtain permission from happy customers to quote them by name or initials in brochures, advertisements, and on the company's Web site.

Don't forget about prospects who have chosen another company to handle their remodeling project. Send them the Lost Bid Questionnaire (2.34). You may discover helpful insights for meeting the expectations of more clients in your market. Moreover, sending a polite note and questionnaire may convince the prospects who rejected your bid that they should hire you for their next job.

Chapter 2 Forms

Marketing

2.1   Sales History and Projection Report (Excel)
2.2   Remodeler's Marketing Plan (Word)
2.3   Marketing Budget (Excel)
2.4   Company Introduction Letter (Word)
2.5   Working in the Neighborhood Letter (Word)
2.6   Press Release Template (Word)
2.7   Referral Thank You Letter (Word)

Tracking Leads

2.9   Lead & Job Tracking Form (Excel)
2.10   Lead & Job Tracking Database Report (Excel)

Qualifying

2.11   Telephone Qualifier Sheet (Excel)
2.12   Telephone Message Procedures (Word)
2.13   Telephone Log (Excel)
2.14   Lead Sheet (Word)
2.15   Client Screener (Word)

Sales Appointments

2.16   Confirmation Letter (Word)
2.17   Preconstruction Site Checklist (Excel)
2.18   Bathroom Remodeling (Word)
2.19   Bathroom Selections (Word)
2.20   Kitchen Design Questionnaire (Word)
2.21   Kitchen Final Selections (Word)
2.22   Kitchen Remodeling Project Guide (Word)
2.23   Aging in Place Audit (Word)
2.24   Remodeling Project Checklist (Word)
2.25   Salesperson's Project Checklist (Word)
2.26   New Job Setup Information (Excel)

Follow-up

2.8   Sales Associate Job Closeout (Word)
2.27   Client Feedback Postcard (Word)
2.28   Client Evaluation of Company Questionnaire 1 (Word)
2.29   Client Evaluation of Company Questionnaire 2 (Word)
2.30   Client Evaluation of Trade Contractor (Word)
2.31   Performance Evaluation–Customer (Word)
2.32   Survey Cover Letter (Word)
2.33   Request for Letter of Referral (Word)
2.34   Lost Bid Questionnaire (Word)

2.1   Sales History and Projection Report

5 Year History

A simple sales projection formula: Annual Sales x Average change in sales = Projected sales
Insert your numbers for a computation

	Year	Year	Year	Year	Year	Projected	
Gross Sales	$ 500,000.00	$ 545,000.00	$ 625,000.00	$ 678,000.00	$ 723,000.00	811,174.79	Last Sales x Avg Increase
Increase/Decrease from previous year		$ 45,000.00	$ 80,000.00	$ 53,000.00	$ 45,000.00		AVERAGE OF INCREASES
Percentage Increase		12.1	7.8	12.8	16.1	12.2	

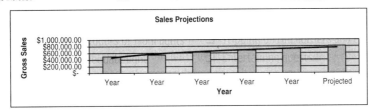

	next year	next year	next year	next year	next year	projected / required
Leads	75	82	87	99	120	135
Increase/Decrease from previous year		7	5	12	21	
Percentage Change		9%	6%	14%	21%	13%

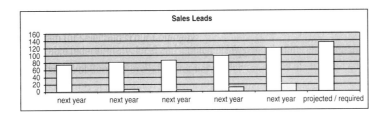

2.2   Remodeler's Marketing Plan

A. Marketing Objective

Our company's marketing objective is:

(List and compare your marketing goals for the next year, then five years out, including dollar volume, profits, market share, customer base/market)

	Year 1	Year 5
Dollar volume:	_____	_____
Profit margin:	_____	_____
Market share:	_____	_____
Customer base:	_____	_____

B. Market Research

1. Our current and potential customers are
Demographics (age, sex, income, occupation, marital status):

_____

Location:

_____

Lifestyle (interests, values):

_____

2. Our current and potential markets are
(Identify major segments as well as small but potentially profitable groups.)

_____

3. Our competitors are (and will be)

_____

4. The market trends that will impact our business are

_____

5. We will position our company as follows:

_____

C. Marketing Strategy

1. Advertising

We will allocate _____ annually for advertising divided among the following media as follows:

a) Create/redesign Web site (%)   d) _____ (%)
b) Advertise in church bulletins (%)   e) _____ (%)
c) _____ (%)   f) _____ (%)

2.2   Remodeler's Marketing Plan (continued)

2. Public relations strategies and events to appeal to our target market will be as follows:

(Although public relations is ongoing, rather than "an event," listing a few specific tasks **with deadlines** for completion and for assessing the results will help you focus staff time and energy. Enlist outside expertise, if possible, through your local Home Builders' Association or other business contacts.)

    a) Work with local newspaper editor to prepare an article about remodeling for home owners. Deadline:

    b) Contact local schools about teaching at "career days." Deadline:

    c) _____

    d) _____

    e) _____

2.3 Marketing Budget

ABD 1/20XX - 12/20XX	January	February	March	April	May	June	July	August	September	October	November	December	Total
PRINT													
Coloradoan (TOMA 1319.99; Inserts 1433.00)	$1,320	$1,320	$2,753	$1,320	$1,320	$1,320	$1,320	$1,320	$2,753	$1,320	$2,753	$1,320	$20,139
Style Media	$0	$0	$0	$0	$0	$0	$0	$0	$0	$0	$0	$0	$0
Steamboat Magazine	$0	$0	$1,440	$0	$0	$1,440	$0	$0	$1,440	$0	$0	$1,440	$5,760
Steamboat Pilot (TOMA)	$654	$654	$654	$654	$654	$654	$654	$654	$654	$654	$654	$654	$7,848
Steamboat At Home Magazine	$454	$0	$0	$0	$0	$0	$0	$0	$0	$0	$0	$0	$454
WEB													
Google/Ad Words	$500	$200	$200	$200	$200	$200	$200	$200	$200	$500	$200	$200	$3,000
iPoint	$0	$150	$150	$150	$150	$150	$150	$150	$150	$150	$150	$150	$1,650
SIGNAGE													
Yard Sign Design	$0	$0	$0	$0	$0	$0	$0	$0	$0	$0	$0	$0	
Yard Sign Production (Adam's van)	$475	$0	$0	$0	$0	$0	$0	$0	$0	$0	$0	$0	$475
Vehicle Sign Production (add CAHB)	$0	$0	$800	$0	$0	$0	$0	$0	$0	$0	$0	$0	$800
OUTDOOR													
Next Media (1125 + tax)	$1,159	$1,159	$1,159	$1,159	$1,159	$1,159	$1,159	$1,159	$1,159	$1,159	$1,159	$1,159	$13,905
EVENTS													
New Home and Remodel Show	$0	$0	$0	$0	$0	$0	$0	$0	$0	$0	$0	$0	$0
COMMERCIAL PLAQUES	$0	$0	$0	$0	$0	$0	$0	$0	$0	$0	$0	$0	$0
COMMERCIAL PROGRAM													
Design, printing, list, postage	$0	$0	$0	$0	$0	$0	$0	$0	$0	$0	$0	$0	$0
Top 25 gifts	$0	$0	$0	$0	$0	$0	$0	$0	$0	$0	$0	$0	$0
PARTNERS REWARDS PROGRAM													
Postcard design, printing	$0	$0	$0	$0	$0	$0	$0	$0	$0	$0	$0	$0	$0
Postage	$0	$0	$0	$0	$0	$0	$0	$0	$0	$0	$0	$0	$0
Travel & gifts	$0	$0	$0	$0	$0	$0	$0	$0	$0	$0	$0	$0	$0
Invitation design and printing	$0	$0	$0	$0	$0	$0	$0	$0	$0	$0	$0	$3,000	$3,000
NEIGHBORHOOD PROGRAM-SS													
Postcard Designs/Printing	$0	$500	$0	$0	$0	$0	$0	$0	$0	$0	$0	$0	$500
Postage	$50	$50	$50	$50	$50	$50	$100	$100	$100	$100	$100	$50	$850
NEIGHBORHOOD PROGRAM-FC													
Post card Design (Miller + 1st,1000 & 3rd-500)	$450	$0	$0	$0	$0	$0	$0	$0	$0	$0	$0	$0	$450
Postcard printing	$300	$0	$0	$0	$0	$0	$0	$0	$0	$0	$0	$0	$300
Postcard postage (2000)	$50	$50	$50	$50	$50	$50	$100	$100	$100	$100	$100	$50	$850
NEWSLETTERS													
External Newsletters (Light Speed printer)	$0	$0	$450	$0	$0	$450	$0	$0	$450	$0	$0	$0	$1,350
Postage (Duncan)	$0	$0	$250	$0	$0	$250	$0	$0	$250	$0	$0	$0	$750
MISC													
Letterhead	$232	$0	$0	$0	$0	$0	$0	$0	$0	$0	$0	$0	$232
Client packets	$0	$0	$0	$0	$0	$0	$0	$0	$0	$0	$0	$0	$0
Gadget Gifts	$0	$0	$0	$0	$0	$0	$0	$0	$0	$0	$0	$0	$0
Gift Quality	$175	$175	$175	$175	$175	$175	$175	$175	$175	$175	$175	$175	$2,100
Qwest	$65	$65	$65	$65	$65	$65	$65	$65	$65	$65	$65	$65	$780
ABD Worker Apparel	$0	$0	$0	$350	$150	$0	$0	$0	$0	$0	$0	$0	$500
Holiday Calendar	$0	$0	$0	$0	$0	$0	$0	$0	$0	$0	$0	$3,200	$3,200
Award Entries	$0	$0	$0	$0	$0	$0	$3,000	$0	$0	$0	$0	$0	$3,000
Professional Pictures/Digigraphics	$200	$0	$0	$85	$350	$155	$0	$150	$0	$170	$0	$0	$1,005
Client Party	$0	$0	$0	$0	$0	$0	$0	$85	$0	$0	$0	$0	$540
Linden Group (3 newsletters only)	$0	$400	$1,000	$400	$400	$1,000	$400	$400	$1,000	$400	$400	$0	$5,800
	$6,084	$4,723	$9,196	$4,658	$4,573	$7,368	$7,323	$4,558	$8,746	$4,793	$5,756	$11,463	$79,238

$79,238

2.4   Company Introduction Letter

Company Name
Company Logo
Company Affiliations

<Date>

<Prospective Customer>
<Address>
<Any town, Any State, Any Zip Code>

Dear <Name>,

We would like to take this opportunity to introduce our company to you. <your company name> has been serving the <your market area> for the past <number of> years.

If you need construction or remodeling/renovation services, please contact us at <insert phone number>. We will be glad to provide you with a no-obligation estimate for all of your building/ remodeling needs.

We are a licensed contractor, and we carry both general liability and workers' compensation insurance.

We have built many successful relationships with our clients. Our customers trust us. We are confident that you will find our record of service, attention to detail, and concern for your safety to be among the best in the Industry. <Add information here about any certifications, designations, or awards.>

We are very interested in building a relationship with you. I've enclosed a copy of our company <brochure/newsletter> for your information.

Again, if we can be of any service to you, please call us at <phone number> or contact us through our Web site at www.<your URL>.com

Sincerely,

<Your Name>
<Your Title>

Address
Phone–Fax
E-mail–Web Site

2.5   Working in the Neighborhood Letter

Company Name
Company Logo
Company Affiliations

<Date>

<Customer's Neighbor's Name>
<Address>
<City, State, Zip>

This letter is to inform you that your neighbors, <INSERT CUSTOMER'S NAME>, have retained us to do an extensive remodel of their home at <INSERT CUSTOMER'S ADDRESS>. We expect to start work on <INSERT PROJECT START DATE>, and complete the project around <INSERT ESTIMATED PROJECT COMPLETION DATE>.

Due to the minimal access to the construction area, we are asking for your patience during the work period. Parking is an issue and we will minimize the amount of traffic; however, it will not be uncommon to have <number of> vehicles on site at any one time. We will contain our construction debris either with an on-site dumpster or by making a trash haul every couple of days.

We will do our best to minimize any inconvenience. However, should you see any of our employees act in an unprofessional manner, please feel free to contact me directly at <INSERT TELEPHONE NUMBER>.

We are a full-service design/build remodeling and custom home building firm. If you have any building or remodeling needs we are currently scheduling projects for <INSERT MONTH AND YEAR>. Please feel free to contact us to assist you.

Thank you,

<INSERT YOUR NAME AND UNIVERSITY OF HOUSING DESIGNATIONS>
<INSERT YOUR TITLE>
<INSERT YOUR COMPANY NAME>

Your Company Name
Phone:
E-mail:
Fax:
Web site:

2.6   Press Release Template

COMPANY NAME
Address, City, State, Zip, Fax, Web Site Address

FOR IMMEDIATE RELEASE   CONTACT: <your name>
                                                                        <your phone>

Asdal Builders of Chester, NJ, wins Green Building Award for Black River Commons

WASHINGTON, May 12—The National Association of Home Builders has named Black River Commons in Chester, NJ as a Green Building Project of the Year. The association honored Asdal Builders LLC, of Chester, NJ, at the 11th Annual NAHB National Green Building Conference in Dallas.

Black River Commons is a collection of one- and two-bedroom townhomes for active adults 55 and better on Main Street in Chester Borough. With residences ranging from 2,000 to 2,900 square feet of space and rents starting from only $2,100 per month, the community is proving to be a money, time and energy-saving alternative to owning a home.

Black River Commons is a prototype for what may well become a growing choice for our senior population. The two buildings are designed with the latest energy-efficient technologies to cut energy costs by thousands per year. The buildings use no fossil fuels—no gas, no oil and no propane. The super-efficient structures utilize the latest construction techniques with cutting edge air sealing techniques, enhanced insulation, a geothermal heating system and solar powered fans.

Each unit at the Black River Commons features a spacious living area with built-in bookshelves; center-island kitchen with wood cabinetry, granite countertops, pantry, and breakfast room; two large bedrooms with ample walk-in closets; full basement with two-thirds finished as a recreation room; walk-up floored attic for storage; a 200 sq. ft. rear patio; and on-site parking. The gently sloping site abuts public lands and has the privacy of an estate just off Main Street.

Bill Asdal, owner of Asdal Builders, has taught numerous seminars on green building through the National Association of Home Builders. He also restored the Raritan Inn Bed & Breakfast, an 1890s Victorian in Califon, NJ, using solar power and geothermal technology. For more information on Black River Commons at Chester, visit www.blackrivercommons.com.

2.7   Referral Thank You Letter

Company Name
Company Logo
Company Affiliations

Date

<Customer Name>
<Customer Address>
<Customer City, State, Zip>

Dear <Customer Name>,

We would like to take this opportunity to thank you for referring <potential customer's name> to us.

We owe our success at *Your Company Name* to friends like you and the referrals that you give. We regard these referrals as endorsements of our craftsmanship and integrity. We take pride in every step of each project—from the initial discussions to the final completion. One of our first goals is to provide superior service to our customers.

In the end, we feel that our technical competence joined with responsible management makes *Your Company Name* stand out from the rest.

We're pleased that you've helped spread the word. We'll do everything possible to meet and exceed your expectations, giving you one more reason to refer family, friends and acquaintances to *Your Company Name*.

Very truly yours,

<Your Name>
<Your Title>

P.S. Please visit our Web site at www.<your URL>.com.

Reply to: Your Company Address
Phone:
Fax:
E-mail:
Web site:

2.8   Sales Associate Job Closeout

Company Name
Company Logo
Company Affiliations

Sales Associate Job Closeout

Production on job is complete. Project manager initials _____

Completed punch List has been signed by the home owner. Project manager initials _____

All invoices are entered to the Job Cost Report. Office manager initials _____

Final Job Cost Report is approved. Office manager initials _____

Final payment has been received _____ Office manager initials_____

Thank-you note sent. Office manager initials _____

	Commission % of Work	Final Sales Price	Incentive Amount
CFO/Owner initials	_____	_____	_____

Referral gift goes to _____

Paid date _____

Check amount _____

Sales associate signature _____

Owner signature _____

Company Address
Phone/Fax
E-mail
Web site

2.9   Lead & Job Tracking Form

Company Name
Company Logo
Company Affiliations

Customer: _____   Lead Number: _____

Address: _____   Date Received: _____

City, State: _____

                               Date Called: _____

Home Phone: _____

Work Phone: _____   Site Visit: _____

Cell phone: _____   Plans Received: _____

E-mail: _____   Estimate Out: _____

Fax Number: _____   Follow-up Call: _____

                               Contract: _____

Type of Project   Permits Applied: _____

Job Site: _____   Permits Released: _____

Architect: _____

Phone Number: _____   Start Of Work: _____

Recommended By: _____ Completion: _____

                               Final Billing: _____

Scope of Work:

Notes:

Directions:

Company Address
Phone
Fax
E-mail
Web site

2.10 Lead & Job Tracking Database Report

Company Name
Company Logo
Company Affiliation

Work	Value	Last Name	First Name	Address	Town	Phone	Work	Date Entered	Follow-up	State	Zip
	Leads										
	$ -										
	Estimates out								Estimate out		
	Site visit								Start		
	$ -										
	Contracts								Start		
	$ -										
	Construction								Balance Due		
	$ -										
	Billed – not collected								Left to Bill		
	$ -										
	To Customer List										
	$ -										

Add leads as they come in. After a site visit move them down and again after the estimate is out. Move them again once contracted and again when the work is in construction. Move them again when billed and lastly to a customer list that holds all contacts.

By tracking the dates of contact and performance some tracking information can be generated. How long did it take to get an estimate out the door?

Company Address
Phone
Fax
E-mail
Web site

2.11   Telephone Qualifier Sheet

Company Name
Company Logo
Company Affiliations

Salesman: _____

Job No. _____

Name: _____

Date: _____

Address: _____

_____

Jobsite location if different:

Lead received by: _____

_____

Source of lead: _____

Phone (H) _____

Phone (W) _____

Any plans for additional work to home?   Yes ☐   No ☐

Who is involved in decision making at the home? _____

How long have you been planning the project? _____

What is your budget for the project?

Type of project:

_____

_____

_____

_____

Getting other bids on this work?

Budget established?

Notes: _____

_____

_____

Directions: _____

_____

_____

_____

Have you visited our Web site?   ☐ Yes   ☐ No

Company Address
Phone
Fax
E-mail
Web site

2.12   Telephone Message Procedures

Company Name
Company Logo
Company Affiliations

Procedure for Taking Telephone Messages

1. Include the caller's name, phone number, message, and the best time to return the call on all messages.
2. Try to address callers' requests before handing them off to other staff members.
3. If you cannot help the caller, and another staff member can, contact the appropriate staff member. Tell the caller that the staff member will return the call within 24 hours, or by the end of the day if the call is urgent.
4. If the caller must speak to the sales or field person, take a message and text, e-mail, or radio it to that person.
5. If the caller will not leave a message, note "called—left no message" in the call log.
6. Mobile phone numbers will only be released with the sales or field person's approval. Even if a sales or field person has given permission to give out the mobile number, ask the caller if there's anything the office staff can do to help first.

Company Address
Phone
Fax
E-mail
Web site

2.13 Telephone Log

Company Name
Address
City, State, Zip
Phone/Fax

Phone Log

Date of Call	Message For	Caller's Name	Caller's Number	Message	Initials

2.14   Lead Sheet

Date Lead Received: Feasibility Appointment:

Name: Design Appointment:
Spouse:

                                                 Directions:

Street:
City:
State: Zip:

                                                 Age of Home: Years in Home:
                                                 Appraised Value:

Name: Name:
Telephone (H):   Telephone (H):
Telephone (W):   Telephone (W):
Work Place: Work Place:
Employer: Employer:
Cell Phone: Cell Phone:
Fax: Fax:
E-mail: E-mail:

Referred By: Type of Project:

- ☐ PAST CLIENT   ☐ ADDITION   ☐ KITCHEN REMODEL
- ☐ REFERRAL: _____ ☐ BASEMENT   ☐ OTHER REMODEL
- ☐ NEWSLETTER/POSTCARDS   ☐ T &M   ☐ REPAIRS
- ☐ HOME SHOW   ☐ BATH   ☐ ROOF
- ☐ OPEN HOUSES   ☐ COMMERCIAL   ☐ SCREEN PORCH
- ☐ JOBSITE/VEHICLE SIGNS ☐ DECK   ☐ WHOLE HOUSE
- ☐ HANDYMAN FLYER   ☐ DESIGN   ☐ WINDOWS & DOORS
- ☐ MAGAZINE ARTICLES/ADS ☐ INSURANCE
- ☐ WEB SITE
- ☐ OTHER:

NOTES:

2.15   Client Screener

Call taken by: Date of call: /   /
Client screened by: Date of screening:
Design/build, estimating, or professional service fee: (circle one) $_____
Ballpark estimate provided by salesperson: $ _____/_____
Date ballpark estimate was provided to client: _____
$ starting point provided to client: _____

Action:

Caller's information   ### Partner/spouse information
Name: Name:
Street Address: City / Zip:

Best way & time to reach
Home #   (   )   Home #   (   )
Work #   (   )   Work #   (   )
Cell #   (   )   Cell #   (   )
E-mail   E-mail

Is there anyone else involved with the decision making?   Spouse   Decorator   Attorney   Other
(Circle and provide contact information.)

Project description/goals of the project: _____
_____
_____
_____
_____
_____

Questions for client (fill in during phone call and score *after* phone call)

	Score:
How did they hear about us and what do they know about us that made them decide to call?	
Past Client	4
Referral Name:	5
Web Site	3
Job Site Signs or Vehicle Signs (*circle one*)	2
Architect/Engineer/Designer	3
Direct Mailer (newsletter/postcard) or Jobsite Neighborhood Mailer (*clarify*)	3
Yellow Pages/Magazine Adv./Other:	2
Associations—Chamber, Rotary, Trades, Suppliers, Etc.	3

2.15   Client Screener (continued)

Sales information	Score*:
Age of home?	+ 10 yrs. (3), + 20 yrs. (5)
How long have you been living there?	3 yrs. or less (2), Less than 10 yrs. (3), 10+ yrs. (4), 20+ yrs. (5)
How long do you plan to live there?	3 or fewer yrs. (2), 10+ yrs. (5)
What is your ideal start date or completion date? _____	30 days (2), 60+ days (5)
What is your budget? $_____	(if realistic) (5)
Need financing?	If yes, recommend a referral.
Have you remodeled / built home before with a contractor?	No (1), Yes (5)
Have you done any remodeling yourself?	No (1), Yes (–7)
Is there a reason you are not working with your previous contractor, (or doing it yourself?)	
Name: _____	
Have you spoken to any other professionals? Names: _____	Yes (0), No (5)
Have you set up any appointments? Y/N	
(Make the last appt.)	
What is most important to you in selecting the company you want to work with?	Quality (2), Trust (5), Price (2)

Office information (fill in and score *after* phone call)

Project type	Score:
Whole House	5
Room Addition	5
Kitchen Remodel	5
Bath Remodel	5
Custom Home/Misc. Remodeling	2

Project location	Score:
Towns close to you	5
More distant towns	2

Design services	Score:
Needs design services	5
Design agreement discussed? (circle) yes no	
Has a design	3
Doesn't need design services	2
Estimate Fee Discussed? (circle) yes no	

Evaluation	Score:
Overall feel of call	Excellent (5), Possible (2), Not likely (1)

Total score: _____ points / 66 points

---

*Numbers in parentheses indicate points to be scored according to answer given.

2.15   Client Screener (continued)

CLIENT NAME: _____

MARKETING TRACKER: Ballpark & Lead Source & Stages: (check off as you do)
$_____   Source:_____   Appt:_____   D/B:_____   Est. Fee: _____
Contract:_____

Checklist for Follow-Up on Leads

Made Sales Appointment/Salesperson _____   Date: Time:
☐ Entered lead into sales tracking software–mailing list and appointment
☐ Input information into marketing tracker (see above)
☐ Created sales folder with marketing packet & put sample client binder with folder
☐ E-mailed appointment confirmation letter to client
☐ Sent thank-you note for referral on: ___/___/____
☐ Sent thank-you gift to referring party when contract was signed on: ___/___/____

2.16   Confirmation Letter

Company Name
Company Logo
Company Affiliations

Date

Your Customer's Name
Your Customers Address
City, State, Zip

Dear ‹*Customer*›,

Thank you for calling on ‹*Your Company Name*› for your project. We are pleased that you thought of us. We look forward to visiting with you on ‹*Date/Time*›.

‹*Your Company Name*› has established a solid reputation for professionalism and integrity since ‹*Year*›. ‹*List professional honors and awards.*›

We take pride in every step of each project—from the initial discussions to final completion. One goal is to provide superior customer service.

For your information, I have enclosed materials about our company and about the remodeling process in general.

Sincerely,

‹*Your Name*›
‹*Title*›

Company Address
Phone
Fax
E-mail
Web site

2.17 Preconstruction Site Checklist

Company Name
Company Logo
Company Affiliations

Date:

Job Name:
Job Address:

Drawings
Permits
Engineering
    Wetlands
    Slopes
Demolition
Variances

Jobsite logistics:
Site:
    Accessibility:

Visable rock	_____
Interior	_____
Exterior	_____
Grade conditions	_____
Distance from drop location	_____

Excavation _____
| Soils stockpiling and relocation | _____ |

Landscaping _____
Trees, shrubs	_____
Lawn	_____
Irrigation systems	_____
Exterior electrical work	_____

Masonry _____
Foundation	_____
Veneer	_____
Walks	_____
Chimney	_____

Exterior Roofing _____
Siding	_____
Flashing	_____
Windows	_____
Deck	_____

2.17   Preconstruction Site Checklist (continued)

Company Name
Company Logo
Company Affiliations

Systems	HVAC	_____
	Electrical	_____
	Plumbing	_____
Flooring		_____
Protection:		_____
	Landscaping	_____
	Dust	_____
	Floors	_____
	Furniture	_____
	Room Separation	_____
Trash Removal:		_____
	Debris Container	_____
	Size Restrictions	_____
	Location	_____
	Accessibility	_____
	Frequency	_____
Parking		_____
	Location	_____
	Hours (restrictions)	_____

2.18   Bathroom Remodeling

When remodeling a bathroom, consider the following items.

(Please check one or more in each category that interests you for further discussion.)

Plumbing fixtures

☐ Toilet (compartmentalized from rest of room?)
☐ Pedestal lavatories quantity: _____
☐ Shower for one person
☐ Shower for two
☐ Standard bathtub
☐ Whirlpool-style bathtub for one
☐ Whirlpool-style bathtub for two
☐ Fixed shower heads, Qty: _____
☐ Body sprays/jets
☐ Bidet
☐ Towel bars, Qty. _____
☐ Faucet finish: chrome, brushed nickel,
   polished brass, chrome and brass combo,
   or other: _____

Cabinetry for vanities

☐ Vanities, qty: _____
☐ Tall cabinet for towels, etc.
☐ Medicine cabinet(s), qty: _____
☐ 3-way mirrors, qty: _____
☐ Natural wood, species: _____
☐ Painted wood, color: _____
☐ Other: _____

Walls / ceilings

☐ Drywall
☐ Plaster
☐ Wood
☐ Other: _____
☐ Keep existing ceiling the way it is.

Countertops for vanities

☐ Ceramic or granite tile
☐ Granite slab
☐ Laminate
☐ Solid surface
☐ Other: _____

Flooring

☐ Ceramic tile
☐ Hardwood, species: _____
☐ Laminate
☐ Vinyl
☐ Other: _____
☐ Keep existing

Lighting, etc.

☐ Exhaust/light(s), qty: _____
☐ Sconces above lav(s), qty: _____
☐ Recessed, general light
☐ Heat lamp(s), qty: _____
☐ Other: _____

Lavatory (sink) material

☐ Porcelain
☐ Integrated solid surface
☐ Stainless
☐ Self-rimming above the counter surface
☐ Under mount
☐ Other: _____

Additional requests

☐ Windows: _____
☐ Doors: _____
☐ Skylights: _____
☐ Solar tubes: _____
☐ Storage/linen closets: _____
☐ Anything else? _____

2.19   Bathroom Selections

Company Name
Company Logo
Company Affiliations

<Date>

<Customer Name>
<Customer Address>
<Customer Phone>

Final Bathroom Selections

Item	Qty	Description	Color	Ordered	Vendor
Vanity					
Counter					
Medicine cabinet					
Tank topper					
Flooring					
Floor grout					
Wall tile					
Wall grout					
Baseboard					
Doors–trim					
Sink					
Toilet					
Bidet					
Tub					
walls					
enclosure					
Shower stall					
Shower door					
Marble					
Toothbrush holder					
Toilet paper holder					
Soap dish					
Towel bar					
Robe hook					

Company Name
Phone–Fax
E-mail–Web site

2.19   Bathroom Selections (continued)

Company Name
Company Logo
Company Affiliations

Item	Qty	Description	Color	Ordered	Vendor
Grab bars					
Splash end					
Fan/light/heater					
Ducting					
Caps: wall/roof					
Wall lights					
Ceiling lights					
GFI					
Mirror					
Sink faucet					
Tub faucet					

Customer Acceptance:

_____ Date _____
_____ Date_____

Company Acceptance:

_____ Date_____

Company Name
Phone–Fax
E-mail–Web site

2.20   Kitchen Design Questionnaire

Company Name
Company Logo
Company Affiliations

<Date>

<Customer Name>
<Address, City, St, Zip>
<Customer Phone/Contact Information>

Kitchen Design Questionnaire

Kitchens are very complex rooms that increasingly serve a variety of functions. To best meet your expectations for your new kitchen, we need to know about your lifestyle, needs and desires.

General Information
- How many members in your household? ___Adults ___Teens ___Children ____Pets ___Seniors
- How long have you lived in your home?
- When was the house built?
- How old is the existing kitchen?
- When would you like to begin the project?
- When would you like it completed?
- What is the budget range you have established for your kitchen project?
- Do you plan to gut the kitchen area?
- Do you plan to keep the same kitchen layout and simply make cosmetic changes? Which elements will remain and which will be replaced?
- What improvements are you looking for in a new kitchen? __ More work space __ Easier to clean __ Upgraded electrical service __ More efficient traffic pattern __ More storage __ Better lighting __ Other, please explain _____ _____

- What do you dislike most about your present kitchen? _____ _____

- What works particularly well in your present kitchen? _____ _____

- List some details of the new kitchen that are important to you. _____ _____ _____

Company Name
Phone—Fax
E-mail—Web site

Company Name
Company Logo
Company Affiliations

Use of Existing Kitchen
• Who is the primary cook?
• Is this person __left-handed __right-handed? How tall is this person? ____
• How many other household members cook? ____
• What are their specific needs if they differ from the general assessment?

_____

Please check if you desire any of the following.
   __Disposal
   __Microwave
   __Trash compactor
   __Icemaker
   __Dishwasher
   __Separate cooktop: Gas __
                      Electric __
                      Downdraft __
                      Updraft __
   __Oven/cooktop combination
   __Refrigerator: Built-in __
                Standard __
   __Freezer: Part of refrigerator __
           Separate unit __
   __Double ovens
   __Second sinks
   __Architectural type stove hood
   __Wine Chiller
   __Appliance drawers (warmer, d/w, microwave, refrigerator, freezer, other)

Where does your family eat?
Kitchen __%   Table __   Counter __
Dining Room __% Table __   Seats __
Family Room __%
Other __%
Changes needed for any of the above items:

_____
_____

Company Name
Phone–Fax
E-mail–Web site

2.20   Kitchen Design Questionnaire (continued)

Company Name
Company Logo
Company Affiliations

Entertaining
__Holidays   __Formal   __Informal
__Business   __Formal   __Informal
__Friends   __Formal   __Informal

Please check the statement below that best describes the way you feel.
__I like to be the only cook in the kitchen with my guests in a separate space that is away from the kitchen.
__I like to be the only cook in the kitchen with my guests close by, with open space to the family room.
__I like my guests to be sitting in the kitchen visiting with me while I cook.
__I like my guests to help me in the kitchen in meal preparation.
__I like my guests to help in the clean-up process after the meal.
__I retain caterers who prepare, serve and clean up all meals for entertainment.

What secondary activities or amenities would you like to have in your kitchen?
__Computer __Eating __Walk-in pantry __Wet bar __Wine storage __Kids' projects
__Laundry __Growing plants __Hobbies __Study __TV/radio __Planning desk __Sewing
__Other

Detail Questions
What small electrical appliances do you use in your kitchen? __Blender __Wok __Toaster
__Coffeepot __Can opener __Electric fry pan __Griddle __Crock-Pot __Food processor
__Other _____

Which items need specialized storage? __Bottles __Breadboard __Breadbox __Cookbooks
__Cutlery __Dishes __Display items __Glassware __Lids __Linen __Plastic __Soft drinks
__Spices __Vegetables __Wine __Other _____

Which items do you recycle? __Paper __Plastic __Glass __Cans
Where do you sort recyclables? __Kitchen __Garage __Utility room __Basement

Company Name
Phone–Fax
E-mail–Web site

2.20   Kitchen Design Questionnaire (continued)

Company Name
Company Logo
Company Affiliations

Where would you like to store the following items?
Code: (B) Base cabinet (W) Wall cabinet (T) Tall cabinet (D) Desk (C) Countertop (AG) Appliance garage
(L) Laundry (O) Outside of kitchen (BC) Bookcase (BA) Basement
___Baking equipment
___Paper products
___Linens
___Cleaning supplies
___Glassware
___Leftover containers
___Fruits/Vegetables (non-refrigerated)
___Iron
___Spices
___Pet foods
___Wrapping materials
___Recycle containers
___Specialty cooking items (wok, etc.)
___Boxed goods
___Canned goods
___Dishes
___Pots and pans
___Serving trays
___Other _____

Decorations & Finishes
- If you are replacing your cabinets, what type of facing material do you prefer?
    ___Wood: Type? _____
    ___Painted ___Stained ___Paint or Stain wash ___Laminate
- What cabinet door styles do you prefer?
    ___Sleek, plain front ___Raised panels ___Arched panels ___Recessed panels ___Glassed fronts
- If you are replacing your countertops, which do you prefer?
    ___Corian ___Laminate ___Tile ___Granite ___Butcher block ___Other _____
- What type of backsplash do you prefer? ___Same as countertop ___Tile ___Corian ___Stainless steel

2.20   Kitchen Design Questionnaire (continued)

Company Name
Company Logo
Company Affiliations

- What floor materials do you prefer? __Sheet vinyl __Tile __Granite __Hardwood __Limestone __Other _____
- What type of feeling would you like your new kitchen space to have? __Formal __Traditional __Family retreat __Strictly functional __Open & airy __Sleek/contemporary __Country __Personal design statement
- What colors do you like? _____
- What colors do you particularly dislike? _____
- What colors are you considering for your new kitchen? _____
- Have you made a sketch of your kitchen or collected pictures of ideas?
- Other design needs or ideas:

_____

_____

_____

It would be helpful to us for you to provide magazine clippings or other items that would illustrate your vision for your new kitchen. We look forward to working with you!

2.21   Kitchen Final Selections

Company Name
Company Logo
Company Affiliations

\<Customer Name\>
\<Customer Address\>
\<Customer Phone\>

Final Kitchen Selections

Item	Qty.	Model, specs.	Selection due date	Installation date	Vendor
Single ovens					
Electric cooktop					
Gas cooktop					
Downdrafts					
Microwave					
Dishwasher					
Refrigerator					
Kitchen sink					
Garbage disposal					
Kitchen faucet					
Kitchen floor					
Cabinets					
Cabinet hardware					
Countertops					
Appliance drawer(s)					

Customer Acceptance:

_____ Date _____

_____ Date _____

Company Acceptance:

_____ Date _____

Company Name
Phone
Fax
E-mail
Web site

2.22   Kitchen Remodeling Project Guide

When remodeling a kitchen, consider the following items.

Please check one or more in each category that interests you.

Appliances
- ☐ Cooktop/range, gas or electric? _____
- ☐ Dishwasher
- ☐ Microwave
- ☐ Oven(s)–gas or electric? _____
- ☐ Range hood
- ☐ Refrigerator
- ☐ Television
- ☐ Trash compactor
- ☐ Disposal
- ☐ Other: _____
- ☐ Keeping these existing appliances:

  _____

Cabinetry
Natural wood, species: _____
- ☐ Painted wood, color: _____
- ☐ Combination: _____
- ☐ Door style: _____
- ☐ Other: _____

Walls/Ceilings
- ☐ Drywall
- ☐ Plaster
- ☐ Wood
- ☐ Other: _____
- ☐ Keep existing ceiling the way it is.

Countertops
- ☐ Ceramic or granite tile
- ☐ Granite slabs
- ☐ Laminate
- ☐ Solid surface
- ☐ Other: _____

Flooring
- ☐ Ceramic tile
- ☐ Hardwood, species: _____
- ☐ Laminate
- ☐ Vinyl
- ☐ Other: _____
- ☐ Keep existing

Lighting
- ☐ Ceiling fan/light(s)
- ☐ Decorative
- ☐ Recessed, general light
- ☐ Task, under-cabinet
- ☐ Other: _____

Plumbing
- ☐ Faucet with pull-out spray
- ☐ Faucet with soap dispenser, instant hot water, etc.
- ☐ Garbage disposal
- ☐ Pot-filler faucet at cooktop
- ☐ Sink (double, single, farm-style) _____
- ☐ Other: _____

Main Sink / Prep sink
- ☐ Porcelain
- ☐ Solid surface
- ☐ Stainless
- ☐ Self-rimming
- ☐ Under-mount
- ☐ Other: _____

Additional requests
- ☐ Windows: _____
- ☐ Doors: _____
- ☐ Skylights: _____
- ☐ Anything else? _____

2.23   Aging in Place Audit

HOME AUDIT–Page 1
Check (✓) any of the following items that present problems

Entry

- ❑ Climbing up the stairs to the front door
- ❑ Going down the stairs from the front door
- ❑ Unlocking the front door
- ❑ Using the door knob
- ❑ Reaching and using the mailbox
- ❑ Walking over the lip at the threshold
- ❑ Seeing in the area

Hallways and Inside Doors

- ❑ Opening and going through doors to rooms
- ❑ Using door knobs
- ❑ Moving between carpeted and non-carpeted areas
- ❑ Seeing because of inadequate lighting
- ❑ Turning on lights in the area being approached

Stairs

- ❑ Slipping on stairs
- ❑ Distinguishing thresholds and edges
- ❑ Tracking over bare treads or other obstacles
- ❑ Balancing support

Bedroom

- ❑ Entering and exiting
- ❑ Privacy
- ❑ Turning lights on and off
- ❑ Using electrical outlets
- ❑ Communication
- ❑ Opening and closing drapes, shades, and/or curtains
- ❑ Opening and closing windows
- ❑ Using the closet (opening/closing, reaching clothes)
- ❑ Finding adequate storage room
- ❑ Tripping on rug corners and edges
- ❑ Seeing because of glare
- ❑ Seeing because of inadequate lighting

Kitchen

- ❑ Turning lights on and off
- ❑ Using electrical outlets
- ❑ Opening and closing windows
- ❑ Seeing because of inadequate lighting
- ❑ Using cabinets, closets, or other storage
- ❑ Using and reaching all parts of the refrigerator/freezer
- ❑ Using counters or other surfaces (preparing meals)
- ❑ Using the oven (door, dials, shelves)
- ❑ Reaching the switch on the range fan
- ❑ Using the stove (dials, reaching burners)
- ❑ Opening cans or bottles
- ❑ Using water taps
- ❑ Cleaning the floor and other surfaces
- ❑ Using the dishwasher
- ❑ Disposing trash/garbage

Bathroom

- ❑ Entering and exiting
- ❑ Privacy
- ❑ Turning lights on and off
- ❑ Using electrical outlets
- ❑ Using cabinets and closets
- ❑ Using the mirror
- ❑ Using water taps
- ❑ Using the sink
- ❑ Using the toilet
- ❑ Using the shower/bathtub
- ❑ Opening and closing the window

2.23   Aging in Place Audit (continued)

HOME AUDIT–Page 2
Check (✓) any of the following items that present problems

Living Room or Family Room

- ❏ Entering the living room
- ❏ Turning lights on and off
- ❏ Using electrical outlets
- ❏ With glare from the outdoors or from lights
- ❏ Seeing because of inadequate light
- ❏ Opening and closing drapes, shades, and/or curtains

- ❏ Opening and closing windows
- ❏ Moving around in the living room
- ❏ Monitoring the heating and cooling system
- ❏ Tripping on rug corners and edges
- ❏ Entertaining guests

2.24   Remodeling Project Checklist

Remodeling Project Checklist—Page 1

Describe your home according to:

3	Number of bedrooms
1 ¾	Number of bathrooms
1	Number of bathtubs
2	Number of showers
Yes	Bedrooms grouped at same end of home
	Bedrooms at different ends of the home
1700	Square footage

When do you want to complete this project?   **My lifetime**

Do you want your plans prepared by:

	An architect
X	A builder contractor
	An interior designer
	Yourself
	Other:

What is your overall estimated budget for this project?

	$12,000-$30,000
	$30,000-$45,000
	$45,000-$60,000
X	$60,000-$80,000
	$80,000-$100,000
	$100,000 or more

Do you want your home to have:

	More room
	Less room
X	Less upkeep
X	Updated features
	Better layout/flow
X	More natural light
	Other:

How long have you lived in your home?   **12 years**

How long do you plan on staying in the remodeled or new house?   **10 years or more**

How many people live in the house on a regular basis?

2	Adults
	Children
occasionally	Extended family

2.24   Remodeling Project Checklist (continued)

Remodeling Project Checklist–Page 2

What are the ages and genders of the family members? Include extended visitors,
(i.e., children in college, grandchildren staying the summer, relatives, saying for holidays).

Age	**48**	Male	**X**	Female	
Age	**48**	Male		Female	**X**
Age		Male		Female	
Age		Male		Female	
Age		Male		Female	
Age		Male		Female	

Are you planning to enlarge your family?   Yes _____   No ____**X**____

Does your family have special needs or physical limitations?   Yes _____   No ____**X**____

   If yes, what are they?   _____

_____

Prioritize the following options:
(1) very important; (2) important; (3) not important

1	Function of space
1	Traffic flow through space
2	Look of space
3	Materials made in USA
3	Brand name of materials
2	Budget flexibility
2	Timeframe of project

What do you like about your home?   **Location**
What do you dislike about your home?   **Small rooms**
What 3 words describe your dream home?   **It's paid for!**

_____

_____

Do you feel your home needs more space?   Yes _____   No ____**X**____

Would you want to move interior walls to enlarge your living space?   Yes ____**X**____   No _____

Are you considering an addition to create more room for your family?   Yes _____   No ____**X**____

Does your home provide you with adequate storage?   Yes ____**X**____   No _____

Remodeling Project Checklist—Page 3

What feeling would you like your home to have?

	Sleek/contemporary
	Warm and cozy
	Country
	Traditional
X	Open and airy
	Formal
	Other

Have you done any drawings of your idea for home improvements?   Yes _____   No __X__

If so, have you had them evaluated by an architect, designer,
or contractor?   Yes _____   No _____

Are you considering making functional improvements to your home? (Check all that apply)

	2nd story addition
	Attic bedroom
	Finished basement
	Deck
X	Adding storage accessories (racks, shelves, pullouts, etc.)
X	Additional countertop space
X	Modern/updated appliances
X	Home office/workspace
X	Exercise/workout room
	Garage
	Roof
x	Energy efficient windows or doors
X	Widen hallways
	Other:

Are you considering making cosmetic improvements to your home? (Check all that apply)

X	Updated windows, doors, cabinets
	Home entertainment areas
X	Master suite
X	Master bath or additional bathroom
	Upgraded deck
	Modern fixtures and amenities
	Update the overall look of your home
	Other:

2.25   Salesperson's Project Checklist

Company Name
Company Logo
Company Affiliations

Date: _____

Job No.: _____

Job Name: _____

Address: _____

_____

Phone: *(home)* _____

Phone: *(work)* _____

☐ Salesperson: _____

☐ Production Mgr: _____

☐ Remodeling
☐ Commercial

Special Arrangements:

☐ Payments   ☐ Vouchers
☐ Lien Waivers   ☐ Other: _____

☐ Certification of Insurance

Referral:

Name _____

Address *(if not client)* _____

_____

Mailing Address: *(if different from invoice)*

_____

_____

_____

Client's PO#: *(if needed for invoice)* _____

Pre-design Meeting:

Date _____   Time _____

☐ Production Manager Notified

Subcontractors:

Needed:	Notified:
_____	_____
_____	_____
_____	_____
_____	_____
_____	_____
_____	_____
_____	_____

Design Fee:	$ _____
Less Anticipated Professional Services/Fee	
Plan Duplication	$ _____
Architectural	$ _____
Interior Decorating	$ _____
% Margin _____ **Gross Profit:**	$ _____

Home Owner's Concerns: _____

_____

_____

Company Address
Phone/Fax
E-mail
Web site

2.26   New Job Setup Information

Company Name
Company Logo
Company Affiliations

Job Number: _____   Date: _____

Job Description: _____

Name: _____

Jobsite Phone: _____   Alarm Co. #: _____

Office Phone: _____   Fax: _____

Job Address: _____

City/State/Zip: _____

JPM: _____   Supervisor: _____

Job Start Date: _____

Estimated Completion Date: _____

Contract Date: _____   Price: _____

Payroll Burden %: _____   Deposit: _____

	State	County	City
Resident Tax Table:	_____	_____	_____

BILLING INFORMATION

TYPE BILLING:

_____ MONTHLY	_____ A.I.A.	_____ DRAW
_____ PROGRESS	_____ PROGRESS	_____ COST PLUS
_____ 10th of MONTH	BILLING	_____ COST PLUS WITH INVOICES
		_____ SERVICE CALL

RETAINAGE AMOUNT: _____

PROFIT PERCENT: _____

REFERRAL GIFT GOES TO: _____

Company Address
Phone
Fax
E-mail
Web site

2.27   Client Feedback Postcard

How Did We Do?

Now that your project has been completed, we'd like to ask you a favor. Please take a moment to rate our performance when remodeling your home. You are a valued client, and your opinion is most important to us. We will use your evaluation to guide us in delivering the best quality service to our clients. Thank you!

Please circle the number that reflects your opinion of our performance in the following areas.

	Unsatisfied		Satisfied		Highly Satisfied
1. Quality of workmanship	1	2	3	4	5
2. Creativity	1	2	3	4	5
3. Problem-solving	1	2	3	4	5
4. Efficiency	1	2	3	4	5
5. Honoring budget	1	2	3	4	5
6. Communication with client	1	2	3	4	5
7. Overall job	1	2	3	4	5

We welcome your comments and suggestions. Please use the space below to write down any thoughts about our company that you wish to share.

Thank you!

<Your Name>

<Your Title>

<Your Company Name>

2.28   Client Evaluation of Company

Survey Questionnaire #1

Company Letterhead

Name (optional): _____

On a scale of 1 to 10, where *1* is *poor* and *10* is *excellent*, please rate each of the following areas.

Rating   **Comments**

During the Project

_____ Job completion schedule   _____

_____ Detail of plans and specs   _____

_____ Allowance amounts   _____

_____ Allowance tracking sheet   _____

_____ Summary of account   _____

_____ Information notebook   _____

_____ Assistance with selections   _____

_____ Change orders' options   _____

_____ Change order pricing   _____

_____ Personnel at jobsite   _____

_____ Cleanliness of jobsite   _____

Communication

_____ Owner   _____

_____ Superintendent   _____

After Project Completion

_____ Walk-through at project
      completion   _____

_____ Cleanliness at move-in   _____

_____ Follow-up on punch list   _____

_____ Personnel providing services
      after move-in   _____

_____ Assistance with problems   _____

2.28   Client Evaluation of Company (continued)

Please rate each of the following by circling the appropriate rating:

	Poor								Excellent	
Communication:										
<Your Company>	1	2	3	4	5	6	7	8	9	10
Electrician	1	2	3	4	5	6	7	8	9	10
Carpenters	1	2	3	4	5	6	7	8	9	10
Flooring	1	2	3	4	5	6	7	8	9	10
Painter	1	2	3	4	5	6	7	8	9	10
Pricing:										
<Your Company>	1	2	3	4	5	6	7	8	9	10
Plumber	1	2	3	4	5	6	7	8	9	10
Electrician	1	2	3	4	5	6	7	8	9	10
Carpenters	1	2	3	4	5	6	7	8	9	10
Flooring Installers	1	2	3	4	5	6	7	8	9	10
Painter	1	2	3	4	5	6	7	8	9	10
Follow-through:										
<Your Company>	1	2	3	4	5	6	7	8	9	10
Plumber	1	2	3	4	5	6	7	8	9	10
Electrician	1	2	3	4	5	6	7	8	9	10
Carpenters	1	2	3	4	5	6	7	8	9	10
Flooring Installers	1	2	3	4	5	6	7	8	9	10
Painter	1	2	3	4	5	6	7	8	9	10
Listened/Incorporated my ideas:										
<Your Company>	1	2	3	4	5	6	7	8	9	10
Plumber	1	2	3	4	5	6	7	8	9	10
Electrician	1	2	3	4	5	6	7	8	9	10
Carpenters	1	2	3	4	5	6	7	8	9	10
Flooring Installers	1	2	3	4	5	6	7	8	9	10
Painter	1	2	3	4	5	6	7	8	9	10
Handled problems with materials:										
<Your Company>	1	2	3	4	5	6	7	8	9	10
Plumber	1	2	3	4	5	6	7	8	9	10
Electrician	1	2	3	4	5	6	7	8	9	10
Carpenters	1	2	3	4	5	6	7	8	9	10
Flooring Installers	1	2	3	4	5	6	7	8	9	10
Painter	1	2	3	4	5	6	7	8	9	10

2.28   Client Evaluation of Company (continued)

	Poor								Excellent	

Handled problems with prices/bills:

<Your Company>	1	2	3	4	5	6	7	8	9	10
Plumber	1	2	3	4	5	6	7	8	9	10
Electrician	1	2	3	4	5	6	7	8	9	10
Carpenters	1	2	3	4	5	6	7	8	9	10
Flooring Installers	1	2	3	4	5	6	7	8	9	10
Painter	1	2	3	4	5	6	7	8	9	10

Performance on the job:

<Your Company>	1	2	3	4	5	6	7	8	9	10
Plumber	1	2	3	4	5	6	7	8	9	10
Electrician	1	2	3	4	5	6	7	8	9	10
Carpenters	1	2	3	4	5	6	7	8	9	10
Flooring Installers	1	2	3	4	5	6	7	8	9	10
Painter	1	2	3	4	5	6	7	8	9	10

Promptness with prices/proposals:

<Your Company>	1	2	3	4	5	6	7	8	9	10
Plumber	1	2	3	4	5	6	7	8	9	10
Electrician	1	2	3	4	5	6	7	8	9	10
Carpenters	1	2	3	4	5	6	7	8	9	10
Flooring Installers	1	2	3	4	5	6	7	8	9	10
Painter	1	2	3	4	5	6	7	8	9	10

Work quality:

<Your Company>	1	2	3	4	5	6	7	8	9	10
Plumber	1	2	3	4	5	6	7	8	9	10
Electrician	1	2	3	4	5	6	7	8	9	10
Carpenters	1	2	3	4	5	6	7	8	9	10
Flooring Installers	1	2	3	4	5	6	7	8	9	10
Painter	1	2	3	4	5	6	7	8	9	10

Overall, reviewing the entire project, please rate the following items:

Remodeling experience	1	2	3	4	5	6	7	8	9	10
Finished product	1	2	3	4	5	6	7	8	9	10
Satisfaction with										
<Your Company Name>	1	2	3	4	5	6	7	8	9	10

Would you remodel again? _____

_____

_____

2.28   Client Evaluation of Company (continued)

Would you remodel another home using <Your Company Name>?   _____

_____

_____

Would you recommend <Your Company Name> to others?   _____

_____

_____

Please write any comments/suggestions below listing changes we could make to improve the
remodeling process and/or the finished product.   _____

_____

_____

_____

_____

_____

_____

_____

_____

_____

2.29   Client Evaluation of Company

Survey Questionnaire #2

Company Letterhead

Client: _____

Project #: _____

1. Were you informed of inconveniences prior to the start of the job? ( ) Yes   ( ) No

    _____
    _____
    _____

2. Are you satisfied with the quality of remodeling work? ( ) Yes   ( ) No

    _____
    _____
    _____

3. Are you happy with the completed project? ( ) Yes   ( ) No
    What if anything would you have done differently? _____

    _____
    _____
    _____

4. Were our employees courteous, helpful, and knowledgeable? ( ) Yes   ( ) No

    _____
    _____
    _____

    Were they respectful of your home? ( ) Yes   ( ) No

    _____
    _____
    _____

    Was there a particular employee whose work was outstanding on this project? ( ) Yes   ( ) No

    _____
    _____
    _____

5. Did the lead carpenter maintain a professional and productive work environment at the jobsite during this project? ( ) Yes   ( ) No

    _____
    _____
    _____

2.29   Client Evaluation of Company (continued)

6. Were the trade contractors professional, prompt, and courteous while working on this project?
( ) Yes   ( ) No

_____

_____

_____

Did you have any problems with any of the trade contractors? ( ) Yes   ( ) No

_____

_____

_____

7. Were the people in our office friendly and efficient? ( ) Yes   ( ) No

_____

_____

_____

8. Were we responsive to your needs? ( ) Yes   ( ) No

_____

_____

_____

9. On a scale of 1 to 10, how would you rate our company's overall performance?
Poor   1   2   3   4   5   6   7   8   9   10   Excellent

_____

_____

_____

10. Was the project started on time? ( ) Yes   ( ) No

11. Were you able to utilize the space on time? ( ) Yes   ( ) No

12. What could <Your Company Name> have done to make your project run more smoothly?

_____

_____

_____

_____

13. May we use you as a reference? ( ) Yes   ( ) No

_____

_____

Person responding: _____   Date: _____

Thank you for your time and assistance in helping us to be a better company!

2.30 Client Evaluation of Trade Contractor

Company Letterhead

1. Are you satisfied with the quality of <Trade Contractors Company Name>'s work?
   [ ] Yes   [ ] No

   _____

   _____

   _____

2. Were <Trade Contractor Name's> employees courteous, helpful and knowledgeable?
   [ ] Yes   [ ] No

   _____

   _____

   _____

3. Were they respectful of your home? [ ] Yes   [ ] No

   _____

   _____

   _____

4. Was there any particular trade contractor that stood out on this project? [ ] Yes   [ ] No

   _____

   _____

   _____

5. Were the trade contractor's employees responsive to your needs? [ ] Yes   [ ] No

   _____

   _____

   _____

6. On a scale of 1 to 10, how would you rate this trade contractors' overall performance?

   Poor 1 2 3 4 5 6 7 8 9 10 Excellent

   Comments: _____

   _____

   _____

7. What could any of the trade contractors have done differently to make your project run more smoothly?

   _____

   _____

   _____

Person responding: _____   Date: _____

Thank you for your time and assistance in helping us to become a better company!

2.31   Performance Evaluation–Customer

Company Name

We would appreciate your honest opinion about your remodeling experience with <Your Company>.
This helps us to know what we're doing right and what we need to improve.

- What made you choose <Your Company Name>?

On a scale of **1** (needs improvement) to **10** (excellent) how do you rate the following:

- Response to your needs/Communication/Keeping you informed: ____

- Timeliness: ____

- Overall Customer Service: ____

- Cleanliness of the Work Site: ____

- Quality of Work: ____

- "Punch List" work completed to your satisfaction & in a timely fashion: ____

- Satisfaction with the Finished Project: ____
  Did we   not meet / meet / surpass   your expectations?

- Value for your Investment: ____

- We care. Did it show? ____

- Quality and professionalism of the Field Team:

  Construction Manager ____   <Your Company> Crew: ____

  Trade Contractors: ____   Anyone you would like to specifically mention? ____

- Quality and professionalism of the Office Team:

  <Name> ____   <Name> ____   <Name> ____   <Name> ____

On a scale of **1** (not at all likely) to **10** (extremely likely), how do you rate the following

- Would you use <Your Company Name> again? ____

- How likely is it that you would recommend <Your Company Name> to a friend or colleague? ____

- Could we use you as a reference?   ☐ Yes   ☐ No

- If yes, could we also use comments from this evaluation on our Web site?   ☐ Yes   ☐ No

---

- Comments/Suggestions for Improvement:

- Compliments/Testimonials:

  Client _____   Date _____

Thank you for helping us to determine what we did right and what we need to do better.
And thank you very much for your business!

2.32   Survey Cover Letter

Company Letterhead

<Date>

<Client's Name>
<Address>
<City, Street, Zip>

Dear <Client's Name>:

Now that the dust has settled and you have had a chance to move into your <describe work completed>, please take a moment to give us your thoughts on what our company did well and where improvement might be needed.

We do our best to provide high-quality service and products for our clients. Our goal is to maintain our current high standards and to be open to any ideas for further improvement. We greatly appreciate your assistance in this endeavor. I can assure you that we will use your insight to improve our customer service, our products, and our business.

I have enclosed a stamped self-addressed envelope for your convenience.

Thank you,

<Your Name>
<Your Title>

2.33   Request for Letter of Referral

**Company Name
Company Logo
Company Affiliations**

\<DATE\>

\<YOUR COMPANY NAME\>
\<YOUR ADDRESS\>

Dear:

In keeping with our commitment to service our clients to the best of our ability, we request your input. Please take a few minutes to share with us your experiences. Thank you in advance for your participation.

As always, we hope you feel completely satisfied with our performance as well as our product. If you are satisfied, please tell your friends about us. If you are not satisfied, please let us know. We rely on your recommendations to build our business and we would be most grateful for a letter of referral that we may enclose with our marketing materials. Again, thank you for your time and we appreciate the opportunity to be of service. We sincerely hope you enjoy your newly remodeled home.

Warm regards,
\<YOUR SIGNATURE AND TITLE\>

Reply to: Your Company Address
Phone:
Fax:
E-mail:
Web site:

2.34　Lost Bid Questionnaire

Company Name
Company Logo
Company Affiliations

Your choice of a Remodeler means a great deal to you, and your opinion means a great deal to us.

We would appreciate your taking a few moments to share your insight with us in regard to our company's structure and practices. Your responses will enable us to better serve you and other clients in the future.

1) How did our company brochure and packet of material represent us?

　　　　　　Poor　1　2　3　4　5　6　7　8　9　10　Excellent

2) What was your first impression of <Your Company Name> when you called the office?

　　　　　　Poor　1　2　3　4　5　6　7　8　9　10　Excellent

3) How thoroughly did our salesman explain the procedures that were to be put into place?

　　　　　　Poor　1　2　3　4　5　6　7　8　9　10　Excellent

4) How satisfied were you with how quickly our salesman got back to you with the proposal and design ideas?

　　　　　　Poor　1　2　3　4　5　6　7　8　9　10　Excellent

5) How would you rate our salesman's overall performance?

　　　　　　Poor　1　2　3　4　5　6　7　8　9　10　Excellent

6) How confident were you that <Your Company Name> could perform to your expectations?

　　　　　　Poor　1　2　3　4　5　6　7　8　9　10　Excellent

7) Would you like to remain on our mailing list?

　　　　　　___ Yes ___ No (if No, why not? _____)

8) Do you know of anyone who may benefit from our services?

　　　　　　Name_____ Phone_____

Address
Phone-Fax
E-mail-Web Site

2.34   Lost Bid Questionnaire (continued)

**Company Name
Company Logo
Company Affiliations**

9) Which of the following reasons led you not to accept our proposal?

___ Had to cancel project.

Why? _____

___ Putting off project until a later date.

Approximate Date: _____

___ Selected another contractor.

Who was the contractor? _____

What was project cost? _____

___ Proposal exceeded budget

___ Proposal did not represent fair value

___ Other _____

We appreciate your time and honesty while answering and returning this questionnaire. Thank you!

Sincerely,

<Your Name>
<Your Company>

Address
Phone–Fax
E-mail–Web Site

Formalizing Client Communication

Effective communication is an implicit theme and explicit goal that underlies and links all of your remodeling company systems. If clients misunderstand decisions or agreements, a project can become ensnarled in problems that erode profits, disappoint or anger clients, and harm your company's reputation.

Written documents are essential to managing customer expectations and eliminating misunderstandings. Therefore, put everything in writing. Memoranda of understanding, minutes of jobsite meetings, and change orders that confirm a selection (even if these changes are done at "no charge") evidence professionalism and help avoid misunderstandings. Using organized written records, you can remind the occasional customer who "forgets" that they need to pay you or that they signed a particular document. This chapter includes a number of sample proposals and contracts.

The Proposal Letter (3.1), to accompany bid submissions, summarizes your standard operating procedures, such as the use of change orders, early on. When clients choose your company to design their project, use the one-page Design Retainer (3.2). When your clients sign a contract, prepare three copies of the Notice of Right to Cancel (3.3). Keep one in the job file and give two to the clients.

Enclose the Predesign Letter (3.4) with the design agreement you send to clients for their approval and signature. The letter thanks the clients and tells them what to do to finalize the agreement. When you send a copy of the signed contract to clients, you should include a Post-contract Letter (3.5), Won Bid Thank You Letter (3.6), or Thank You Letter (3.7) which reiterate your commitment to respond to the clients' needs in accordance with the contract you have signed.

Other written documents set the ground rules for how your company works, specifying, for example, the crew's work hours and the person to contact in case of an after-hours emergency. If you are billing a project based on time and materials, summarize your price and billing policies for clients with an informational sheet such as Time and Materials Terms and Pricing (3.8).

Before starting production, meet with the clients to complete the following:

- Environmental Protection Agency (EPA) booklet on lead paint, Lead Hazard Notification Receipt (3.9) and Lead Notification and Waiver of Testing (3.10). You can download the booklet at http://www.epa.gov/lead/pub/renovation.htm. To comply with laws regarding lead paint disclosure and remediation, you will need these documents. Obtain the client's signature on the general acknowledgments sheet and/or on the more specific sheet declining lead paint testing.
- Mold Disclaimer (3.11). This document informs clients about the potential problems of mold in the home. After reviewing the information with them, ask the clients to sign the disclosure and disclaimer agreement on the second page, which limits your company's liability for mold-related problems.
- Preconstruction Orientation Checklist (3.12). This document includes information about client preferences that your crew and trade contractors will need to know when accessing a property. It also includes guidelines for the clients. Give a copy of each signed form to the clients and keep copies in the job folder, which is discussed in more detail in chapter 5.
- Emergency Information Sheet (3.13), which defines "emergency" and provides contact information.

Another important function of client communication is to obtain consents and approvals from the clients for work to be done and products you will purchase for them. Virtually every document describing work to be performed should have space for the clients' signatures. At project completion, signatures on the Job Completion–Home Owner Sign-off (3.14) indicate agreement that your work is done, and that final payment is due. Present the Certificate of Satisfaction and Payment Authorization (3.15) to clients for their signature upon completion of insurance-based work. This form states the terms of your company's warranty as well.

A tightly woven communications system enables you to manage all parties throughout the remodeling project—an advantage for you and a source of reassurance to clients that you are organized and have the job under control. Explain to your clients that you share their objectives to complete the project according to plan, on budget, on schedule, and with as few problems as possible. Tell them that your communications system is designed to achieve your common objectives. Customer-oriented planning forms, product selection sheets, and a schedule for particular decisions and product selections deadlines will help customers fulfill their responsibilities in keeping a project on track. Fill in the contact information on the Product Selection Tracking Form (*see* chapter 5) that becomes part of the Job Folder and work with the clients on this document when they are selecting products for their project. Alert vendors that your clients will be calling or visiting them.

Of course, even the most attentive clients are susceptible to "selective memory syndrome." Clearly communicate in writing specifics of all agreements and important conversations about project plans, including decisions on design options, products, and scheduling issues such as a demand to cease work during children's nap time. This will protect you from the words uttered by a client that send chills down many a remodeler's spine: "But I thought you said. . . ."

One way to alleviate "selective memory syndrome" is to use a Project Communication Sheet (3.16) with date and signature lines next to each entry. Jot down each significant exchange of information with clients and decisions clients have made. Maintain the sheet in the job folder discussed in chapter 5. Used with sensitivity, records like these can help stave off unpleasant conflicts over project details.

When clients have questions or raise issues, address them immediately rather than postponing discussing them. Even if your response is not what the clients want to hear—the cabinet delivery is late, for example—responding quickly and directly may defuse tension. One remodeler solicits a 1-to-10 rating of each client's frame of mind at weekly company staff meetings to spot problems that may be brewing, even if customers have not mentioned them yet.

Use the sample letters to request payments from clients when overdue invoices accumulate. The Collection Letter (3.17) is a gentle reminder and should be used first. If the clients fail to respond, you can send them Collection Letter 2 (3.18). Occasionally a client will request a Waiver Release of Lien (3.19) stipulating that the remodeler has paid all bills that may be due or owed related to their project.

Contracts

Clear, comprehensive contracts are not only legal agreements. They should include attachments that define the project and how it will be carried out, such as plans and specifications, a site plan noting access and storage areas, and company policies regarding customer responsibilities. Share relevant portions of the contracts with members of your team, including construction supervisors, crews, and trade contractors.

Changes in law, in the business environment, or in your company's experiences require you to revise your contracts from time to time. Have an attorney familiar with the remodeling industry periodically review your contracts and other legal documents to ensure that they comply with applicable laws, and check the wording of dispute resolution provisions, particularly those in standard contracts you may have adopted from other sources, to assure that they protect your company as much as possible. Ensure that your contracts defend your right to collect for services rendered and accurately represent all of your company's policies, procedures, and commitments.

Your system should allow adequate time to review agreements and contracts with clients so that everyone involved with a project clearly understands what to expect. This up-front time commitment will avoid headaches down the road. At contract signing, bring closure to all project planning discussions and articulate a collective understanding of what is being built and how.

Each sample client contract in *The Paper Trail* was written for use with a particular kind of project or price structure. Find the right one to match your business operations. Any contract should be reviewed by your local attorney for compliance with state laws and to incorporate additional protections for your firm. Keep the terms in the Design Retainer Addendum (3.20) in mind as you build your custom contract from among the examples provided. The following contracts are included in this book:

- Build-Remodel Contract (3.21)
- Design-Build Construction Agreement (3.22)
- Design-Build Guaranteed Maximum Price Construction Agreement (3.23)
- Build-Only Construction Agreement (3.24)
- Build-Only Guaranteed Maximum Price (3.25)
- Preliminary Design-Build (3.26)
- Professional Services Agreement (3.27)
- Predesign Contract (3.28)
- Design Contract (3.29)

Section 6.03 of the Design-Build and Build-Only construction agreements includes a clause discussing material prices increases as well as two alternatives for wording an escalation clause. Use the provision that best suits your needs and delete the other two options. In addition, a Third-Party Financing Addendum (3.30) explains that you will be reimbursed for bank fees related to third-party financing arrangements. Finally, some remodelers include disclaimers such as the Concrete Flatwork Disclaimer (3.31) that release them from claims for damage that may occur to existing driveways.

If your contracts reference *Residential Construction Performance Guidelines for Professional Builders & Remodelers*, be sure you are familiar with and have the most recent edition of this publication. You can also provide your client with a consumer version of the guidelines.

Your written communications with clients have multiple purposes. One is to exchange specific information, such as contact names, after-hours emergency procedures, product selections, and contract terms. Another is to convey the general message, consistently, that your company is managing the remodeling project with professionalism, competence, and care. By issuing thorough, well-written documents every step of the way you will deliver the latter message clearly while building a record of the job for future use.

Chapter 3 Forms

Letters

3.1   Proposal Letter (Word)
3.4   Predesign Letter (Word)
3.5   Post-contract Letter (Word)
3.6   Won Bid Thank You Letter (Word)
3.7   Thank You Letter (Word)

Contracts

3.2   Design Retainer (Word)
3.3   Notice of Right to Cancel (Word)
3.20   Design Retainer Addendum (Word)
3.21   Build-Remodel Contract (Word)
3.22   Design-Build Construction Agreement (Word)
3.23   Design-Build Maximum Price Construction Contract (Word)
3.24   Build-Only Construction Agreement (Word)
3.25   Build-Only Guaranteed Maximum Price Construction Agreement (Word)
3.26   Preliminary Design-Build Agreement (Word)
3.27   Professional Services Agreement (Word)
3.28   Predesign Contract (Word)
3.29   Design Contract (Word)

Addenda

3.30   Third-Party Financing Addendum (Word)
3.31   Concrete Flatwork Disclaimer (Word)

Preconstruction and Project Documents

3.8   Time and Materials Terms and Pricing (Word)
3.9   Lead Hazard Notification Receipt (PDF)
3.10   Lead Notification and Waiver of Testing (Word)
3.11   Mold Disclaimer (Word)
3.12   Preconstruction Orientation Checklist (Word)

Payment

3.1   Proposal Letter

Company Name
Company Logo
Company Affiliations

<Date>

<Customer>
<Address>
<City, State, Zip>

Dear <Customer Name>,

Thank you for the opportunity to work with you in preparing an estimate of costs and outline of our services. Attached is our proposal for the work as detailed. A sample contract addendum is attached for your review. It outlines our expectations during the construction process. Before work can begin on your project, both parties to the contract must sign the final set of plans. Thereafter, any deviation will constitute a change of work order. It is our intention to provide you with the very best in quality construction services. We continually endeavor to deliver what we have promised and when we have promised it.

We are pleased to be of service. Please do not hesitate to call with any questions or comments. We look forward to a collaborative review of the enclosures to answer any questions and fine-tune your vision of the work and our proposal.

Sincerely,

<Your Name>
<Your Title>

Company Address
Phone–Fax
E-mail–Web site

3.2   Design Retainer

Company Name
Company Logo
Company Affiliations

CLIENT:_____

ADDRESS: _____

We [Client] retain [Your Company Name] to define and clarify a project consistent with our request, and develop investment options based on preliminary parameters. The design retainer fee [Fee] is to engage [Your Company Name] to create final (permit ready) construction documents and to establish a firm contract price. Documents may include, but are not limited to plans, elevations, and specifications.

If Client elects not to enter into a construction contract, the Fee shall be non-refundable and the plans remain the sole property of [Your Company Name] and may not be used or relied upon by Client or any third parties. _____(initial) The design fee is separate from the construction contract and no credit will be issued against future work for this design initiative.

The Fee covers costs incurred by[Your Company Name] in carrying out the terms of this Agreement.

Copies of plans and specifications will be provided upon signing of the construction contract.

PROJECT SCOPE:

_____
_____
_____
_____

PRELIMINARY INVESTMENT RANGE: $ _____   to $ _____
                                    _____   _____

Completion date of initial design: _____

DESIGN RETAINER
Paid on signing: $ _____
Paid on deliver of design $_____

NOTE: Should the scope of the project change in the design phase, an addendum will be provided to modify the budget, and may be subject to additional charges.

_____   _____
Owner   [Your Company Name]

_____   _____
Owner   Date

Company Address
Phone
Fax
E-mail
Web site

3.3   Notice of Right to Cancel

Company Name
Company Logo
Company Affiliations

DESCRIPTION OF GOODS SOLD AND/OR SERVICES TO BE PERFORMED

_____

_____

_____

Per Specifications

NOTICE OF CANCELLATION   Date _____

(ENTER DATE OF TRANSACTION)

YOU MAY CANCEL THIS TRANSACTION, WITHOUT ANY PENALTY OR OBLIGATIONS, WITHIN THREE BUSINESS DAYS FROM THE ABOVE DATE.

IF YOU CANCEL, ANY PROPERTY TRADED IN, ANY PAYMENTS MADE BY YOU UNDER THE CONTRACT OR SALE, AND ANY NEGOTIABLE INSTRUMENT EXECUTED BY YOU WILL BE RETURNED WITHIN ____ BUSINESS DAYS FOLLOWING RECEIPT BY THE SELLER OF YOUR CANCELLATION NOTICE, AND ANY SECURITY INTEREST ARISING OUT OF THE TRANSACTION WILL BE CANCELLED.

IF YOU CANCEL, YOU MUST MAKE AVAILABLE TO THE SELLER AT YOUR RESIDENCE, IN SUBSTANTIALLY AS GOOD CONDITION AS WHEN RECEIVED, ANY GOODS DELIVERED TO YOU UNDER THIS CONTRACT OR SALE; OR YOU MAY IF YOU WISH, COMPLY WITH THE INSTRUCTIONS OF THE SELLER REGARDING THE RETURN SHIPMENT OF THE GOODS AT THE SELLER'S EXPANSE AND RISK.

IF YOU DO NOT AGREE TO RETURN THE GOODS TO THE SELLER OR IF THE SELLER DOES NOT PICK THEM UP WITHIN 20 DAYS OF THE DATE OF YOUR NOTICE OF CANCELLATION, YOU MAY RETAIN OR DISPOSE OF THE GOODS WITHOUT ANY FURTHER OBLIGATION.

TO CANCEL THIS TRANSACTION, MAIL OR DELIVER A SIGNED AND DATED COPY OF THIS CANCELLATION NOTICE OR ANY OTHER WRITTEN NOTICE, OR SEND A TELEGRAM TO:

_____

(NAME OF SELLER)

AT _____

(ADDRESS OF SELLER'S PLACE OF BUSINESS)

NOT LATER THAN MIDNIGHT OF _____.

(DATE)

I HEREBY CANCEL THIS TRANSACTION

_____

(DATE)   (BUYER'S SIGNATURE)

Company Address
Phone/Fax
E-mail
Web site

3.3   Notice of Right to Cancel (continued)

Company Name
Company Logo
Company Affiliations

OR CBB # _____   LICENSE # _____

IMPORTANT INFORMATION ABOUT YOUR RIGHT OF CANCELLATION

"YOU, THE BUYER, MAY CANCEL THIS TRANSACTION AT ANY TIME PRIOR TO MIDNIGHT OF THE THIRD BUSINESS DAY AFTER THE DATE OF THIS TRANSACTION. SEE THE ATTACHED NOTICE OF CANCELLATION FORM FOR AN EXPLANATION OF THIS RIGHT."

CUSTOMER ACKNOWLEDGES THE RECEIPT OF TWO COPIES OF THIS "NOTICE OF RIGHT OF CANCELLATION."

SIGNATURE OF CUSTOMER _____   DATE _____   , 20 ____

SIGNATURE OF CUSTOMER _____   DATE _____   , 20 ____

ADDRESS _____

_____

| CITY | COUNTY | STATE | ZIP CODE |

Company Address
Phone/Fax
E-mail
Web site

3.4   Predesign Letter

Company Name
Company Logo
Company Affiliations

‹Date›

‹Customer Name›
‹Customer Address›
‹City, State, Zip›

Dear ‹Customer›,

Thank you for selecting *‹Your Company Name›* to work with you on preliminary drawings for ‹insert type of work› at your home.

I've enclosed two copies of our design agreement for your review. Please sign one copy and return it to our office with a check for the retainer amount as indicated.

Please feel free to call me anytime if you have questions, or would like to make an appointment to meet at my office.

Thanks once again. We look forward to working with you on the design and construction of your project.

Sincerely,

‹Your Name›
‹Your Title›

Reply to: Your Company Name
Phone:
Fax:
E-mail:
Web site:

3.5   Post-Contract Letter

Company Name
Company Logo
Company Affiliations

\<Date>

\<Customer>
\<Address>
\<City, St, Zip>

Dear \<Customer Name>,

Thank you for choosing our company for your remodeling project. It is our intention to provide you with the very best in quality construction services. We continually endeavor to deliver what we have promised and when we have promised it. Here are a few ways that you can help us to help you.

Although we consider our project group among the very best in the region, unfortunately no one can predict with full accuracy the "absolute cost" of and "exact time to complete" a custom building project. Conditions may be discovered along the way that will require additional decision-making and additional time to address. This in turn requires a good deal of communication among all of us, including you.

Our project managers are always available to explain, listen, recommend, and take appropriate action. Please be sure to give us all of your contact numbers and information so that we can reach you promptly.

Completing your project on time is our primary goal. However, inclement weather may cause delays. Please understand that delivery schedules and trade contractor availability are not always in our control. We always strive to resolve delays and we do our best to work around them if possible.

If some portion of the project is to be furnished directly by you, such as specialty fixtures or perhaps your own tradesmen, we will need to coordinate the schedules for them with our production schedule. It is important that you are fully aware that these portions of your project cannot be completed without your diligence and cooperation, and therefore may delay the completion date. We warrant no work that we do not supply nor complete.

Also, please be aware that safety is a top priority on our projects. We will take appropriate safety measures, and we ask that you keep children and pets out of the affected areas.

We are pleased to be of service. Please do not hesitate to call with any questions or comments.

Sincerely,

\<Your Name>
\<Your Title>

Company Address
Phone–Fax
E-mail–Web site

3.6   Won Bid Thank You Letter

Company Name
Company Logo
Company Affiliations

<Date>

<Name>
<Address>
<City, St, Zip>

Dear <Name>,

We have received your signed proposal and appreciate your confidence and patronage of our company. The paperwork is being processed in our office. Our job superintendent will contact you shortly to schedule the work.

You have selected a long established company in the <Your community>community. You can be assured that we will do the utmost to expedite the work and do a professional job to your satisfaction.

Thank you again for selecting <*Your Company*>.

Sincerely yours,

<Your Name>
<Your Title>

Company Address
Phone
Fax
E-mail
Web site

3.7   Thank You Letter

Company Name
Company Logo
Company Affiliations

\<Date\>

Mr. & Mrs. _____
Address
City, State Zip

Dear ___ and ___,

THANK YOU for selecting \<Your Company Name\> to help with your project. We are all looking forward to the work that lies ahead.

In choosing \<Your Company Name\>, you've invited us into your home—and that is precisely how our employees will approach this project. There will be some disruption, certainly, but at all times we'll respect your property and treat you with courtesy. By doing so, we hope to make the remodeling experience for you both pleasurable and satisfying.

A successful project depends on effective communication. If you have questions or concerns as the job progresses, please voice them. Your primary contact will be _____, our Production Coordinator. _____ has extensive industry experience. I'm sure you will find him to be both eager to work and attentive to your needs.

If for some reason ____ is unavailable, please call our office. We'll do everything we can to address your concern or to respond to your request.

Again, thank you for choosing \<Your Company Name\>.

Very truly yours,

\<Your Name\>
\<Your Title\>

Company Address
Phone/Fax
E-mail
Web site

3.8   Time and Materials Terms and Pricing

Company Name
Company Logo
Company Affiliations

Time and Materials Terms and Pricing

CONTRACT AMOUNT: THE CONTRACTOR MAY HAVE SUBMITTED AN ESTIMATE OF COST TO COMPLETE THE PROJECT. PAYMENT BY THE OWNER WILL BE BASED ON THE FOLLOWING CRITERIA. THE TERM "ACTUAL COST OF THE WORK" SHALL MEAN COSTS NECESSARILY INCURRED BY THE CONTRACTOR IN THE PROPER PERFORMANCE OF THE WORK. COSTS TO BE REIMBURSED ARE AS FOLLOWS:

LABOR: THE CONTRACTOR WILL BE COMPENSATED FOR WAGES OF CONSTRUCTION WORKERS DIRECTLY EMPLOYED BY THE CONTRACTOR, TO PERFORM THE WORK AT THE FOLLOWING HOURLY RATES: OVERTIME HOURS WILL BE CALCULATED AT __ TIMES THE HOURLY RATE.

ARCHITECT	__.00 PER HOUR
DESIGNER	__.00 PER HOUR
PROJECT MANAGER/LEAD CARPENTER	__.00 PER HOUR
CARPENTERS	__.00 PER HOUR
SUPPORT CARPENTERS	__.00 PER HOUR

MATERIALS: THE CONTRACTOR'S INVOICED COSTS, INCLUDING TRANSPORTATION, FOR MATERIALS AND SUPPLIES TO BE INCORPORATED IN THE COMPLETED CONSTRUCTION, SUBSTANTIATED BY INVOICES.

SUB-CONTRACTORS: PAYMENTS MADE BY THE CONTRACTOR TO SUBCONTRACTORS IN ACCORDANCE WITH THE REQUIREMENTS OF THE SUBCONTRACTS.

EQUIPMENT RENTAL: THE RENTAL CHARGES FOR CONSTRUCTION MACHINERY AND EQUIPMENT SHALL BE PAID FOR AT AGREED UPON RATES SUBSTANTIATED BY INVOICES.

OTHER COSTS: THE CONTRACTOR WILL BE PAID FOR OTHER COSTS INCURRED IN THE PERFORMANCE OF THE WORK IF AND TO THE EXTENT APPROVED IN ADVANCE AND IN WRITING BY THE OWNER.

ADMINISTRATION FEE: THE CONTRACTOR WILL BE PAID THE TOTAL OF ALL COSTS AS QUALIFIED ABOVE, PLUS A MARGIN FOR ADMINISTRATION AND BUILDER'S FEE (THIS FEE IS CALCULATED BY TAKING THE TOTALS OF THE ABOVE ITEMS AND DIVIDING BY .70).

SALES TAX: THE CONTRACTOR WILL BE PAID THE AMOUNT OF <CITY, STATE> SALES TAX LEVIED ON ALL LABOR, MATERIALS AND THE BUILDER'S FEE. SALES TAX PAID BY SUBCONTRACTORS AND SUPPLIERS WILL BE CONSIDERED TO BE INCLUDED IN THEIR INVOICES AS NOTED.

PROGRESS PAYMENTS: CONTRACTOR SHALL SUBMIT AN APPLICATION FOR PAYMENT ONCE EVERY TWO (2) WEEKS WITH COPIES OF REIMBURSABLE INVOICES. APPLICATION FOR PAYMENT TO BE MADE BASED ON PROGRESS AND MATERIALS DELIVERED TO THE JOBSITE. PAYMENT TO BE MADE TO THE CONTRACTOR NO LATER THAN 7 DAYS FROM DATE SUBMITTED.

Company Address
Phone
Fax
E-mail
Web site

3.9   Lead Hazard Notification Receipt

Effective until April 2010.

Confirmation of Receipt of Lead Pamphlet

☐ I have received a copy of the pamphlet, *Renovate Right: Important Lead Hazard Information for Families, Child Care Providers and Schools* informing me of the potential risk of the lead hazard exposure from renovation activity to be performed in my dwelling unit. I received this pamphlet before the work began.

_____   _____
Printed name of recipient   Date

_____
Signature of recipient

Self-Certification Option (for tenant-occupied dwellings only)—
If the lead pamphlet was delivered but a tenant signature was not obtainable, you may check the appropriate box below.

☐ **Refusal to sign**—I certify that I have made a good faith effort to deliver the pamphlet, *Renovate Right: Important Lead Hazard Information for Families, Child Care Providers and Schools*, to the rental dwelling unit listed below at the date and time indicated and that the occupant refused to sign the confirmation of receipt. I further certify that I have left a copy of the pamphlet at the unit with the occupant.

☐ **Unavailable for signature**—I certify that I have made a good faith effort to deliver the pamphlet, *Renovate Right: Important Lead Hazard Information for Families, Child Care providers and Schools*, to the rental dwelling unit listed below and that the occupant was unavailable to sign the confirmation of receipt. I further certify that I have left a copy of the pamphlet at the unit by sliding it under the door.

_____   _____
Printed name of person certifying   Attempted delivery date and time lead
                                                                              pamphlet delivery

_____
Signature of person certifying lead pamphlet delivery

_____

_____
Unit Address

Note Regarding Mailing Option—As an alternative to delivery in person, you may mail the lead pamphlet to the owner and/or tenant. Pamphlet must be mailed at least 7 days before renovation (Document with a certificate of mailing from the post office).

3.9   Lead Hazard Notification Receipt (continued)

Company Name
Address
City, St, Zip
Phone
Fax

Date:

To: <Supplier/Contact>

From: <Estimator's Name>

Quote needed by:

1000	Windows & Doors	
	windows	Andersen w/ grilles and screens
		(7) 2817
		(8) 3052
		(2) 3032
		(1) 2032
		(3) 3042
		(4) 3046
		(1) 4446
		(2) 1046 side lts
	skylights	
	storm windows/doors	
	exterior doors	
	interior/closet doors	paint grade hollow core wood, flush
		(1) 3/0 × 6/8
		(1) 2/8 × 6/8
	sliding glass/French doors	Andersen brass hardware, grilles & screens when avail.
		(2) FWO060611APLR
		(3) FWG 6068L
		(1) ELFW6006 above
	garage doors	
	hardware	
	installation	

3.10   Lead Notification and Waiver of Testing

Company Name
Company Logo
Company Affiliations

Lead Paint Notification/Receipt/Release

We are parties to a construction contract with **<Your Company Name>** regarding work to be done to the property at _____ .

We understand that there may be building components that are coated with lead; and as a result, persons and/or pets may have been exposed to lead while inhabiting this structure.

We understand that the work to be done may disturb such building components and create additional risk of lead exposure.

<Your Company Name> has proposed that all inhabitants of this structure undergo blood tests to establish existing lead levels, and that an atomic absorption test be conducted to ascertain the lead level present in building components and home furnishings.

We have declined this proposal.

Knowing that our decision will make it difficult, if not impossible, to determine in the future whether any lead exposure could be attributable to the prior inhabitation of this structure rather than the current work being performed, we hereby release **<Your Company Name>,** its officers, directors, shareholders, employees, agents, successors and assigns, from any liability whatsoever to the undersigned and our children for lead exposure which may result from its work; and we assume all associated risks and agree to indemnify, defend and hold harmless **<Your Company Name>** from any and all such claims.

I have received a copy of the lead information pamphlet, informing me of the potential risk of lead hazard exposure in my dwelling unit. I received this pamphlet before work began.

Date: _____   _____

Date: _____   _____

Company Address
Phone
Fax
E-mail
Web site

3.11   Mold Disclaimer

Notice, Disclosure, and Disclaimer

What Home Owners Should Know about Mold

Mold. Mold is a type of fungus. It occurs naturally in the environment, and it is necessary for the natural decomposition of plant and other organic material. It spreads by means of microscopic spores borne on the wind. It is found everywhere life can be supported. Residential home construction is not, and cannot be, designed to exclude mold spores. If the growing conditions are right, mold can grow in your home. Most home owners are familiar with mold growth in the form of bread mold and mold that may grow on bathroom tile.

In order to grow, mold requires a food source. This might be supplied by items found in the home, such as fabric, carpet or even wallpaper, or by building materials, such as drywall, wood and insulation, to name a few. Also, mold growth requires a temperate climate. The best growth occurs at temperatures between 40°F and 100°F. Finally, mold growth requires moisture. Moisture is the only mold growth factor that can be controlled in a residential setting. By minimizing moisture, a home owner can reduce or eliminate mold growth.

Moisture in the home can have many causes. Spills, leaks, overflows, condensation, and high humidity are common sources of home moisture. Good housekeeping and home maintenance practices are essential in the effort to prevent or eliminate mold growth. If moisture is allowed to remain on the growth medium, mold can develop within 24 to 48 hours.

Consequences of mold. All mold is not necessarily harmful, but certain strains of mold have been shown to have adverse health effects in susceptible persons. The most common effects are allergic reactions, including skin irritation, watery eyes, runny nose, coughing, sneezing, congestion, sore throat and headache. Individuals with suppressed immune systems may risk infections. Some experts contend that mold causes serious symptoms and diseases which may even be life threatening. However, experts disagree about the level of mold exposure that may cause health problems, and about the exact nature and extent of the health problems that may be caused by mold. The Centers for Disease Control states that a causal link between the presence of toxic mold and serious health conditions has not been proven.

What the home owner can do. The home owner can take positive steps to reduce or eliminate the occurrence of mold growth in the home, and thereby minimize any possible adverse effects that may be caused by mold. These steps include the following:

1. Regular vacuuming and cleaning will help reduce mold levels. Mild bleach solutions or most tile cleaners are effective in eliminating or preventing mold growth.

2. Keep the humidity in the home low. Vent clothes dryers to the outdoors. Ventilate kitchens and bathrooms by opening the windows, by using exhaust fans, or by running the air conditioning to remove excess moisture in the air, and to facilitate evaporation of water from wet surfaces.

3.11   Mold Disclaimer (continued)

3. Promptly clean up spills, condensation and other sources of moisture. Thoroughly dry any wet surfaces or material. Do not let water pool or stand in your home. Promptly replace any materials that cannot be thoroughly dried, such as drywall or insulation.

4. Inspect for leaks on a regular basis. Look for discolorations or wet spots. Repair any leaks promptly. Take notice of musty odors, and any visible signs of mold.

5. Should mold develop, thoroughly clean the affected area with a mild solution of bleach. First, test to see if the affected material or surface is color safe. Porous materials, such as fabric, upholstery or carpet should be discarded. If mold growth becomes severe, call on the services of a qualified professional cleaner.

Disclaimer and Waiver.

Whether or not you as a home owner experience mold growth depends to a great degree on how you manage and maintain your home. Our responsibility as a home builder must be limited to things that we can control. As explained in our express warranty, provided by separate instrument, we will repair or replace defects in our construction (defects defined as a failure to comply with reasonable standards of residential construction) for a period of _____ years. We, the builder, will not be responsible for any damages caused by mold that may be associated with defects in our construction, to include but not be limited to property damage, personal injury, loss of income, emotional distress, death, loss of use, loss of value, and adverse health effects, or any other effects. **ANY IMPLIED WARRANTIES, INCLUDING AN IMPLIED WARRANTY OF WORKMANLIKE CONSTRUCTION, AN IMPLIED WARRANTY OF HABITABILITY, OR AN IMPLIED WARRANTY OF FITNESS FOR A PARTICULAR USE, ARE HEREBY WAIVED AND DISCLAIMED.**

This notice, disclosure, and disclaimer agreement is hereby appended to and made a part of the contract of sale. The consideration for this agreement shall be the same consideration as stated in the contract of sale. Should any term or provision of this agreement be ruled invalid or unenforceable by a court of competent jurisdiction, the remainder of this agreement shall nonetheless stand in full force and effect.

I acknowledge receipt of the notice, disclosure and disclaimer agreement. I have carefully read and reviewed its terms, and I agree to its provisions.

_____	_____	_____	_____
Buyer	Date	Seller	Date
_____	_____	_____	_____
Buyer	Date	Seller	Date

3.12   Preconstruction Orientation Checklist

Company Name
Company Logo
Company Affiliations

Preconstruction Orientation Checklist

Client: _____   Date: _____

Have you carefully reviewed all documents associated with your project? Do you understand and agree with what has been approved, including the Contract, Plans, General Specifications, Addendums, Terms and Conditions and Change Orders if applicable?   [ ] Yes   [ ] No

Questions you may have:

_____

_____

_____

Have you removed all personal property, valuables and breakables in and around the immediate vicinity of the work area?   [ ] Yes   [ ] No

Do you wish to designate any items scheduled for demolition that you do not want to be hauled? [ ] Yes   [ ] No

The starting time will vary from craft to craft, however the approximate starting time will be 8:00 a.m. and quitting time will be approximately 4:30 p.m. In order to have access to the project during construction, a key box will be placed on or near an entrance. Only representatives of **<Your Company Name>** will have a key or combination to open the box and obtain the key to the home.

Notes: _____

We proposed to place a company sign in your yard so that our people and suppliers can readily identify the project location. Also, we propose to send a mailing to local neighbors informing them of our presence in the neighborhood and spelling out any conditions such as hammering and sawing.

In order to maintain the safety and security of your children and or pets during the course of the remodeling project we need to be aware of any special instructions:

_____

The designated toilet facility shall be: _____

_____

Company Address
Phone–Fax
E-mail–Web site

3.12   Preconstruction Orientation Checklist (continued)

Company Name
Company Logo
Company Affiliations

From time to time, our craftsmen on the project may need to use the phone to order supplies. The designated telephone location shall be: _____

_____

Also, a designated communication area should be determined. This area is where notes, invoices, and checks can be left to assure proper communication continues on the project. The designated communication area shall be: _____

_____

If permissible with you, craftsmen are allowed to smoke (outside) during breaks when property disposing of cigarettes or other waste materials.
Notes: _____

If access to neighboring property is required, has written permission been obtained? [ ] Yes [ ] No

Have you notified your insurance company?   [ ] Yes   [ ] No

Have you notified your security company?   [ ] Yes   [ ] No

From time to time in a remodeling project it may become necessary to make additions or deletions to the scope of the project. When these changes result in a change of cost, a Change Order form will be used. Whenever possible the cost of the change will be determined <u>before</u> the change is made. There are circumstances where the change may have to be done on a time and material basis.

All product selections, including colors, styles and/or finishes should have been selected and recorded on the "Product Selection Sheets".

Payment Schedule:
1st _____
2nd_____
3rd _____
4th _____

Because draws are due upon presentation, will you need a few days advance notice in order to transfer funds and ensure timely payments?
[ ] Yes, I would like ____ days notice.   [ ] No, advance notice is not necessary.

We will supply you with lien waivers after each progress payment and at the final payment.
Notes: _____

Company Address
Phone-Fax
E-mail-Web site

3.12   Preconstruction Orientation Checklist (continued)

Company Name
Company Logo
Company Affiliations

Approximate starting date: _____

Approximate completion date: _____

Do you wish to have a regularly scheduled meeting with your Project Manager?

If so when? _____ or [ ] Meet on an as-needed basis

This schedule is only estimated and can change due to weather, product and labor availability, change orders or any other condition that may arise that affects the delay of the project.

Should you ever have any concerns or questions, please voice your concerns at your earliest convenience. We will, in turn, keep you advised of our progress and/or delays that may cause problems or misunderstandings.

We appreciate the opportunity to serve your needs.

Company Name:

By: _____   Date _____

Owner(s):

By: _____   Date _____

By: _____   Date _____

Company Address
Phone–Fax
E-mail–Web site

3.13   Emergency Information Sheet

Company Name
Company Logo
Company Affiliations

What to Do in Case of an After Hours Emergency

We want your construction project to flow as smoothly as possible. However, sometimes things just don't go as planned. What happens if there is an emergency after work hours or on a weekend?

What is an emergency?
- No electrical power or electricity not working in critical areas of your home
- A water leak that is causing immediate damage to ceilings, walls and/or floors
- No heat on a cold day or no air conditioning on a hot day
- Any life-threatening situation

What is not an emergency?
- Information you want to relay to <Your Company Name> or questions you may have that can be directed to the appropriate person the next workday
- New ideas or changes to the work you'd like to have implemented

Who should you contact in case of emergency?
1. Call the appropriate company for the situation:

Trade	Company name	Emergency Phone number
	<Your Company Name>	_____
Electric	_____	_____
Plumbing	_____	_____
HVAC (Heating/Air)	_____	_____
_____	_____	_____

You will not be charged for the services provided if it is determined that the emergency was caused by <Your Company Name> or any of its trade contractors.

2. If you cannot reach the appropriate tradesperson listed above, please call our emergency number, also listed above. If you still cannot reach someone within a reasonable amount of time, please contact an emergency company of your choice. You will be reimbursed for the cost if it is determined that the emergency was caused by <Your Company Name> or any of its trade contractors.

3. If the emergency is NOT obviously caused by any of the trades listed above, please call our emergency number and we will determine the next course of action.

We respect our employees' personal time and ask that you do not call anyone at home except in the most dire circumstances.

Thank you for your understanding.

Company Address
Phone/Fax
E-mail
Web site

3.14   Job Completion—Home Owner Sign-Off

Company Name
Company Logo
Company Affiliations

Job Completion—Home Owner Sign-Off

PROJECT NAME	
ADDRESS	
CLIENT(S)	

I understand that my project is substantially complete and the one-year [Your Company Name] warranty period begins now. I have inspected the job with the [Your Company Name] representative, and we agree that the following punch list items remain. [Your Company Name] will complete these items per our contract. I agree to pay all invoices, withholding no more than 1-½ times the value of incomplete punch list items.

[Your Company] Representative		Client(s)	
Date		Date	

Item No.	Description	Completed [Your Company]	Client

Do you have any questions on the care or operation of any items supplied to the job?
Please contact us if you have any issues with the work we have performed or any items with the scope of work.

Certificate of Acceptance

I agree that the punch list items have been completed to my satisfaction. Any additional work will be scheduled as a new job.

[Your Company] Representative		Client(s)	
Date		Date	

Initial   Initial

Company Address
Phone/Fax
E-mail
Web site

3.15   Certificate of Satisfaction and Payment Authorization

Company Name
Company Logo
Company Affiliation

Certificate of Satisfaction and Payment Authorization

That portion of the restoration for which <Your Company Name> is responsible has been restored to our satisfaction, and we hereby release and discharge <Insurance Company Name> from all claims and demands for that portion of the loss or damage handled by <Your Company Name> which occurred on or about the ___ of _____, ___, and authorize the payment of the cost of such restoration to <Your Company Name>, whose receipt for same shall be a complete release for said period of loss or damage.

<Your Company Name> guarantees all workmanship for a period of one year from the date of first occupancy or final municipal inspection. All materials used are covered by normal guarantees, if any, provided by the manufacturer and/or supplier.

_____
Date

_____
Owner

_____   Emergency Work

_____   Entire Job

Company Address
Phone/Fax
E-mail
Web site

3.16   Project Communication Sheet

Company Name
Company Logo
Company Affiliations

This form is used in the field to record all significant conversations, decisions. Keep in job folder in field.

Date: _____

Job Name: _____

Job Location: _____

Date of Contact	Description of Conversation	Person Talked To	Our Employee Name

Company Address
Phone/Fax
E-mail—Web site

3.17   Collection Letter 1

Company Name
Company Logo
Company Affiliations

Date

Mr. and Mrs. Customer
123 Main Street
Anytown, USA 12345

Dear Mr. and Mrs. Customer,

Ref. Project:

This is a friendly reminder that you have an overdue invoice with a balance of $<Insert Amount>. If you have any questions about the amount owed, please give us a call and we'll be happy to discuss it with you. If you've already sent your payment, please disregard this reminder.

We appreciate your continuing business, and we look forward to hearing from you shortly.

Sincerely,

Owner's Name
Title

Company Address
Phone
Fax
E-mail
Web site

3.18 Collection Letter 2

Company Name
Company Logo
Company Affiliations

Date

Mr. and Mrs. Customer
123 Main Street
Anytown, USA 12345

Dear Mr. and Mrs. Customer:

The following invoices are past due:

Inv. No.	Inv. Date	Due Date	Inv. Amount	Balance

Please send your payment in full immediately or call us to discuss the matter.

If we do not hear from you within 7 days, we will be forced to refer your account to our collection agency. This will have a negative effect on your credit rating.

Sincerely,

Owner's Name
Title

Company Address
Phone
Fax
E-mail
Web site

3.19   Waiver Release of Lien

Company Name
Company Logo
Company Affiliations

I, <Your Name>, being duly sworn according to law, depose and state that I am the <Your Company Title> of **<Your Company Name>,** the prime contractor for a(n) <project description> for _____ (hereinafter referred to as Owner), located at _____.

Undersigned warrants that he has already paid in full all of his laborers, subcontractors, and materials suppliers for all work, materials, equipment or services provided for or to the above referenced project up to the date of this waiver.

The undersigned hereby waives, releases and relinquishes all claims, or fights of lien upon the described premises for labor and material, general supervision of construction, or otherwise as of the last billing date with the exception of our final invoice in the amount of $_____ dated __-__-___.

DATED AND SIGNED THIS _____ DAY OF _____, 20xx.

By _____

<Your Name and Company Title>

STATE OF _____ }

COUNTY OF _____ }

On the _____day of _____, 20xx_, before me, a Notary Public, in and for the jurisdiction aforesaid, personally appeared before me, who being sworn by me first, duly acknowledged and declared that he/she is the person who signed the foregoing document and that the statements therein contained are true.

NOTARY PUBLIC_____

My commission expires_____

(Notary Seal)

Company Address
Phone
Fax
E-mail
Web Site

3.20   Design Retainer Addendum

Company Name
Company Logo
Company Affiliations

Addendum to Design Retainer Agreement

CLIENT:_____

ADDRESS: _____

_____has entered into a design retainer agreement with [*Your Company Name*] on _____ . This agreement was to develop a project as outlined with the scope of a specific budget range.

The scope of the project has changes as follows:_____
_____
_____
_____
_____
_____

This will require additional: ____ Design   ____ Engineering   ____ Code Appeals
                                  ____ Cost Analysis

An additional development fee of _____ Is required. This fee is accepted on the same terms as the original retainer. The fee will be deducted from the contract amount when all documents have been signed. The design will remain the property of [*Your Company Name*] if you do not proceed with the project.

Signed _____   Date _____

_____   Date _____
        Client(s)

Signed _____   Date _____
        [*Your Company*] Representative

Company Address
Phone
Fax
E-mail
Web site

3.21   Build-Remodel Contract

Company Name
Company Logo
Company Affiliations

Remodeling/New Home Agreement

<NOTE TO USER (TO BE DELETED BY USER BEFORE COMPLETING CONTRACT): DEPENDING ON WHETHER YOU ARE USING THIS DOCUMENT FOR NEW CONSTRUCTION OR REMODELING, NOT ALL PROVISIONS WILL APPLY.>

This AGREEMENT is made this the __ day of _____, 20xx__, by and between **<Your company Name>**, a <Your State> corporation, hereinafter sometimes referred to as "Builder", and **<CLIENTS' NAME, ADDRESS, CITY, STATE & ZIP CODE>**, hereinafter sometimes referred to as "Owners".

Builder is in the business of home building, construction, and general contracting in the _____ market. Said builder is a licensed general contractor (lic. #_____) and this can be confirmed by contacting the State of _____. Owners, **Clients' Name,** own a parcel of land, and structure(s) thereon, located in **City, State,** and more particularly known as **Clients' Address,** hereinafter sometimes referred to as the "Lot".

Owners desire to improve said lot/structure by completion of a project more particularly described in **SCHEDULE A,** attached hereto and thereby made a part hereof, and hereinafter sometimes referred to as the "Project"; and, trusting in the skill and expertise of Builder, wishes for Builder to do the construction.

The parties, therefore, agree to the following terms and conditions, including the Acknowledgments contained in Schedule B, included herein by reference. Builder will start the project on or about _____, **20xx__,** and will complete the project on or about _____, **20xx__.**

1. Construction: Builder will complete the project following and in accordance with plans and construction schedule delivered to it by Owners, which may be attached hereto as **SCHEDULE B** and may thereby be made a part hereof.

2. Consideration: Builder and Owners have discussed and agreed upon a general budget for the project. Each party understands that variables in construction conditions, materials, or costs may alter the magnitude of the budget. Owners agree to compensate Builder with payment pursuant to the scheduled payment plan attached hereto as **SCHEDULE C** and thereby made a part hereof.

3. Owners' Covenant: Owners covenant that they own the Lot and residence in fee and that the Builder's construction thereupon will violate the rights of no individual or entity having or claiming right, title or interest in or to the Lot. Owners will pay Builder sums for all bills incurred by Builder related to materials, permits, and labor on the project.

4. Builder's Covenants: The Builder will use its best efforts to complete the construction of the project by the completion date. However, if reasons beyond the Builder's control cause an unavoidable delay in the progress of construction (including, but not limited to, such factors as the unavailabil-

3.21   Build-Remodel Contract (continued)

Company Name
Company Logo
Company Affiliations

ity of materials, inclement weather, strikes, changes in governmental regulation, acts of governmental agencies or their employees, acts of God, or the failure of the architect or Client to perform their responsibilities in a timely manner under this Agreement), the Builder may request, in writing, an extension of the date of completion of the project.

The Builder will use its best efforts to complete the construction of the project by the completion date. However, if reasons beyond the Builder's control cause an unavoidable delay in the progress of construction (including, but not limited to, such factors as the unavailability of materials, inclement weather, strikes, changes in governmental regulation, acts of governmental agencies or their employees, acts of God, or the failure of the architect or Client to perform their responsibilities in a timely manner under this Agreement), the Builder may request, in writing, an extension of the date of completion of the project.

Builder will carry general liability insurance coverage and worker's compensation coverage; and generally promises to indemnify and hold Owners harmless for personal injury or property damage incident to Builder's work on the project on the Lot, which damage is not occasioned by the act or failure to act of Owners, their employees, agents, or invitees. If Owners have made payment to Builder as contemplated hereunder, Builder indemnifies and promises to hold Owners harmless for any claim or lien which may be asserted by any subcontractor, worker, or other entity or individual related to this project. Builder guarantees that all materials used in the project shall be in accordance with the requirements of code and regulatory authorities in the **City of _____, and County of _____, State,** and with any requirement promulgated or imposed by any lending institution which makes any mortgage or construction loan to Owners.

5. Lien: Owners grant Builder a lien upon the Lot and structures thereon for the value of the labor and materials contributed by the Builder, its employees, agents or subcontractors to the said realty. Said lien shall be released upon payment in full by Owners. See **SCHEDULE D** attached hereto.

6. Contract Changes: Our clients are reminded/advised that employees and specialty trades are on your job as agents of <Your Company Name>. Any task requiring our specialty trades or employees shall be performed strictly in compliance with our additional work order form. Any changes in this Agreement, or changes in the plans submitted to Builder by Owners, or significant changes necessitated in the methodology to be utilized by Builder in the project, must be agreed upon by the parties in writing. The parties will adjust the budget of the project to account for any costs incident to said changes contemplated and agreed upon by the parties prior to commencement of construction. Owners shall bear all costs incurred in changes which are contemplated and agreed upon after the commencement of construction. It shall be understood that every change will extend the length of construction. All charges related to the additional work order are payable at the time of signing the additional work order. Failure to comply with these procedures renders this contract null and void. See **SCHEDULE E** attached hereto.

3.21   Build-Remodel Contract (continued)

Company Name
Company Logo
Company Affiliations

7. Warranty: Upon completion of all improvements, the Contractor and Owner shall together per-form one "walk-through" inspection of the property and prepare a one-time only punch list of items requiring attention consistent with the Residential Construction Performance Guidelines: Contractor and Consumer References, 3rd Edition; the Contractor shall repair such items within a reasonable time thereafter. See **SCHEDULE F** attached hereto.

8. Default: In the event of default hereunder, the defaulting party agrees to pay, as a portion of those damages recoverable at law or in equity, all reasonable attorney fees, costs, and expenses incurred by the non-defaulting party in securing a remedy.

9. Assignment: This Agreement shall not be assigned or alienated by either party without the express written agreement of the parties.

10. Right of Rescission: This agreement may be rescinded by either party within three (3) business days from the date of execution of this agreement.

11. Notice to the Owners:

   A. Do not sign this contract if blank. You are entitled to a copy of the contract at the time you sign.
   B. Before construction begins, The Builder will present to you Schedule D, which shall signed and dated.

Schedule B:

1. EXISTING CONDITIONS: We make no representation of existing conditions and assume no respon-sibility of condition for any of the Owner's equipment that may or may not be relocated or affected by our work, unless such conditions are caused by an act of negligence on our part.

2. HIDDEN DEFECTS: It is acknowledged that hidden structural defects, faulty wiring, substandard plumbing, or other defective components of the existing house may need to be updated or replaced in order to properly complete the above-quoted work, and further acknowledge that the expense, if any, will be the responsibility of the property Owner.

3. DESTRUCTIVE INSPECTIONS: We have made thorough visual inspections of the existing structure and have made our analysis of the building methods and locations of covered systems. We have not made destructive inspections (that is, removing floors, walls, sidings, or other coverings) to reveal possible unknowns. In the event of a discovery of an unknown element, i.e. termite dam-age or water damage (not an oversight on our part), any additional costs involved shall be a cost incurred by the property Owner.

4. UNDERGROUND INSPECTIONS: It is unknown, by all parties, if any underground obstructions other than those stated in the text of this contract exist. If any such obstructions are found i.e. under-ground septic tank and/or field lines and must be removed from the site work area, the move-

3.21   Build-Remodel Contract (continued)

Company Name
Company Logo
Company Affiliations

ment of such obstructions causes an increase in the cost of the contract, then those costs shall be incurred by the property Owner. This provision shall not apply to anticipated roots of trees. It is acknowledged that there has been no soil stabilization test done on the subject site. If a test is requested by the Owner or by local authorities (for example, the Building Department), <**Your Company Name**> shall have such a test performed by a licensed engineer. All costs involved in this testing shall be the responsibility of the property Owner.

5. DELIVERIES: It is acknowledged that <**Your Company Name**> shall need to have heavy trucks picking up and delivering materials for the above-described work. The property Owner acknowledges this fact and releases <**Your Company Name**> from liability for possible damage to landscape; sprinklers; driveways (e.g. cracking or sinking); or sidewalks, where applicable, except in cases of gross negligence.

6. ADVERTISING: It is acknowledged that <**Your Company Name**> shall install a yard sign to facilitate delivery of materials, as well as to advertise. <**Your Company Name**> shall have the right to photograph its work and use the photographs for promotional purposes in brochures and in other advertising media. <**Your Company Name**> shall not advertise client names unless prior approval has been obtained from the client. We shall add client names to the current Past Clients List to be provided to potential clients, on request, as references.

7. UTILITIES: <**Your Company Name**> has not included costs for electrical, water, sewage, gas or telephone. It is understood that <**Your Company Name**> shall have full use of the Owner's utilities during the process of construction and that the Owner shall bear the costs of those utilities above and beyond the contract price agreed upon in this contract. Any long distance or directory-assistance calls made by <**Your Company Name**> shall be reimbursed to the Owner.

8. ALLOWANCE: The term "allowance" may be used in categories describing the scope of work or materials where the actual item or service to be provided has not yet been fully determined or has not yet been fully detailed in the plans. Whenever costs are more or less than allowances, the contract price will be adjusted accordingly by change order.

The parties have agreed to the terms hereof and executed this Agreement on the day and date written above.

OWNERS: BUILDER:

_____   _____

_____

(Please consider inserting the file language from The Paper Trail titled CONTRACT ADDENDUM which covers additional contracting contingencies.)

3.21   Build-Remodel Contract (continued)

Company Name
Company Logo
Company Affiliations

OUR CONTRACT SPECIFICALLY EXCLUDES ANYTHING NOT WRITTEN IN SCHEDULE A BELOW.

SCHEDULE A
Project description

3.21   Build-Remodel Contract (continued)

Company Name
Company Logo
Company Affiliations

<u>SCHEDULE B</u>
Project plans and specifications

3.21   Build-Remodel Contract (continued)

Company Name
Company Logo
Company Affiliations

SCHEDULE C

PAYMENT SCHEDULE

JOB: <NAME>
         <ADDRESS>
         <City, St, Zip>

NOTE: FAILURE TO MAKE PAYMENT WITHIN THREE (3) DAYS OF RECEIPT OF INVOICE CONSTITUTES
         A BREACH OF THIS CONTRACT AND THE BUILDER RESERVES THE RIGHT TO STOP ALL WORK.
         IN THE EVENT THIS OCCURS ADDITIONAL COSTS WILL BE INCURRED AND LEVIED AGAINST
         THE OWNER.

         PAYMENT NO. 1:   UPON SIGNING OF CONTRACT
                            IN THE AMOUNT OF $_____

         PAYMENT NO. 2:   UPON COMMENCEMENT OF FRAMING
                            IN THE AMOUNT OF $_____

         PAYMENT NO. 3:   UPON COMMENCEMENT OF SHEETROCK
                            IN THE AMOUNT OF $_____

         PAYMENT NO. 4:   UPON COMMENCEMENT OF TILE WORK
                            IN THE AMOUNT OF $_____

         PAYMENT NO. 5:   UPON COMMENCEMENT OF TRIM OUT II–
                            MOULDING STAGE IN THE AMOUNT OF $_____

         PAYMENT NO. 6:   UPON SUBSTANTIAL COMPLETION
                            IN THE AMOUNT OF $_____

              TOTAL $_____

*Substantial completion is defined as the following: we have received a sign-off on each item of our
quality control walk-through list. The quality control walk-through is conducted when we feel we
are completed. A one time walk-through with the client is performed in order to catch any item or
items the client may have concern about. Any items coming to our or the client's attention after the
quality control walk-through become warranty items and will be handled in a manner consistent
with our warranty policy. The owner will receive a copy of the signed-off Quality Control List at the
Job Closeout Ceremony.

3.21   Build-Remodel Contract (continued)

Company Name
Company Logo
Company Affiliations

SCHEDULE D

Delivered this _____ day of _____, 20xx__, by **<Your Company Name**>, Contractor. The above captioned contractor hereby gives notice to the owner of the property to be improved, that said contractor is about to begin improving said property according to the terms and conditions of the contract and that:

1. There shall be a right of lien upon said real property and building for the improvements made in favor of the contractor, <Your Company Name>, who does the work, or furnishes the materials for such improvements for a duration of one (1) year after the work is finished or materials furnished.

2. Upon final payment, in full, <Your Company Name>, Inc. shall present a notarized lien release, dissolving our right of lien, to the owner of said improved property.

_____

for <Your Company Name>   Date

_____

Property Owner   Date

_____

Property Owner   Date

3.21   Build-Remodel Contract (continued)

Company Name
Company Logo
Company Affiliations

SCHEDULE E

ADDITIONAL WORK ORDER

Job: _____

Date: _____

Additional Work to be Performed: _____

_____

_____

_____

_____

NOTE: THIS ADDITIONAL WORK ORDER WILL EXTEND THE LENGTH OF CONSTRUCTION BY _____ DAYS.

This work will be completed by _____.

Cost of Additional Work $_____   (To Be Collected In Full At Time of Execution of this Document)

Property Owner: _____

_____

Signature   Date

_____

for <Your Company Name>   Position   Date

3.21   Build-Remodel Contract (continued)

Company Name
Company Logo
Company Affiliations

SCHEDULE F

WARRANTY

OWNER:_____   DATE:_____

<Your Company Name> hereby warrants that the construction work performed at the above location is free from defects due to noncompliance with the Performance Standards referenced to and incorporated into this Limited Warranty for a period of one year from the date of substantial completion, date of commencement of use, or date of notice of completion, whichever occurs first.

The limited warranty is extended to the above-named Owner or Owners (referred to collectively as "Owner"), while occupying the house as a resident during the coverage period. This warranty is extended to the original Owner only and is not transferable to subsequent owners.

NOTE: Consequential and incidental damages are excluded and there are limitations in the duration of implied warranties.

NOTE TO OWNER: All homes go through a period of settlement and as the seasons change periods of expansion or contraction will occur. As a result, the home will experience minor material changes which are unavoidable and are considered normal. The Owner should also be aware that he/she is responsible for proper home maintenance such as maintaining contractor grades around the house. Damage caused by Owner negligence, improper maintenance or changes, alterations or additions performed by anyone other than the Contractor, his/her employees, or subcontractors directed by builder is excluded from the warranty.

It will be helpful to the Owner's home maintenance program to keep a color chart of the different materials used on the home and a small supply of corresponding colored paint, stain, grout, etc. for easy touch-up.

This limited warranty is subject to the following conditions:

This warranty covers the property above for as long as the said property remains in the possession of the Owner named above.

The construction work has not been subject to misuse, abuse, accident or neglect.

The construction work has not been modified, altered, defaced, worked on or repaired in any way by others.

The Owner will notify contractor of any defect within 10 days of discovery of that defect.

The Owner shall give the contractor the first opportunity to:

1) inspect the defect claimed, and
2) to effect the repair, replacement or payment of reasonable sums to affect those repairs.

Approximately eleven (11) months after final payment we will call to see if you have any warranty items that need to be addressed. If there are such items we will schedule a time to complete them.

3.22   Design-Build Construction Agreement

CONSTRUCTION AGREEMENT BETWEEN
GENERAL CONTRACTOR AND OWNER DESIGN BUILD

THIS AGREEMENT, is made and entered into this____day of_____, 20____, by and between _____, a_____, ("Contractor") and_____, a_____, ("Owner").

RECITALS:

WHEREAS, Owner has title or an agreement to acquire title to certain real property as described in Exhibit A ("Property");

WHEREAS, Owner desires that certain improvements be made on said real property, the scope and purposes as generally outlined in the specifications and plan as described in Exhibit B ("Project");

WHEREAS, Contractor desires to provide certain architectural, engineering and construction services to complete Project for Owner and shall complete detailed specifications and plans, to be set forth in Exhibit C; and

WHEREAS, Contractor and Owner desire to set forth in writing the term and conditions of their Agreement and intend to be legally bound by their Agreement.

NOW, THEREFORE, for and in consideration of the above premises, and of the following terms, conditions and mutual covenants of Contractor and Owner as hereinafter stated, IT IS HEREBY AGREED:

SECTION 1
OWNER'S OBLIGATIONS

1.01 <u>Project</u>.   Owner shall provide Property for Project. Owner shall furnish at Owner's expense certified surveys describing the physical characteristics, soil reports, legal restrictions, utility locations and legal description; and an ALTA title policy or other title report acceptable to Contractor. Contractor shall be entitled to rely upon the accuracy and the completeness of such information furnished by Owner.

1.02 <u>Other Requirements</u>.   Owner shall furnish at Owner's expense all necessary approvals; easements; assessments; expenses; building, use or occupancy and other governmental permits and licenses required for the construction; use or occupancy of permanent structures of Project; any bonds that may be required; and any legal services that may be required to obtain such items.

1.03 <u>Owner's Participation</u>.   Owner shall timely furnish Contractor complete information regarding Owner's requirements for Project. Owner shall designate in writing a representative who shall have authority to approve Change Orders and to furnish information on a timely basis. Owner shall promptly give notice to Contractor of any known fault or defect in Project or nonconformance with Project requirements.

3.22   Design-Build Construction Agreement (continued)

1.04 <u>Funding</u>.   Prior to Contractor commencing construction and at any subsequent time requested by Contractor, Owner shall furnish evidence acceptable to Contractor that sufficient funds are available and committed for the entire Cost of Project as set forth in Section 4. If such evidence is not furnished to Contractor, Section 8.02 shall apply.

1.05 <u>Safety</u>.   Owner shall require and cause all of Owner's tenants (if any) and all contractors separately hired by Owner to abide by and fully adhere to all applicable federal, state and local safety laws and regulations and to comply with Contractor's request for the elimination or abatement of safety hazards. Owner shall indemnify and hold Contractor harmless from all claims and damages arising from safety hazards caused by Owner's tenants and by separate contractors employed by Owner. Owner shall be responsible for the elimination or abatement of safety hazards created at Project by other persons employed by Owner as separate contractors or by Owner's tenants. Owner shall cause such separate contractors and such tenants to coordinate and cooperate with Contractor in all other respects of construction.

1.06 <u>Subcontractors</u>.   Owner shall not have a contractual relationship with Contractor's subcontractors and Owner shall communicate with such subcontractors through Contractor.

SECTION 2
CONTRACTOR'S OBLIGATIONS

2.01 <u>Design and Engineering</u>.   Based upon Owner's requirements, Contractor shall perform the necessary design and engineering and shall prepare detailed construction drawings and specifications to be set forth in Exhibit C (to be signed by Owner and Contractor). Construction of Project shall be in accordance with these drawings and specifications and with any subsequent drawings and specifications as approved in writing by Owner and Contractor. The drawings and specifications shall remain the property of Contractor and are not to be used by Owner for other projects without the written consent of Contractor.

2.02 <u>Construction</u>.   Contractor shall be responsible for the construction of Project and shall provide all supervision, labor, materials, tools, machinery, equipment and other items necessary for the completion of Project. Contractor shall use Contractor's best efforts to complete construction at the earliest possible time and shall at all times furnish sufficient materials and labor to assure an efficient completion of Project. Contractor is experienced and qualified to perform the work provided for herein and shall finance its own operations hereunder. Contractor shall operate as an independent contractor and not as an agent of Owner.

2.03 <u>Completion Date</u>.   The work to be performed under this Agreement shall be substantially completed on or before the_____day of, _____ 20_____(Completion Date) as set forth in Paragraph 5.01, subject however, to delays beyond the Contractor's control. In the event the work to be performed under this Agreement shall not be substantially completed by the Completion Date, then there shall be a penalty of _____.

3.22   Design-Build Construction Agreement (continued)

2.04 <u>Accounting</u>.   Contractor shall keep detailed records necessary for financial accounting of Project. Owner shall have access to Contractor's records, drawings, receipts and similar data relating to Project. Contractor shall specifically itemize all changes in Cost of Project and all Change Orders. Contractor shall maintain all records for a period of three years after Final Payment or longer where required by law.

2.05 <u>Safety</u>.   Contractor shall take precautions for the safety of Contractor's employees and shall comply with applicable provisions of federal, state and local safety laws to prevent accidents or injury to persons on Project.

2.06 <u>Subcontracts</u>.   All construction that Contractor does not perform shall be performed by subcontractors. The term "Subcontractor" shall not include any separate contractor employed by Owner or such separate contractors' subcontractors. Contractor shall be responsible for the management of subcontractors in the performance of their work. Contractor shall cause all subcontractors to indemnify and hold harmless Owner and Contractor from all claims for bodily injury and property damage that may arise, other than property damage required to be insured by Owner as set forth in Section 7.02.

2.07 <u>Clean Conditions</u>.   Contractor shall maintain Project free from the accumulation of construction waste and rubbish. Upon completion of Project, Contractor shall deliver Project in a "clean" condition, free from all trash, rubbish, debris, Contractor's tools, construction equipment and machinery, surplus materials and inventory.

2.08 <u>Warranties</u>.   Contractor warrants that all materials and equipment furnished shall be new, unless otherwise specified, and that all construction shall be of good quality, free from improper workmanship and defective materials and in conformance with the drawings and specifications. Contractor warrants that title to all work, materials and equipment shall pass to Owner upon delivery to Owner free and clear of all liens, claims, security interests or encumbrances ("Liens"). Contractor shall correct all work performed by Contractor which proves to be defective in material and workmanship within a period of one year from the date of completion. Upon written notice of such defects, Contractor shall, at Contractor's option, either make necessary repairs or request Owner to make such repairs at Contractor's expense. Contractor will secure required certificates of inspection, testing or approval and any and all express warranties from manufacturers, suppliers and subcontractors, and deliver same to Owner.

2.09 <u>Manufactured Equipment</u>.   Contractor shall guarantee manufactured equipment for ninety (90) days after initial use. Contractor shall collect all warranties and equipment manuals and deliver same to Owner. Contractor shall assist Owner's maintenance personnel with the testing and initial start up of such systems and equipment.

3.22   Design-Build Construction Agreement (continued)

SECTION 3
MUTUAL REPRESENTATIONS

3.01 <u>Litigation</u>.   Contractor and Owner hereby warrant and represent that neither is a party to or threatened with any litigation proceeding or controversy before any Court or administrative agency nor in default with respect to any judgment, order, writ, injunction, decree, rule, or regulation before any Court or administrative agency which might result in any adverse effect on representations, statements and conditions set forth in this Agreement.

3.02 <u>Conflicts</u>.   The execution of this Agreement by Contractor and Owner will not violate or conflict with or result in a breach of or constitute a default under any agreement or instrument which they may be bound. No consent of any third party not a party to this Agreement is required.

3.03 <u>Accuracy of Information</u>.   Contractor and Owner hereby warrant and represent that this Agreement does not contain any intentionally false statements and that this Agreement does not omit any material facts.

3.04 <u>Authorization</u>.   Contractor and Owner have the requisite power and authority for execution of this Agreement.

3.05 <u>Legal Responsibilities</u>.   Contractor and Owner shall comply, abide by and fully adhere with all applicable federal, state, local and municipal laws, regulations and ordinances applicable to any responsibilities of Contractor and Owner hereunder.

SECTION 4
FEES AND COSTS

4.01 <u>Contractor's Fee</u>.   Owner shall pay Contractor for the cost of Project as defined in Section 4.02 ("Cost of Project"). Owner shall pay Contractor compensation for services a fee ("Contractor's Fee") in addition to payments for Cost of Project. Contractor's Fee shall be _____

_____

_____.

4.02 <u>Cost of Project</u>.   Cost of Project shall include:

(a) Architectural, engineering and consulting fees incurred in design and construction of Project;

(b) Wages for Contractor's employees under (1) applicable collective bargaining agreements, if any, and (2) under salary or wage schedule agreed upon by Owner and Contractor;

(c) Salaries of Contractor's employees when stationed at the field office, and employees from the main office performing functions related to Project;

(d) Cost of all employee benefits and taxes for unemployment compensation and social security (all such cost based on wages or salaries paid to Contractor's employees);

(e) Reasonable transportation, travel, hotel and relocation expenses of Contractor's employees connected with Project;

3.22   Design-Build Construction Agreement (continued)

(f) Cost of all materials, supplies and equipment for Project and cost of transportation and storage;

(g) Payments to subcontractors for work performed pursuant to this Agreement;

(h) Cost, including transportation and maintenance, of all temporary facilities and hand tools which are employed or consumed;

(i) Rental charges for machinery and equipment, whether rented from Contractor or others, including installations, repairs, replacements, removal, transportation and delivery costs, at rental rates consistent with those prevailing in the area;

(j) Cost of premiums for all insurance and performance bonds which Contractor is required to obtain or that is deemed necessary by Contractor;

(k) Sales, use, gross receipts or similar taxes related to Project;

(l) Permit fees, licenses, tests, royalties, damages for infringement of patents (and costs of defending suits thereof), and deposits lost for causes other than Contractor's gross negligence;

(m) Losses, expenses or damages to the extent not compensated by insurance or otherwise (including settlements made with the written approval of Owner), and the cost of corrective work;

(n) Expenses such as telegrams, long-distance telephone calls, telephone service at the site and similar minor cash items connected with Project;

(o) Cost of removal of all trash and construction debris;

(p) Cost incurred due to an emergency affecting safety of persons and property;

(q) Cost of accounting services required herein;

(r) Legal fees reasonably and properly resulting from actions taken by Contractor on behalf of Owner or Project; and

(s) All costs directly incurred in Project and not included in Contractor's Fee as set forth in Section 4.03.

4.03 Non Cost Items: The following items are specifically excluded from Cost of Project (as set forth in Section 4.02). Such costs are included in Contractor's Fee:

(a) Salaries or other compensation of Contractor's employees at the principal office other than as described in Section 4.02;

(b) General operating expenses of Contractor's principal office other than Project's field office;

(c) Any part of Contractor's capital expenses, including interest on Contractor's capital directly related to Project; and

(d) Overhead or general expenses of any kind, except as may be expressly set forth in Section 4.02.

3.22   Design-Build Construction Agreement (continued)

SECTION 5

PAYMENTS

5.01 <u>Time Schedule</u>.   Construction of Project shall commence on or about the _____day of _____, 20 ___("Commencement Date"). Substantial completion of Project shall occur on the _____day of _____, 20 _____("Completion Date"). Contractor shall prepare an estimated progress schedule for Project which shall set forth the dates for the commencement and completion of the various stages of construction. The schedule and Completion Date may be revised as provided in Section 6.

5.02 <u>Progress Payments</u>.   On or before the _____day of each month after Commencement Date, Contractor shall submit to Owner an application for progress payment ("Application for Progress Payment") in such detail reasonably required by Owner and based on the construction completed, along with the proportionate amount of Contractor's Fee for such period, such aggregate amount hereinafter referred to as "Progress Payment." Within ten days after receipt of said monthly Application for Progress Payment, Owner shall pay Contractor the appropriate amount for which Application for Progress Payment is made.

5.03 <u>Retainage</u>.   Owner may retain ten percent (10%) of the amount of each monthly Progress Payment to assure performance of this Agreement. A reduction in the amount of funds retained shall be paid to Contractor if Owner and Contractor agree that satisfactory progress is being maintained in the construction of Project.

5.04 <u>Final Payment</u>.   The final payment, ("Final Payment") shall be due and payable when Project is substantially completed and (1) delivered to Owner ready for occupancy or (2) when Owner occupies Project, whichever event occurs first, ("Substantial Completion"); PROVIDED, HOWEVER, in the event that there should remain minor items to be completed, then and in that event Contractor and Owner shall list such items and Contractor shall deliver a written guarantee to complete said items within a reasonable time thereafter. Owner may retain a sum equal to One Hundred Fifty Percent (150%) of the estimated costs of completing any unfinished items; PROVIDED, HOWEVER, that each unfinished item and the estimated cost of completing each unfinished item shall be listed separately. Thereafter, Owner shall pay Contractor on a monthly basis the amount retained for such unfinished items as said items are completed for the previous month. Contractor shall provide Owner with a Certificate of Completion and Application for Final Payment prior to Owner's Final Payment to Contractor.

5.05 <u>Inspection</u>.   Progress Payments to Contractor shall not be construed as an absolute acceptance by Owner of the construction completed to the date of such Progress Payments except as to matters that are open and obvious. During the construction period, Owner shall exercise reasonable diligence in discovering and promptly reporting to Contractor all materials and labor which are not in accordance with drawings and specifications. Upon Completion Date, Owner shall diligently inspect all work for improper workmanship or defective materials, including work not open and obvious upon inspection during construction.

3.22   Design-Build Construction Agreement (continued)

5.06 <u>Payments Due and Unpaid</u>.   In the event Owner should fail to pay Contractor at the time that the payment of any amount becomes due under the terms of this Agreement, then and in that event Contractor may, and at any time thereafter, serve written notice that Contractor will stop work within five days after receipt of the notice by Owner. After the expiration of said five day period, Contractor shall have the right to stop all work on Project until payment of said unpaid amount has been paid to Contractor. Payments due to Contractor and unpaid shall bear interest at the highest legal commercial rate.

5.07 <u>Waiver of Claims</u>.   The making of Final Payment shall constitute a waiver of all claims by Owner except those rising from unsettled liens, improper workmanship and defective materials appearing within one year after Completion Date, except those previously made in writing and unsettled. The acceptance of Final Payment shall constitute a waiver of all claims by Contractor except those previously made in writing and unsettled as of this date.

5.08 <u>Discounts</u>.   All discounts for prompt payment shall accrue to Owner when paid directly by Owner or from a fund made available by Owner to Contractor for such payments. To the extent that such is paid with funds of Contractor, all cash discounts shall accrue to Contractor. All trade discounts, rebates and refunds, and all returns from sale of surplus materials and equipment, shall be credited to Cost of Project.

5.09 <u>Royalties and Patents</u>.   Contractor shall pay all royalties and license fees for materials, methods and systems. Contractor shall defend all suits or claims for infringement of any patent rights except when a particular design, process or product is specified by Owner.

SECTION 6
CONTINGENCIES

6.01 <u>Change Orders</u>.   All changes to Project shall be authorized by a written change order authorizing such change and signed by Contractor and Owner ("Change Order"). Each Change Order shall be numbered and dated, and shall clearly itemize the amount attributable to Cost of Project and Contractor's Fee and shall reflect any change in Completion Date. The value of the work added or omitted in a Change Order shall be agreed upon by Owner and Contractor. A Change Order shall be signed by Contractor and Owner prior to Contractor proceeding with the work set forth in the Change Order.

6.02 <u>Events Beyond Control</u>: Cost of Project shall be increased by a reasonable amount and Completion Date shall be extended by a reasonable period upon the occurrence of events beyond Contractor's control as agreed upon by Owner and Contractor. Such additional costs and fee adjustments required by any event beyond Contractor's control shall be evidenced by a written Change Order executed within a thirty day period after such event occurs. Such events shall include, but not be limited to, the following: (1) an act or neglect by Owner or by third persons not under the control of Contractor; (2) changes required to comply with new laws, rules or regulations; (3) labor disputes; (4) earthquakes, tornado, windstorms, floods or other actions of the elements; (5) war; (6) fire;

3.22   Design-Build Construction Agreement (continued)

(7) concealed and unknown conditions below the surface of the ground or concealed and unknown conditions in an existing structure at variance with the conditions indicated by the drawings and specifications, information furnished by Owner, or of an unusual nature differing materially from those ordinarily encountered and generally recognized as inherent in work of the character provided for in this Agreement; or (8) any cause beyond Contractor's control which Contractor could not have reasonably foreseen.

6.03 Material Price Increase:

Owner understands and agrees that a material allowance amount has been estimated and included to cover the entire expense of the {SPECIFY MATERIAL(s)} for this job. This amount is included to set the price on those materials in anticipation of potential material price increases beyond {CONTRACTOR}'s control. The MATERIAL ALLOWANCE AMOUNT IS: ${SPECIFY AMOUNT}.

{CONTRACTOR} will notify owner immediately during the job if material price increases cause the cost of {SPECIFY MATERIAL(s)} for this job to exceed the MATERIAL ALLOWANCE AMOUNT. The Owner may then, at his option, terminate this contract by providing within (#) business days both written notice of termination to the Builder and payment to the Builder for all costs expended in performance of the contract up to the date of termination, plus payment of ${SPECIFY AMOUNT} based on the percent of completion. If Owner fails to terminate this agreement upon notice of the material price increases within (#) business days, {CONTRACTOR} may proceed to purchase the {SPECIFY MATERIAL(s)} at the increased price, and the Owner shall be required to pay the increased cost as provided herein.

Final review of all specified material invoices will be reviewed by Owner and {CONTRACTOR} within 24 hours of job completion and the final price for the {SPECIFY MATERIAL(s)} will be calculated, along with (%) for administrative fees, and will paid to {CONTRACTOR} by Owner in addition to the final payment for the job.

<ALTERNATE LANGUAGE: ESCALATION CLAUSES>

Escalation Clause for Panelized Lumber

Option One

The house will require approximately _____ square feet of_____ (describe material: plywood, OSB, other). As of the date of this contract, the Builder's cost of _____ (describe material) is_____(price) per thousand square feet, based on _____(describe basis for determining cost: name of supplier). The stated consideration to be paid under this contract is based on current material costs without margin for fluctuations in the price of _____ (describe material). The current market for _____ (describe material) is considered to be volatile, and sudden price increases could occur. The Builder does agree to use his best efforts to obtain the lowest possible price from available building material suppliers. But, should there be an increase in the price

3.22   Design-Build Construction Agreement (continued)

of _____ (describe material) purchased after execution of this contract for use in the construction of this house, in order to avoid inequities, the Owner agrees to pay this cost increase to the Builder. Any claim by the Builder for payment of a cost increase, as provided above, shall require written notice delivered by the Builder to the Owner stating both the increased cost and the source of supply, supported by invoices or bills of sale.

Special Circumstances—Right of Termination

Should there be a rise in the cost of _____(describe material), exclusive of any other price changes, that would cause the total contract price to increase by more than _____(%) percent, the Builder shall, before making any additional purchase of _____ (describe material), provide to the Owner a written statement expressing both the percentage increase of the contract price and the dollar amount of the increase. The Owner may then, at his option, terminate this contract by providing within _____ business days both written notice of termination to the Builder and payment to the Builder for all costs expended in performance of the contract up to the date of termination, plus payment of a prorated percentage of profits based on the percent of completion. Should both notice of termination and full payment, as provided above, not be forthcoming within _____ business days, the Builder may proceed to purchase the _____(describe material) at the increased price, and the Owner shall be required to pay the increased cost as provided herein.

Escalation Clause for Panelized Lumber

Option Two

The house will require approximately _____ panels of_____ (describe material: plywood, OSB, other). As of the date of this contract, the Builder's cost of _____ (describe material) is_____(price) per panel, based on _____ _____(describe basis for determining cost: name of supplier). The stated consideration to be paid under this contract is based on current material costs without margin for fluctuations in the price of _____(describe material). The current market for _____ (describe material) is considered to be volatile, and sudden price increases could occur. The Builder does agree to use his best efforts to obtain the lowest possible price from available building material suppliers. But, should there be an increase in the price of _____ (describe material) purchased after execution of this contract for use in the construction of this house, in order to avoid inequities, the Owner agrees to pay this cost increase to the Builder. Any claim by the Builder for payment of a cost increase, as provided above, shall require written notice delivered by the Builder to the Owner stating both the increased cost and the source of supply, supported by invoices or bills of sale.

Special Circumstances—Right of Termination

Should there be a rise in the cost of _____(describe material), exclusive of any other price changes, that would cause the total contract price to increase by more than _____(%) percent,

3.22   Design-Build Construction Agreement (continued)

the Builder shall, before making any additional purchase of _____ (describe material), provide to the Owner a written statement expressing both the percentage increase of the contract price and the dollar amount of the increase. The Owner may then, at his option, terminate this contract by providing within _____ business days both written notice of termination to the Builder and payment to the Builder for all costs expended in performance of the contract up to the date of termination, plus payment of a prorated percentage of profits based on the percent of completion. Should both notice of termination and full payment, as provided above, not be forthcoming within _____ business days, the Builder may proceed to purchase the _____ (describe material) at the increased price, and the Owner shall be required to pay the increased cost as provided herein.

6.04 <u>Emergencies</u>.   In an emergency affecting the safety of persons or property, Contractor shall act, in Contractor's sole discretion, to prevent threatened damage, injury or loss. Any increase in the Cost of Project or extension of Completion Date on account of emergency work shall be determined as provided in Section 6.02 and 6.03.

SECTION 7
INSURANCE/INDEMNITY

7.01 <u>Contractor</u>.   Contractor shall purchase and maintain the following insurance:

(a) Workers' Compensation Insurance that shall comply with the state law of the site of the Project relating to compensation of injured workmen; and

(b) Comprehensive General Liability Insurance, for not less than such reasonable limits of liability as may be required by Owner. Such insurance policies shall contain a provision that the policies will not be canceled or not renewed until at least sixty days written notice has been given to Owner and Contractor. Certificates of Insurance showing such coverages to be in force shall be filed with Owner prior to commencement of the work.

7.02 <u>Owner</u>.   Owner shall purchase and maintain "All Risk" Builder's Risk Insurance. Owner shall purchase and maintain property insurance in a form acceptable to Contractor upon the entire Project for the full cost of replacement. This insurance shall include as named insureds Owner and Contractor and shall insure against loss from the perils of fire, extended coverage, and shall include insurance for physical loss or damage including theft, vandalism, malicious mischief, collapse, flood, earthquake, and damage resulting from defective design, workmanship or material. Owner will increase limits of coverage, if necessary, to reflect estimated replacement cost. Owner will be responsible for any co-insurance penalties or deductibles.

7.03 <u>Waiver of Subrogation</u>.   Owner and Contractor waive all rights against each other, Subcontractors and Sub-subcontractors for damages caused by perils covered by insurance provided by Owner, except such rights as they may have to the proceeds of such insurance. Contractor shall require waivers from all Subcontractors and Sub-subcontractors.

7.04 <u>Indemnity</u>.   Owner hereby indemnifies Contractor against all liabilities, claims and demands for negligent acts or personal injury or property damage arising out of or caused by any

3.22   Design-Build Construction Agreement (continued)

act or omission of Owner, Owner's separate Contractors and separate Sub-subcontractors, Owner's agents and employees arising from the commencement of construction until final completion. Contractor hereby indemnifies Owner against all liabilities, claims and demands for negligent acts or personal injury or property damage arising out of or caused by any act or omission of Contractor, Contractor's separate contractors and separate Sub- subcontractors, agents and employees arising from the commencement of construction until final completion. Contractor and Owner agree to use proper care not to cause damage to any adjoining or adjacent property. Contractor shall indemnify and hold Owner harmless from any liabilities, claims or demands for damage to such adjoining or adjacent property caused by Contractor. Contractor will not be liable for any damages resulting from the owner's negligence.

SECTION 8
TERMINATION

8.01 <u>Termination by Owner</u>.   In the event Contractor should at any time fail to perform the work with promptness or diligence, then and in that event Owner shall have the right to terminate this Agreement unless the Contractor begins to remedy such failure within ten days after receiving the Owner's notice of intent to terminate. In the event of termination by Owner, Owner shall pay Contractor for all work performed, all obligations incurred by Contractor which cannot be canceled, and the proportionate amount of Contractor's Fee.

8.02 <u>Termination by Contractor</u>.   In the event (1) the work should be stopped for a period of ten days by Owner, (2) Owner should fail to pay Contractor any sum then payable and due Contractor, or (3) Owner should fail for ten days to perform any other obligation hereunder, then and in that event Contractor five days after notice is sent to Owner stop work or terminate this Agreement and recover from Owner payment for all work performed, all obligations incurred by Contractor which cannot be canceled, all loss sustained upon Project or material, Contractor's Fee on the Cost of Project incurred, and any other expense, loss or damage which Contractor may sustain.

8.03 <u>Termination Without Cause</u>.   If the work should be stopped for a period of thirty days by any public law, regulation, acts of public officials or other causes not the fault of Owner or Contractor, then either Owner or Contractor shall have the right and option, upon ten day's notice to the other, to terminate this Agreement, in which event Owner shall pay Contractor for all Cost of Project, all obligations incurred by Contractor which cannot be canceled, all loss sustained upon the Project or materials, and the proportionate amount of Contractor's Fee.

SECTION 9
MISCELLANEOUS PROVISIONS

9.01 <u>Arbitration</u>.   Subsequent to the execution of this Agreement by the parties hereto, all claims, disputes, differences, controversies and questions that may arise concerning the matters and obligations set forth in this Agreement, or for the construction or application of this Agreement,

3.22   Design-Build Construction Agreement (continued)

or concerning any liabilities created hereunder, or any act or omission of any party hereto, shall be subject to arbitration in accordance with the rules and regulations then in force of the American Arbitration Association. The prevailing party shall be entitled to their costs including reasonable attorney's fees; PROVIDED, HOWEVER, this clause shall not limit the right of any party to seek temporary injunctive relief where an unacceptable interim period may exist between the time the decision to arbitrate is made and the earliest time at which arbitration can be commenced.

9.02   Time of Essence.   Time is of the essence of this Agreement.

9.03   Attorney's Fees.   Any party who unreasonably fails to perform any covenant of this Agreement as determined by the arbitrator shall pay to the other party the amounts of all attorney's fees and expenses incurred or sustained by such other party in enforcing performance by the other party.

9.04   Notices.   Any notices or other communication to be given under this Agreement to any party hereto shall be mailed certified mail, return receipt requested, addressed to such party as follows:

Contractor:_____

_____

_____

Owner:_____

_____

_____

A change of such mailing address by either party shall be made by giving notice to the other party in accordance with this Section. Such notice or other communication shall be deemed to have been given when so served, or upon the expiration of seventy-two (72) hours after such mailing, as the case may be.

9.05   Entire Agreement.   This Agreement constitutes the entire Agreement between the parties hereto and none of the parties shall be bound by any promises, representations or agreements except as are herein expressly set forth.

9.06   Amendments.   This Agreement can be amended, modified or supplemented only by a written document signed by the parties hereto. Any purported oral amendment, modification or supplement shall be void.

9.07   Filing of Agreement.   This is a confidential Agreement among the parties hereto and this Agreement shall not be filed of record with any city, county, state or federal authority.

9.08   Assignment.   The parties hereto shall not have the power or right to assign their respective duties and obligations hereunder unless such assignment is agreed to in writing by the parties hereto, or is provided otherwise herein.

9.09   Applicable Law.   This Agreement shall be construed according to the laws of the State of _____ regardless of where such Agreement is signed or the site of Project.

3.22   Design-Build Construction Agreement (continued)

9.10 <u>Unenforceable Provisions</u>.   If any portion of this Agreement shall be held to be void or unenforceable, the balance thereof shall nevertheless be carried into effect.

9.11 <u>Benefit</u>.   This Agreement shall be binding upon the parties, their heirs, legal representatives, successors and permitted assigns.

9.12 <u>Preamble Clauses</u>.   The preamble clauses hereto are hereby incorporated into this Agreement as though fully rewritten herein at length.

9.13 <u>Descriptive Headings</u>.   The descriptive paragraph headings contained herein are for convenience only and are not intended to include or conclusively define all the subject matter in the paragraphs accompanying such headings and, accordingly, such headings should not be resorted to for interpretation of this Agreement.

9.14 <u>Interpretation</u>.   Any words used herein shall be interpreted as singular or plural, and any pronouns used herein shall be interpreted as masculine, feminine or neuter, as the context so requires.

9.15 <u>Exhibits</u>.   All Exhibits attached hereto are made a part hereof by reference and are hereby incorporated into this Agreement as though fully rewritten herein at length.

9.16 <u>Acknowledgments</u>.   Each of the parties to this Agreement hereby acknowledges that such party has received a fully executed copy of this Agreement and further acknowledges that such party has carefully reviewed the representations, terms and conditions contained herein.

IN WITNESS WHEREOF, the parties have entered into this Agreement the day and year first above written.

"Contractor"

_____

By_____

Title_____

"Owner"

_____

By_____

Title_____

3.23   Design-Build Maximum Price Construction Contract

CONSTRUCTION AGREEMENT BETWEEN GENERAL CONTRACTOR AND OWNER DESIGN BUILD GUARANTEED MAXIMUM PRICE

THIS AGREEMENT, is made and entered into this____day of_____, 20___, by and between_____, a_____, ("Contractor") and_____, a_____, ("Owner").

RECITALS:

WHEREAS, Owner has title or an agreement to acquire title to certain real property as described in Exhibit A ("Property");

WHEREAS, Owner desires that certain improvements be made on said real property, the scope and purposes as generally outlined in the specifications and plan as described in Exhibit B ("Project");

WHEREAS, Contractor desires to provide certain architectural, engineering and construction services to complete Project for Owner and shall complete detailed specifications and plans, to be set forth in Exhibit A (list of documents to be provided).

WHEREAS, Contractor and Owner desire to set forth in writing the terms and conditions of their Agreement and intend to be legally bound by their Agreement.

NOW, THEREFORE, for and in consideration of the above premises, and of the following terms, conditions and mutual covenants of Contractor and Owner as hereinafter stated, IT IS HEREBY AGREED:

SECTION 1
OWNER'S OBLIGATIONS

1.01 Project.   Owner shall provide Property for Project. Owner shall furnish at Owner's expense certified surveys describing the physical characteristics, soil reports, legal restrictions, utility locations and legal description; and an American Land Title Association title policy or other title report acceptable to Contractor. Contractor shall be entitled to rely upon the accuracy and the completeness of such information furnished by Owner.

1.02 Other Requirement.   Owner shall furnish at Owner's expense all necessary approvals; easements; assessments; expenses; building, use or occupancy and other governmental permits and licenses required for the construction; use or occupancy of permanent structures of Project; any bonds that may be required; and any legal services that may be required to obtain such items.

1.03 Owner's Participation.   Owner shall timely furnish Contractor complete information regarding Owner's requirements for Project. Owner shall designate in writing a representative who shall have authority to approve Change Orders and to furnish information on a timely basis. Owner

3.23 Design-Build Maximum Price Construction Contract (continued)

shall promptly give notice to Contractor of any known fault or defect in Project or nonconformance with Project requirements.

1.04 <u>Funding</u>.   Prior to Contractor commencing construction and at any subsequent time requested by Contractor, Owner shall furnish evidence acceptable to Contractor that sufficient funds are available and committed for the entire Guaranteed Maximum Price as set forth in Section 4.02. If such evidence is not furnished to Contractor, Section 8.02 shall apply.

1.05 <u>Safety</u>.   Owner shall require and cause all of Owner's tenants and all contractors separately hired by Owner to abide by and fully adhere to all applicable federal, state and local safety laws and regulations and to comply with Contractor's request for the elimination or abatement of safety hazards. Owner shall indemnify and hold Contractor harmless from all claims and damages arising from safety hazards caused by Owner's tenants and by separate contractors employed by Owner, including, but not limited to, multiemployer citations issued by the United States Occupational Safety and Health Administration. Owner shall be responsible for the elimination or abatement of safety hazards created at Project by other persons employed by Owner as separate contractors or by Owner's tenants. Owner shall cause such separate contractors and such tenants to coordinate and cooperate with Contractor in all other respects of construction.

1.06 <u>Subcontractors</u>.   Owner shall not have a contractual relationship with Contractor's subcontractors and Owner shall communicate with such subcontractors through Contractor.

SECTION 2
CONTRACTOR'S OBLIGATIONS

2.01 <u>Design and Engineering</u>.   Based upon Owner's requirements, Contractor shall perform the necessary design and engineering and shall prepare detailed construction drawings and specifications to be set forth in Exhibit A (list of documents to be provided). Construction of Project shall be in accordance with these drawings and specifications and with any subsequent drawings and specifications as approved in writing by Owner and Contractor. The drawings and specifications shall remain the property of Contractor and are not to be used by Owner for other projects without the written consent of Contractor.

2.02 <u>Construction</u>.   Contractor shall be responsible for the construction of Project and shall provide all supervision, labor, materials, tools, machinery, equipment and other items necessary for the completion of Project. Contractor shall use Contractor's best efforts to complete construction at the "earliest possible time" and shall at all times furnish sufficient materials and labor to assure an efficient completion of Project. Contractor is experienced and qualified to perform the work provided for herein and shall finance its own operations hereunder. Contractor shall operate as an independent contractor and not as an agent of Owner.

2.03 <u>Completion Date</u>.   The work to be performed under this Agreement shall be substantially completed on or before the_____day of_____, 20___ (Completion Date) as set forth

3.23   Design-Build Maximum Price Construction Contract (continued)

in Paragraph 5.01, subject however, to delays beyond the Contractor's control. In the event the work to be performed under this Agreement shall not be substantially completed by the Completion Date, then there shall be liquidated damages of_____.

2.04 <u>Accounting</u>.   Contractor shall keep detailed records necessary for financial accounting of Project. Owner shall have access to Contractor's records, drawings, receipts and similar data relating to Project. Contractor shall specifically itemize all changes in Cost of Project and all Change Orders. Contractor shall maintain all records for a period of three years after Final Payment or longer where required by law.

2.05 <u>Safety</u>.   Contractor shall comply with applicable provisions of federal, state and local safety laws for the safety of Contractor's employees and to prevent accidents or injury to persons on Project.

2.06 <u>Subcontracts</u>.   All construction that Contractor does not perform shall be performed by subcontractors. The term "Subcontractor" shall not include any separate contractor employed by Owner or such separate contractors' subcontractors. Contractor shall be responsible for the management of subcontractors in the performance of their work. Contractor shall cause all subcontractors to indemnify and hold harmless Owner and Contractor from all claims for bodily injury and property damage that may arise out of the subcontractor's work, other than property damage required to be insured by Owner as set forth in Section 7.02.

2.07 <u>Clean Conditions</u>.   Contractor shall maintain Project free from the accumulation of construction waste and rubbish. Upon completion of Project, Contractor shall deliver Project in a "clean" condition, free from all trash, rubbish, debris, Contractor's tools, construction equipment and machinery, surplus materials and inventory.

2.08 <u>Warranties</u>.   Contractor warrants that all materials and equipment furnished shall be new, unless otherwise specified, and that all construction shall be of good quality, free from improper workmanship and in conformance with the drawings and specifications. Contractor warrants that title to all work, materials and equipment shall pass to Owner upon delivery to Owner free and clear of all liens, claims, security interests or encumbrances ("Liens"). Contractor shall correct all work performed by Contractor which is reported and proves to be defective in material and workmanship within a period of one year from the date of completion. Upon written notice of such defects, Contractor shall, at Contractor's option, either make necessary repairs or request owner to make such repairs at Contractor's expense. Contractor will secure required certificates of inspection, testing or approval and any and all express warranties from manufacturers, suppliers and subcontractors, and deliver same to Owner.

2.09 <u>Manufactured Equipment</u>.   Contractor shall guarantee manufactured equipment for ninety (90) days after initial use. Contractor shall collect all warranties and equipment manuals and deliver same to Owner. Contractor shall assist Owner's maintenance personnel with the testing and initial start up of such systems and equipment.

3.23 Design-Build Maximum Price Construction Contract (continued)

SECTION 3
MUTUAL REPRESENTATIONS

3.01 <u>Litigation</u>.   Contractor and owner hereby warrant and represent that neither is a party to or threatened with any litigation proceeding or controversy before any Court or administrative agency nor in default with respect to any judgment, order, writ, injunction, decree, rule, or regulation before any Court or administrative agency which might result in any adverse effect on representations, statements and conditions set forth in this Agreement.

3.02 <u>Conflicts</u>.   The execution of this Agreement by Contractor and Owner will not violate or conflict with or result in a breach of or constitute a default under any agreement or instrument which they may be bound. No consent of any third party not a party to this Agreement is required.

3.03 <u>Accuracy of Information</u>.   Contractor and Owner hereby warrant and represent that this Agreement does not contain any false statements and that this Agreement does not omit any material facts.

3.04 <u>Authorization</u>.   Contractor and Owner have the requisite power and authority for execution of this Agreement.

3.05 <u>Legal Responsibilities</u>.   Contractor and Owner shall comply, abide by and fully adhere with all applicable federal, state, local and municipal laws, regulations and ordinances applicable to any responsibilities of Contractor and Owner hereunder.

SECTION 4
FEES AND COSTS

4.01 <u>Contractor's Fee</u>.   Owner shall pay Contractor for the cost of Project as defined in Section 4.03 ("Cost of Project"). Owner shall pay Contractor compensation for services a fee ("Contractor's Fee") in addition to payments for Cost of Project. Contractor's Fee shall be

_____

_____

4.02 <u>Guaranteed Maximum Price</u>.   Contractor guarantees to Owner that the maximum price for (1) Cost of Project and (2) Contractor's Fee ("Guaranteed Maximum Price") shall not exceed_____ Dollars ($_____), unless by Change Order per Section 6.01 or Events Beyond Control per Section 6.02. In the event that Cost of Project and Contractor's Fee should exceed Guaranteed Maximum Price, then and in that event Contractor shall absorb such excess.

4.03 <u>Cost of Project</u>.   Cost of Project shall include:

(a) Architectural, engineering and consulting fees incurred in design and construction of Project;

(b) Wages for Contractor's employees under (1) applicable collective bargaining agreements, if any, and (2) under salary or wage schedule agreed upon by Owner and Contractor;

3.23 Design-Build Maximum Price Construction Contract (continued)

(c) Salaries of Contractor's employees when stationed at the field office, and employees from the main office performing functions related to Project;

(d) Cost of all employee benefits and taxes for unemployment compensation and social security (all such cost based on wages or salaries paid to Contractor's employees);

(e) Reasonable transportation, travel, hotel and relocation expenses of Contractor's employees connected with Project;

(f) Cost of all materials, supplies and equipment for Project and cost of transportation and storage;

(g) Payments to subcontractors for work performed pursuant to this Agreement;

(h) Cost, including transportation and maintenance, of all temporary facilities and hand tools which are employed or consumed;

(i) Rental charges for machinery and equipment, whether rented from Contractor or others, including installations, repairs, replacements, removal, transportation and delivery costs, at rental rates consistent with those prevailing in the area;

(j) Cost of premiums for all insurance and performance bonds which Contractor is required to obtain or that is deemed necessary by Contractor;

(k) Sales, use, gross receipts or similar taxes related to Project;

(l) Permit fees, licenses, tests, royalties, damages for infringement of patents (and costs of defending suits thereof), and deposits lost for causes other than Contractor's gross negligence;

(m) Losses, expenses or damages to the extent not compensated by insurance or otherwise (including settlements made with the written approval of Owner), and the cost of corrective work;

(n) Expenses such as telegrams, long-distance telephone calls, telephone service at the site and similar minor cash items connected with Project;

(o) Cost of removal of all trash and construction debris;

(p) Cost incurred due to an emergency affecting safety of persons and property;

(q) Cost of accounting services required herein;

(r) Legal fees reasonably and properly resulting from actions taken by Contractor on behalf of Owner or Project; and

(s) All costs directly incurred in Project and not included in Contractor's Fee as set forth in Section 4.04.

4.04 Non Cost Items: The following items are specifically excluded from Cost of Project (as set forth in Section 4.03). Such costs are included in Contractor's Fee:

(a) Salaries or other compensation of Contractor's' employees at the principal office other than as described in Section 4.03;

(b) General operating expenses of Contractor's principal office other than Project's field office;

3.23   Design-Build Maximum Price Construction Contract (continued)

(c) Any part of Contractor's capital expenses, including interest on Contractor's capital directly related to Project;

(d) Overhead or general expenses of any kind, except as may be expressly set forth in Section 4.03; and

(e) All Costs of Project in excess of Guaranteed Maximum Price.

SECTION 5

PAYMENTS

5.01 Time Schedule.   Construction of Project shall commence on or about the_____ day of_____, 20__("Commencement Date"). Substantial completion of Project shall occur on the_____day of_____, 20__("Completion Date"). Contractor shall prepare an estimated progress schedule for Project which shall set forth the dates for the commencement and completion of the various stages of construction. The schedule and Completion Date may be revised as provided in Section 6.

5.02 Progress Payments.   On or before the_____day of each month after Commencement Date, Contractor shall submit to Owner an application for progress payment ("Application for Progress Payment") in such detail reasonably required by Owner and based on the construction completed, along with the proportionate amount of Contractor's Fee for such period, such aggregate amount hereinafter referred to as "Progress Payment." Within ten days after receipt of said monthly Application for Progress Payment, Owner shall pay Contractor the appropriate amount for which Application for Progress Payment is made.

5.03 Retainage.   Owner may retain ten percent (10%) of the amount of each monthly Progress Payment to assure performance of this Agreement. A reduction in the amount of funds retained shall be paid to Contractor if Owner and Contractor agree that satisfactory progress is being maintained in the construction of Project.

5.04 Final Payment.   The final payment, ("Final Payment") shall be due and payable when (1) the Project is delivered to Owner ready for occupancy or (2) when Owner occupies Project, whichever event occurs first, ("Substantial Completion"); PROVIDED, HOWEVER, in the event that there should remain minor items to be completed, then and in that event Contractor and Owner shall list such items and Contractor shall deliver a written guarantee to complete said items within a reasonable time thereafter. Owner may retain a sum equal to One Hundred Fifty Percent (150%) of the estimated costs of completing any unfinished items; PROVIDED, HOWEVER, that each unfinished item and the estimated cost of completing each unfinished item shall be listed separately. Thereafter, Owner shall pay Contractor on a monthly basis the amount retained for such unfinished items as said items are completed for the previous month. Contractor shall provide Owner with a Certificate of Completion and Application for Final Payment prior to Owner's Final Payment to Contractor.

5.05 Inspection.   Progress Payments to Contractor shall not be construed as an absolute acceptance by Owner of the construction completed to the date of such Progress Payments except as to matters that are open and obvious. During the construction period, Owner shall exercise rea-

3.23 Design-Build Maximum Price Construction Contract (continued)

sonable diligence in discovering and promptly reporting to Contractor all materials and labor which are not in accordance with drawings and specifications. Upon Completion Date, Owner shall diligently inspect all work for improper workmanship or defective materials, including work not open and obvious upon inspection during construction.

5.06 <u>Payments Due and Unpaid</u>.   In the event Owner should fail to pay Contractor at the time that the payment of any amount becomes due under the terms of this Agreement, then and in that event Contractor may, and at any time thereafter, serve written notice that Contractor will stop work within five days after receipt of the notice by Owner. After the expiration of said five day period, Contractor shall have the right to stop all work on Project until payment of said unpaid amount has been paid to Contractor. Payments due to Contractor and unpaid shall bear interest at the highest legal commercial rate.

5.07 <u>Waiver of Claims</u>.   The making of Final Payment shall constitute a waiver of all claims by Owner except those rising from unsettled liens, and latent defects in workmanship and/or materials appearing within one year after Completion Date, except those previously made in writing and unsettled. The acceptance of Final Payment shall constitute a waiver of all claims by Contractor except those previously made in writing and unsettled.

5.08 <u>Discounts</u>.   All discounts for prompt payment shall accrue to Owner when paid directly by Owner or from a fund made available by Owner to Contractor for such payments. To the extent that such is paid with funds of Contractor, all cash discounts shall accrue to Contractor. All trade discounts, rebates and refunds, and all returns from sale of surplus materials and equipment, shall be credited to Cost of Project.

5.09 <u>Royalties and Patents</u>.   Contractor shall pay all royalties and license fees for materials, methods and systems. Contractor shall defend all suits or claims for infringement of any patent rights except when a particular design, process or product is specified by Owner.

SECTION 6

CONTINGENCIES

6.01 <u>Change Orders</u>.   All changes to Project shall be authorized by a written change order authorizing such change and signed by Contractor and Owner ("Change Order"). Each Change Order shall be numbered and dated, and shall clearly itemize the amount attributable to (1) Cost of Project, (2) Contractor's Fee and (3) Guaranteed Maximum Price and shall reflect any change in Completion Date. The value of the work added or omitted in a Change Order shall be agreed upon by Owner and Contractor, and the amount thereof added to or deducted from the Guaranteed Maximum Price. A Change Order shall be signed by Contractor and Owner prior to Contractor proceeding with the work set forth in the Change Order.

6.02 <u>Events Beyond Control</u>: The Guaranteed Maximum Price shall be increased by a reasonable amount and Completion Date shall be extended by a reasonable period upon the occurrence of events beyond Contractor's control as agreed upon by Owner and Contractor. Such additional

3.23   Design-Build Maximum Price Construction
Contract (continued)

costs and fee adjustments required by any event beyond Contractor's control shall be evidenced by a written Change Order executed within a thirty day period after such event occurs. Such events shall include, but not be limited to the following: (1) an act or neglect by Owner or by third persons not under the control of Contractor; (2) changes required to comply with new laws, rules or regulations; (3) labor disputes; (4) earthquakes, tornado, windstorms, floods or other actions of the elements; (5) war; (6) fire; (7) concealed and unknown conditions below the surface of the ground or concealed and unknown conditions in an existing structure at variance with the conditions indicated by the drawings and specifications, information furnished by Owner, or of an unusual nature differing materially from those ordinarily encountered and generally recognized as inherent in work of the character provided for in this Agreement; or (8) any cause beyond Contractor's control which Contractor could not have reasonably foreseen.

6.03 <u>Emergencies</u>.   In an emergency affecting the safety of persons or property, Contractor shall act, in Contractor's sole discretion, to prevent threatened damage, injury or loss. Any increase in the Guaranteed Maximum Price or extension of Completion Date on account of emergency work shall be determined as provided in Section 6.02.

SECTION 7
INSURANCE/INDEMNITY

7.01 <u>Contractor</u>.   Contractor shall purchase and maintain the following insurance:

(a) Workers' Compensation Insurance that shall comply with the state law of the site of the Project relating to compensation of injured workmen; and

(b) Comprehensive General Liability Insurance, for not less than such reasonable limits of liability as may be required by Owner. Such insurance policies shall contain a provision that the policies will not be canceled or not renewed until at least sixty days written notice has been given to Owner and Contractor. Certificates of Insurance showing such coverage to be in force shall be filed with Owner prior to commencement of the work.

7.02 <u>Owner</u>.   Owner shall purchase and maintain "All Risk" Builder's Risk Insurance. Owner shall purchase and maintain property insurance in a form acceptable to Contractor upon the entire Project for the full cost of replacement. This insurance shall include as named insureds Owner and Contractor and shall insure against loss from the perils of fire, extended coverage, and shall include insurance for physical loss or damage including theft, vandalism, malicious mischief, collapse, flood, earthquake, and damage resulting from defective design, workmanship or material. Owner will increase limits of coverage, if necessary, to reflect estimated replacement cost. Owner will be responsible for any co-insurance penalties or deductibles.

7.03 <u>Waiver of Subrogation</u>.   Owner and Contractor waive all rights against each other, Subcontractors and Sub- subcontractors for damages caused by perils covered by insurance provided by Owner, except such rights as they may have to the proceeds of such insurance. Contractor shall require waivers from all Subcontractors and Sub-subcontractors.

3.23   Design-Build Maximum Price Construction Contract (continued)

7.04 <u>Indemnity</u>.   Owner hereby indemnifies Contractor against all liabilities, claims and demands for negligent acts or personal injury or property damage arising out of or caused by any act or omission of Owner, Owner's separate Contractors and separate Sub-subcontractors, Owner's agents and employees arising from the commencement of construction until final completion. Contractor hereby indemnifies Owner against all liabilities, claims and demands for negligent acts or personal injury or property damage arising out of or caused by any act or omission of Contractor, Contractor's separate contractors and separate Sub-subcontractors, agents and employees arising from the commencement of construction until final completion. Contractor and Owner agree to use proper care not to cause damage to any adjoining or adjacent property. Contractor shall indemnify and hold Owner harmless from any liabilities, claims or demands for damage to such adjoining or adjacent property caused solely by Contractor.

SECTION 8
TERMINATION

8.01 <u>Termination by Owner</u>.   In the event Contractor should at any time fail to perform the work with promptness or diligence, then and in that event Owner shall have the right to terminate this Agreement after ten days notice to Contractor (unless within said ten day period Contractor begins to remedy such failure). In the event of termination by Owner, Owner shall pay Contractor for all work performed, all obligations incurred by Contractor which cannot be canceled, and the proportionale amount of Contractor's Fee.

8.02 <u>Termination by Contractor</u>.   In the event (1) the work should be stopped for a period of ten days by Owner, (2) Owner should fail to pay Contractor any sum then payable and due Contractor, or (3) Owner should fail for ten days to perform any other obligation hereunder, then and in that event Contractor may after five days notice to Owner stop work or terminate this Agreement and recover from Owner payment for all work performed, all obligations incurred by Contractor which cannot be canceled, all loss sustained upon Project or material, Contractor's Fee on the Cost of Project incurred, and any other expense, loss or damage which Contractor may sustain.

8.03 <u>Termination Without Cause</u>.   If the work should be stopped for a period of thirty days by any public law, regulation, acts of public officials or other causes not the fault of Owner or Contractor, then either Owner or Contractor shall have the right and option, upon ten day's notice to the other, to terminate this Agreement, in which event Owner shall pay Contractor for all Cost of Project, all obligations incurred by Contractor which cannot be canceled, all loss sustained upon the Project or materials, and the proportionate amount of Contractor's Fee.

3.23   Design-Build Maximum Price Construction Contract (continued)

SECTION 9
MISCELLANEOUS PROVISIONS

9.01 <u>Arbitration</u>.   Subsequent to the execution of this Agreement by the parties hereto, all claims, disputes, differences, controversies and questions which may arise concerning the matters and obligations set forth in this Agreement, or for the construction or application of this Agreement, or concerning any liabilities created hereunder, or any act or omission of any party hereto, shall be subject to arbitration in accordance with the rules and regulations then in force of the American Arbitration Association. The prevailing party, as specifically determined by the Arbitrator, shall be entitled to their costs including reasonable attorney's fees; PROVIDED, HOWEVER, this clause shall not limit the right of any party to period may exist between the time the decision to arbitrate is made and the earliest time at which arbitration can be commenced.

9.02 <u>Time of Essence</u>.   Time is of the essence of this Agreement.

9.03 <u>Attorney's Fees</u>.   Any party who unreasonably fails to perform any covenant of this Agreement shall pay to the other party the amounts of all attorney's fees and expenses incurred or sustained by such other party in enforcing performance by the other party.

9.04 <u>Notices</u>.   Any notices or other communication to be given under this Agreement to any party hereto shall be mailed certified mail, return receipt requested, addressed to such party as follows:

Contractor _____

_____

_____

Owner _____

_____

_____

A change of such mailing address by either party shall be made by giving notice to the other party in accordance with this Section. Such notice or other communication shall be deemed to have been given when so served, or upon the expiration of seventy-two (72) hours after such mailing, as the case may be.

9.05 <u>Entire Agreement</u>.   This Agreement constitutes the entire Agreement between the parties hereto and none of the parties shall be bound by any promises, representations or agreements except as are herein expressly set forth.

9.06 <u>Amendments</u>.   This Agreement can be amended, modified or supplemented only by a written document signed by the parties hereto. Any purported oral amendment, modification or supplement shall be void.

9.07 <u>Filing of Agreement</u>.   This is a confidential Agreement among the parties hereto and this Agreement shall not be filed of record with any city, county, state or federal authority.

3.23   Design-Build Maximum Price Construction Contract (continued)

9.08 <u>Assignment</u>.   The parties hereto shall not have the power or right to assign their respective duties and obligations hereunder unless such assignment is agreed to in writing by the parties hereto, or is provided otherwise herein.

9.09 <u>Applicable Law</u>.   This Agreement shall be construed according to the laws of the State of_____, regardless of where such Agreement is Signed or the site of project.

9.10 <u>Unenforceable Provisions</u>.   If any portion of this Agreement shall be held to be void or unenforceable, the balance thereof shall nevertheless be carried into effect.

9.11 <u>Benefit</u>.   This Agreement shall be binding upon the parties, their heirs, legal representatives successors and permitted assigns.

9.12 <u>Preamble Clauses</u>.   The preamble clauses hereto are hereby incorporated into this Agreement as though fully rewritten herein at length.

9.13 <u>Descriptive Heading</u>.   The descriptive paragraph headings contained herein are for convenience only and are not intended to include or conclusively define all the subject matter in the paragraphs accompanying such headings band, accordingly, such headings should not be resorted to for interpretation of this Agreement.

9.14 <u>Interpretation</u>.   Any words used herein shall be interpreted as singular or plural, and any pronouns used herein shall be interpreted as masculine, feminine or neuter, as the context so requires.

9.15 <u>Exhibits</u>.   All Exhibits attached hereto are made a part hereof by reference and are hereby incorporated into this Agreement as though fully rewritten herein at length.

9.16 <u>Acknowledgments</u>.   Each of the parties to this Agreement hereby acknowledges that such party has received a fully executed copy of this Agreement and further acknowledges that such party has carefully reviewed the representations, terms and conditions contained herein.

IN WITNESS WHEREOF, the parties have entered into this Agreement the day and year first above written.

"Contractor"

_____

By_____

Title_____

"Owner"

_____

By_____

Title_____

3.24   Build-Only Construction Agreement

CONSTRUCTION AGREEMENT BETWEEN
GENERAL CONTRACTOR AND OWNER
BUILD ONLY

THIS AGREEMENT, is made and entered into this_____day of_____, 20____, by and between_____, a_____, ("Contractor") and_____, a_____, ("Owner").

RECITALS:

WHEREAS, Owner has title or an agreement to acquire title to certain real property as described in Exhibit A ("Property");

WHEREAS, Owner desires that certain improvements be made on said real property, the scope and purposes as generally outlined in the specifications and plan as described in Exhibit B ("Project");

WHEREAS, Contractor desires to provide certain architectural, engineering and construction services to complete Project for Owner and shall complete detailed specifications and plans, to be set forth in Exhibit C; and

WHEREAS, Contractor and Owner desire to set forth in writing the terms and conditions of their Agreement and intend to be legally bound by their Agreement.

NOW, THEREFORE, for and in consideration of the above premises, and of the following terms, conditions and mutual covenants of Contractor and Owner as hereinafter stated, IT IS HEREBY AGREED:

SECTION 1
OWNER'S OBLIGATIONS

1.01 <u>Project</u>.   Owner shall provide Property for Project. Owner shall furnish at Owner's expense certified surveys describing the physical characteristics, soil reports, legal restrictions, utility locations and legal description; and an ALTA title policy or other title report acceptable to Contractor. Contractor shall be entitled to rely upon the accuracy and the completeness of such information furnished by Owner.

1.02 <u>Design and Engineering</u>.   Owner has furnished Contractor with Owner's design, engineering and detailed construction drawings and specifications as set forth in Exhibit C (to be signed by Owner and Contractor). Construction of Project shall be in accordance with these drawings and specifications and with any subsequent drawings and specifications as approved in writing by Owner and Contractor. The drawings and specifications shall remain the property of Contractor and are not to be used by Owner for other projects without the written consent of Contractor.

1.03 <u>Other Requirements</u>.   Owner shall furnish at Owner's expense all necessary approvals; easements; assessments; expenses; building, use or occupancy and other governmental permits

3.24   Build-Only Construction Agreement (continued)

and licenses required for the construction; use or occupancy of permanent structures of Project; any bonds that may be required; and any legal services that may be required to obtain such items.

1.04 <u>Owner's Participation</u>.   Owner shall timely furnish Contractor complete information regarding Owner's requirements for Project. Owner shall designate in writing a representative who shall have authority to approve Change Orders and to furnish information on a timely basis. Owner shall promptly give notice to Contractor of any known fault or defect in Project or nonconformance with Project requirements.

1.05 <u>Funding</u>.   Prior to Contractor commencing construction and at any subsequent time requested by Contractor, Owner shall furnish evidence acceptable to Contractor that sufficient funds are available and committed for the entire Cost of Project as set forth in Section 4. If such evidence is not furnished to Contractor, Section 8.02 shall apply.

1.06 <u>Safety</u>.   Owner shall require and cause all of Owner's tenants and all contractors separately hired by Owner to abide by and fully adhere to all applicable federal, state and local safety laws and regulations and to comply with Contractor's request for the elimination or abatement of safety hazards. Owner shall indemnify and hold Contractor harmless from all claims and damages arising from safety hazards caused by Owner's tenants and by separate contractors employed by Owner. Owner shall be responsible for the elimination or abatement of safety hazards created at Project by other persons employed by Owner as separate contractors or by Owner's tenants. Owner shall cause such separate contractors and such tenants to coordinate and cooperate with Contractor in all other respects of construction.

1.07 <u>Subcontractors</u>.   Owner shall not have a contractual relationship with Contractor's subcontractors and Owner shall communicate with such subcontractors through Contractor.

SECTION 2
CONTRACTOR'S OBLIGATIONS

2.01 <u>Construction</u>.   Contractor shall be responsible for the construction of Project and shall provide all supervision, labor, materials, tools, machinery, equipment and other items necessary for the completion of Project. Contractor shall use Contractor's best efforts to complete construction by the completion date and shall at all times furnish sufficient materials and labor to assure an efficient completion of Project. Contractor is experienced and qualified to perform the work provided for herein and shall finance its own operations hereunder. Contractor shall operate as an independent contractor and not as an agent of Owner.

2.02 <u>Completion Date</u>.   The work to be performed under this Agreement shall be substantially completed on or before the_____day of_____, 20___(Completion Date) as set forth in Paragraph 5.01, subject however, to delays beyond the Contractor's control. In the event the work to be performed under this Agreement shall not be substantially completed by the Completion Date, then there shall be a penalty of_____.

3.24   Build-Only Construction Agreement (continued)

2.03 <u>Accounting</u>.   Contractor shall keep detailed records necessary for financial accounting of Project. Owner shall have access to Contractor's records, drawings, receipts and similar data relating to Project. Contractor shall specifically itemize all changes in Cost of Project and all Change Orders. Contractor shall maintain all records for a period of three years after Final Payment or longer where required by law.

2.04 <u>Safety</u>.   Contractor shall take precautions for the safety of Contractor's employees and shall comply with applicable provisions of federal, state and local safety laws to prevent accidents or injury to persons on Project.

2.05 <u>Subcontracts</u>.   All construction that Contractor does not perform shall be performed by subcontractors. The term "subcontractor" shall not include any separate contractor employed by Owner or such separate contractors' subcontractors. Contractor shall be responsible for the management of subcontractors in the performance of their work. Contractor shall cause all subcontractors to indemnify and hold harmless Owner and Contractor from all claims for bodily injury and property damage that may arise, other than property damage required to be insured by Owner as set forth in Section 7.02.

2.06 <u>Clean Conditions</u>.   Contractor shall maintain Project free from the accumulation of construction waste and rubbish. Upon completion of Project, Contractor shall deliver Project in a "clean" condition, free from all trash, rubbish, debris, Contractor's tools, construction equipment and machinery, surplus materials and inventory.

2.07 <u>Warranties</u>.   Contractor warrants that all materials and equipment furnished shall be new, unless otherwise specified, and that all construction shall be of good quality, free from improper workmanship and defective materials and in conformance with the drawings and specifications. Contractor warrants that title to all work, materials and equipment shall pass to Owner upon delivery to Owner free and clear of all liens, claims, security interests or encumbrances ("Liens"). Contractor shall correct all work performed by Contractor which is reported and proves to be defective in material and workmanship within a period of one year from the date of completion. Upon written notice of such defects, Contractor shall, at Contractor's option, either make necessary repairs or request Owner to make such repairs at Contractor's expense. Contractor will secure required certificates of inspection, testing or approval and any and all express warranties from manufacturers, suppliers and subcontractors, and deliver same to Owner.

2.08 <u>Manufactured Equipment</u>.   Contractor shall guarantee manufactured equipment for ninety (90) days after initial use. Contractor shall collect all warranties and equipment manuals and deliver same to Owner. Contractor shall assist Owner's maintenance personnel with the testing and initial start up of such systems and equipment.

3.24   Build-Only Construction Agreement (continued)

SECTION 3
MUTUAL REPRESENTATIONS

3.01 <u>Litigation</u>.   Contractor and Owner hereby warrant and represent that neither is a party to or threatened with any litigation proceeding or controversy before any Court or administrative agency nor in default with respect to any judgment, order, writ, injunction, decree, rule, or regulation before any Court or administrative agency which might result in any adverse effect on representations, statements and conditions set forth in this Agreement.

3.02 <u>Conflicts</u>.   The execution of this Agreement by Contractor and Owner will not violate or conflict with or result in a breach of or constitute a default under any agreement or instrument which they may be bound. No consent of any third party not a party to this Agreement is required.

3.03 <u>Accuracy of Information</u>.   Contractor and Owner hereby warrant and represent that this Agreement does not contain any intentionally false statements and that this Agreement does not omit any material facts.

3.04 <u>Authorization</u>.   Contractor and Owner have the requisite power and authority for execution of this Agreement.

3.05 <u>Legal Responsibilities</u>.   Contractor and Owner shall comply, abide by and fully adhere with all applicable federal, state, local and municipal laws, regulations and ordinances applicable to any responsibilities of Contractor and Owner hereunder.

SECTION 4
FEES AND COSTS

4.01 <u>Contractor's Fee</u>.   Owner shall pay Contractor for the cost of Project as defined in Section 4.02 ("Cost of Project"). Owner shall pay Contractor a fee as compensation for services ("Contractor's Fee") in addition to payments for Cost of Project. Contractor's Fee shall be_____

_____.

4.02 <u>Cost of Project</u>.   Cost of Project shall include:

(a) Architectural, engineering and consulting fees incurred in design and construction of Project;

(b) Wages for Contractor's employees under (1) applicable collective bargaining agreements, if any, and (2) under salary or wage schedule agreed upon by Owner and Contractor;

(c) Salaries of Contractor's employees when stationed at the field office, and employees from the main office performing functions related to Project;

(d) Cost of all employee benefits and taxes for unemployment compensation and social security (all such cost based on wages or salaries paid to Contractor's employees);

3.24   Build-Only Construction Agreement (continued)

(e) Reasonable transportation, travel, hotel and relocation expenses of Contractor's employees connected with Project;

(f) Cost of all materials, supplies and equipment for Project and cost of transportation and storage;

(g) Payments to subcontractors for work performed pursuant to this Agreement;

(h) Cost, including transportation and maintenance, of all temporary facilities and hand tools which are employed or consumed;

(i) Rental charges for machinery and equipment, whether rented from Contractor or others, including installations, repairs, replacements, removal, transportation and delivery costs, at rental rates consistent with those prevailing in the area;

(j) Cost of premiums for all insurance and performance bonds which Contractor is required to obtain or that is deemed necessary by Contractor;

(k) Sales, use, gross receipts or similar taxes related to Project;

(l) Permit fees, licenses, tests, royalties, damages for infringement of patents (and costs of defending suits thereof), and deposits lost for causes other than Contractor's gross negligence;

(m) Losses, expenses or damages to the extent not compensated by insurance or otherwise (including settlements made with the written approval of Owner), and the cost of corrective work;

(n) Expenses such as telegrams, long-distance telephone calls, telephone service at the site and similar minor cash items connected with Project;

(o) Cost of removal of all trash and construction debris;

(p) Cost incurred due to an emergency affecting safety of persons and property;

(q) Cost of accounting services required herein;

(r) Legal fees reasonably and properly resulting from actions taken by Contractor on behalf of Owner or Project; and

(s) All costs directly incurred in Project and not included in Contractor's Fee as set forth in Section 4.03.

4.03 Non Cost Items: The following items are specifically excluded from Cost of Project (as set forth in Section 4.02). Such costs are included in Contractor's Fee:

(a) Salaries or other compensation of Contractor's employees at the principal office other than as described in Section 4.02;

(b) General operating expenses of Contractor's principal office other than Project's field office;

(c) Any part of Contractor's capital expenses, including interest on Contractor's capital directly related to Project; and

(d) Overhead or general expenses of any kind, except as may be expressly set forth in Section 4.02.

3.24   Build-Only Construction Agreement (continued)

SECTION 5
PAYMENTS

5.01 <u>Time Schedule</u>.   Construction of Project shall commence on or about the_____day of_____, 20____("Commencement Date"). Substantial completion of Project shall occur on the_____day of_____, 20____("Completion Date"). Contractor shall prepare an estimated progress schedule for Project which shall set forth the dates for the commencement and completion of the various stages of construction. The schedule and Completion Date may be revised as provided in Section 6.

5.02 <u>Progress Payments</u>.   On or before the_____day of each month after Commencement Date, Contractor shall submit to Owner an application for progress payment ("Application for Progress Payment") in such detail reasonably required by Owner and based on the construction completed, along with the proportionate amount of Contractor's Fee for such period, such aggregate amount hereinafter referred to as "Progress Payment." Within ten days after receipt of said monthly Application for Progress Payment, Owner shall pay Contractor the appropriate amount for which Application for Progress Payment is made.

5.03 <u>Retainage</u>.   Owner may retain ten percent (10%) of the amount of each monthly Progress Payment to assure performance of this Agreement. A reduction in the amount of funds retained shall be paid to Contractor if Owner and Contractor agree that satisfactory progress is being maintained in the construction of Project.

5.04 <u>Final Payment</u>.   The final payment, ("Final Payment") shall be due and payable when Project is substantially completed and (1) delivered to Owner ready for occupancy or (2) when Owner occupies Project, whichever event occurs first, ("Substantial Completion"); PROVIDED, HOWEVER, in the event that there should remain minor items to be completed, then and in that event Contractor and Owner shall list such items and Contractor shall deliver a written guarantee to complete said items within a reasonable time thereafter. Owner may retain a sum equal to One Hundred Fifty Percent (150%) of the estimated costs of completing any unfinished items; PROVIDED, HOWEVER, that each unfinished item and the estimated cost of completing each unfinished item shall be listed separately. Thereafter, Owner shall pay Contractor on a monthly basis the amount retained for such unfinished items as said items are completed for the previous month. Contractor shall provide Owner with a Certificate of Completion and Application for Final Payment prior to Owner's Final Payment to Contractor.

5.05 <u>Inspection</u>.   Progress Payments to Contractor shall not be construed as an absolute acceptance by Owner of the Construction completed to the date of such Progress Payments except as to matters that are open and obvious. During the construction period, Owner shall exercise reasonable diligence in discovering and promptly reporting to Contractor all materials and labor which are not in accordance with drawings and specifications. Upon Completion Date, Owner shall diligently inspect all work for improper workmanship or defective materials, including work not open and obvious upon inspection during construction.

3.24   Build-Only Construction Agreement (continued)

5.06 <u>Payments Due and Unpaid</u>.   In the event Owner should fail to pay Contractor at the time that the payment of any amount becomes due under the terms of this Agreement, then and in that event Contractor may, and at any time thereafter, serve written notice that Contractor will stop work within five days after receipt of the notice by Owner. After the expiration of said five day period, Contractor shall have the right to stop all work on Project until payment of said unpaid amount has been paid to Contractor. Payments due to Contractor and unpaid shall bear interest at the highest legal commercial rate.

5.07 <u>Waiver of Claims</u>.   The making of Final Payment shall constitute a waiver of all claims by Owner except those rising from unsettled liens, improper workmanship and defective materials appearing within one year after Completion Date, except those previously made in writing and unsettled. The acceptance of Final Payment shall constitute a waiver of all claims by Contractor except those previously made in writing and unsettled.

5.08 <u>Discounts</u>.   All discounts for prompt payment shall accrue to Owner when paid directly by Owner or from a fund made available by Owner to Contractor for such payments. To the extent that such is paid with funds of Contractor, all cash discounts shall accrue to Contractor. All trade discounts, rebates and refunds, and all returns from sale of surplus materials and equipment, shall be credited to Cost of Project.

5.09 <u>Royalties and Patents</u>.   Contractor shall pay all royalties and license fees for materials, methods and systems. Contractor shall defend all suits or claims for infringement of any patent rights except when a particular design, process or product is specified by Owner.

SECTION 6
CONTINGENCIES

6.01 <u>Change Orders</u>.   All changes to Project shall be authorized by a written change order authorizing such change and signed by Contractor and Owner ("Change Order"). Each Change Order shall be numbered and dated, and shall clearly itemize the amount attributable to Cost of Project and Contractor's Fee and shall reflect any change in Completion Date. The value of the work added or omitted in a Change Order shall be agreed upon by Owner and Contractor. A Change Order shall be signed by Contractor and Owner prior to Contractor proceeding with the work set forth in the Change Order.

6.02 <u>Events Beyond Control</u>: Cost of Project shall be increased by a reasonable amount and Completion Date shall be extended by a reasonable period upon the occurrence of events beyond Contractor' control as agreed upon by Owner and Contractor. Such additional costs and fee adjustments required by any event beyond Contractor's control shall be evidenced by a written Change Order executed within a thirty day period after such event occurs. Such events shall include, but not be limited to, the following: (1) an act or neglect by Owner or by third persons not under the control of Contractor; (2) changes required to comply with new laws, rules or regulations; (3) labor disputes; (4) earthquakes, tornado, windstorms, floods or other actions of the elements; (5) war;

3.24   Build-Only Construction Agreement (continued)

(6) fire; (7) concealed and unknown conditions below the surface of the ground or concealed and unknown conditions in an existing structure at variance with the conditions indicated by the drawings and specifications, information furnished by Owner, or of an unusual nature differing materially from those ordinarily encountered and generally recognized as inherent in work of the character provided for in this Agreement; or (8) any cause beyond Contractor's control which Contractor could not have reasonably foreseen.

6.03 Material Price Increase:

Owner understands and agrees that a material allowance amount has been estimated and included to cover the entire expense of the {SPECIFY MATERIAL(s)} for this job. This amount is included to set the price on those materials in anticipation of potential material price increases beyond {CONTRACTOR}'s control. The MATERIAL ALLOWANCE AMOUNT IS: ${SPECIFY AMOUNT}.

{CONTRACTOR} will notify owner immediately during the job if material price increases cause the cost of {SPECIFY MATERIAL(s)} for this job to exceed the MATERIAL ALLOWANCE AMOUNT. The Owner may then, at his option, terminate this contract by providing within (#) business days both written notice of termination to the Builder and payment to the Builder for all costs expended in performance of the contract up to the date of termination, plus payment of ${SPECIFY AMOUNT} based on the percent of completion. If Owner fails to terminate this agreement upon notice of the material price increases within (#) business days, {CONTRACTOR} may proceed to purchase the {SPECIFY MATERIAL(s)} at the increased price, and the Owner shall be required to pay the increased cost as provided herein.

Final review of all specified material invoices will be reviewed by Owner and {CONTRACTOR} within 24 hours of job completion and the final price for the {SPECIFY MATERIAL(s)} will be calculated, along with (%) for administrative fees, and will paid to {CONTRACTOR} by Owner in addition to the final payment for the job.

<ALTERNATE LANGUAGE COVERING ESCALATION CLAUSES>

Escalation Clause for Panelized Lumber

Option One

The house will require approximately _____ square feet of_____ (describe material: plywood, OSB, other). As of the date of this contract, the Builder's cost of _____ (describe material) is_____(price) per thousand square feet, based on _____(describe basis for determining cost: name of supplier). The stated consideration to be paid under this contract is based on current material costs without margin for fluctuations in the price of _____ (describe material). The current market for _____ (describe material) is considered to be volatile, and sudden price increases could occur. The Builder does agree to use his best efforts to obtain the lowest possible price from available building material suppliers. But, should there be an increase in the price of _____ (describe material) purchased after execution of this contract for use in the construction of this house, in order to avoid inequities, the Owner agrees

3.24   Build-Only Construction Agreement (continued)

to pay this cost increase to the Builder. Any claim by the Builder for payment of a cost increase, as provided above, shall require written notice delivered by the Builder to the Owner stating both the increased cost and the source of supply, supported by invoices or bills of sale.

Special Circumstances—Right of Termination

Should there be a rise in the cost of _____(describe material), exclusive of any other price changes, that would cause the total contract price to increase by more than _____(%) percent, the Builder shall, before making any additional purchase of _____ (describe material), provide to the Owner a written statement expressing both the percentage increase of the contract price and the dollar amount of the increase. The Owner may then, at his option, terminate this contract by providing within _____ business days both written notice of termination to the Builder and payment to the Builder for all costs expended in performance of the contract up to the date of termination, plus payment of a prorated percentage of profits based on the percent of completion. Should both notice of termination and full payment, as provided above, not be forthcoming within _____ business days, the Builder may proceed to purchase the _____ (describe material) at the increased price, and the Owner shall be required to pay the increased cost as provided herein.

Escalation Clause for Panelized Lumber

Option Two

The house will require approximately _____ panels of_____ (describe material: plywood, OSB, other). As of the date of this contract, the Builder's cost of _____ (describe material) is_____(price) per panel, based on _____ _____(describe basis for determining cost: name of supplier). The stated consideration to be paid under this contract is based on current material costs without margin for fluctuations in the price of _____ (describe material). The current market for _____ (describe material) is considered to be volatile, and sudden price increases could occur. The Builder does agree to use his best efforts to obtain the lowest possible price from available building material suppliers. But, should there be an increase in the price of _____ (describe material) purchased after execution of this contract for use in the construction of this house, in order to avoid inequities, the Owner agrees to pay this cost increase to the Builder. Any claim by the Builder for payment of a cost increase, as provided above, shall require written notice delivered by the Builder to the Owner stating both the increased cost and the source of supply, supported by invoices or bills of sale.

Special Circumstances—Right of Termination

Should there be a rise in the cost of _____(describe material), exclusive of any other price changes, that would cause the total contract price to increase by more than _____(%) percent, the Builder shall, before making any additional purchase of _____ (describe material), provide to the Owner a written statement expressing both the percentage increase of the contract price and the dollar amount of the increase. The Owner may then, at his option, terminate

3.24   Build-Only Construction Agreement (continued)

this contract by providing within _____ business days both written notice of termination to the Builder and payment to the Builder for all costs expended in performance of the contract up to the date of termination, plus payment of a prorated percentage of profits based on the percent of completion. Should both notice of termination and full payment, as provided above, not be forthcoming within _____ business days, the Builder may proceed to purchase the _____ (describe material) at the increased price, and the Owner shall be required to pay the increased cost as provided herein.

6.04 <u>Emergencies</u>.   In an emergency affecting the safety of persons or property, Contractor shall act, in Contractor's sole discretion, to prevent threatened damage, injury or loss. Any increase in the Cost of Project or extension of Completion Date on account of emergency work shall be determined as provided in Section 6.02 and 6.03.

SECTION 7

INSURANCE/INDEMNITY

7.01 <u>Contractor</u>.   Contractor shall purchase and maintain the following insurance:

(a) Workers' Compensation Insurance that shall comply with the state law of the site of the Project relating to compensation of injured workmen; and

(b) Comprehensive General Liability Insurance, for not less than such reasonable limits of liability as may be required by Owner. Such insurance policies shall contain a provision that the policies will not be canceled or not renewed until at least sixty days written notice has been given to Owner and Contractor. Certificates of Insurance showing such coverages to be in force shall be filed with Owner prior to commencement of the work.

7.02 <u>Owner</u>.   Owner shall purchase and maintain "All Risk" Builder's Risk Insurance. Owner shall purchase and maintain property insurance in a form acceptable to Contractor upon the entire Project for the full cost of replacement. This insurance shall include as named insureds Owner and Contractor and shall insure against loss from the perils of fire, extended coverage, and shall include insurance for physical loss or damage including theft, vandalism, malicious mischief, collapse, flood, earthquake, and damage resulting from defective design, workmanship or material. Owner will increase limits of coverage, if necessary, to reflect estimated replacement cost. Owner will be responsible for any co-insurance penalties or deductibles.

7.03 <u>Waiver of Subrogation</u>.   Owner and Contractor waive all rights against each other, Subcontractors and Sub-subcontractors for damages caused by perils covered by insurance provided by Owner, except such rights as they may have to the proceeds of such insurance. Contractor shall require waivers from all Subcontractors and Sub-subcontractors.

7.04 <u>Indemnity</u>.   Owner hereby indemnifies Contractor against all liabilities, claims and demands for negligent acts or personal injury or property damage arising out of or caused by any act or omission of Owner, Owner's separate Contractors and separate Sub-subcontractors, Owner's agents and employees arising from the commencement of construction until final completion.

3.24   Build-Only Construction Agreement (continued)

Contractor hereby indemnifies Owner against all liabilities, claims and demands for negligent acts or personal injury or property damage arising out of or caused by any act or omission of Contractor, Contractor's separate contractors and separate Sub-subcontractors, agents and employees arising from the commencement of construction until final completion. Contractor and Owner agree to use proper care not to cause damage to any adjoining or adjacent property. Contractor shall indemnify and hold Owner harmless from any liabilities, claims or demands for damage to such adjoining or adjacent property caused by Contractor.

SECTION 8
TERMINATION

8.01 Termination by Owner.   In the event Contractor should at any time fail to perform the work with promptness or diligence, then and in that event Owner shall have the right to terminate this Agreement unless the contractor begins to remedy such failure within ten days after receiving the Owner's notice of intent to terminate. In the event of termination by Owner, Owner shall pay Contractor for all work performed, all obligations incurred by Contractor which cannot be canceled, and the proportionate amount of Contractor's Fee.

8.02 Termination by Contractor.   In the event (1) the work should be stopped for a period of ten days by Owner, (2) Owner should fail to pay Contractor any sum then payable and due Contractor, or (3) Owner should fail for ten days to perform any other obligation hereunder, then and in that event Contractor may after five days after notice is sent to Owner stop work or terminate this Agreement and recover from Owner payment for all work performed, all obligations incurred by Contractor which cannot be canceled, all loss sustained upon Project or material, Contractor's Fee on the Cost of Project incurred, and any other expense, loss or damage which Contractor may sustain.

8.03 Termination Without Cause.   If the work should be stopped for a period of thirty days by any public law, regulation, acts of public officials or other causes not the fault of Owner or Contractor, then either Owner or Contractor shall have the right and option, upon ten days' notice to the other, to terminate this Agreement, in which event Owner shall pay Contractor for all Cost of Project, all obligations incurred by Contractor which cannot be canceled, all loss sustained upon the Project or materials, and the proportionate amount of Contractor's Fee.

SECTION 9
MISCELLANEOUS PROVISIONS

9.01 Arbitration.   Subsequent to the execution of this Agreement by the parties hereto, all claims, disputes, differences, controversies and questions which may arise concerning the matters and obligations set forth in this Agreement, or for the construction or application of this Agreement, or concerning any liabilities created hereunder, or any act or omission of any party hereto, shall be subject to arbitration in accordance with the rules and regulations then in force of the American Arbitration Association. The prevailing party shall be entitled to their costs including reasonable

3.24   Build-Only Construction Agreement (continued)

attorney's fees; PROVIDED, HOWEVER, this clause shall not limit the right of any party to seek temporary injunctive relief where an unacceptable interim period may exist between the time the decision to arbitrate is made and the earliest time at which arbitration can be commenced.

9.02 <u>Time of Essence</u>.   Time is of the essence of this Agreement.

9.03 <u>Attorney's Fees</u>.   Any party who unreasonably fails to perform any covenant of this Agreement as determined by the arbitrator shall pay to the other party the amounts of all attorney's fees and expenses incurred or sustained by such other party in enforcing performance by the other party.

9.04 <u>Notices</u>.   Any notices or other communication to be given under this Agreement to any party hereto shall be mailed certified mail, return receipt requested, addressed to such party as follows:

Contractor _____

_____

_____

Owner _____

_____

_____

A change of such mailing address by either party shall be made by giving notice to the other party in accordance with this Section. Such notice or other communication shall be deemed to have been given when so served, or upon the expiration of seventy-two (72) hours after such mailing, as the case may be.

9.05 <u>Entire Agreement</u>.   This Agreement constitutes the entire Agreement between the parties hereto and none of the parties shall be bound by any promises, representations or agreements except as are herein expressly set forth.

9.06 <u>Amendments</u>.   This Agreement can be amended, modified or supplemented only by a written document signed by the parties hereto. Any purported oral amendment, modification or supplement shall be void.

9.07 <u>Filing of Agreement</u>.   This is a confidential Agreement among the parties hereto and this Agreement shall not be filed of record with any city, county, state or federal authority.

9.08 <u>Assignment</u>.   The parties hereto shall not have the power or right to assign their respective duties and obligations hereunder unless such assignment is agreed to in writing by the parties hereto, or is provided otherwise herein.

9.09 <u>Applicable Law</u>.   This Agreement shall be construed according to the laws of the State of_____regardless of where such Agreement is signed or the site of Project.

9.10 <u>Unenforceable Provisions</u>.   If any portion of this Agreement shall be held to be void or unenforceable, the balance thereof shall nevertheless be carried into effect.

3.24   Build-Only Construction Agreement (continued)

9.11 <u>Benefit</u>.   This Agreement shall be binding upon the parties, their heirs, legal representatives, successors and permitted assigns.

9.12 <u>Preamble Clauses</u>.   The preamble clauses hereto are hereby incorporated into this Agreement as though fully rewritten herein at length.

9.13 <u>Descriptive Headings</u>.   The descriptive paragraph headings contained herein are for convenience only and are not intended to include or conclusively define all the subject matter in the paragraphs accompanying such headings and, accordingly, such headings should not be resorted to for interpretation of this Agreement.

9.14 <u>Interpretation</u>.   Any words used herein shall be interpreted as singular or plural, and any pronouns used herein shall be interpreted as masculine, feminine or neuter, as the context so requires.

9.15 <u>Exhibits</u>.   All Exhibits attached hereto are made a part hereof by reference and are hereby incorporated into this Agreement as though fully rewritten herein at length.

9.16 <u>Acknowledgments</u>.   Each of the parties to this Agreement hereby acknowledges that such party has received a fully executed copy of this Agreement and further acknowledges that such party has carefully reviewed the representations, terms and conditions contained herein.

IN WITNESS WHEREOF, the parties have entered into this Agreement the day and year first above written.

"Contractor"

_____

By_____

Title_____

"Owner"

_____

By_____

Title_____

3.25   Build-Only Guaranteed Maximum Price

CONSTRUCTION AGREEMENT BETWEEN OWNER AND GENERAL CONTRACTOR BUILD ONLY GUARANTEED MAXIMUM PRICE

THIS AGREEMENT, is made and entered into this _____ day of _____, 20____, by and between _____, a _____, ("Owner") and _____, a _____, ("Contractor").

RECITALS:

WHEREAS, Owner has title or an agreement to acquire title to certain real property as described in Exhibit A ("Property");

WHEREAS, Owner desires that certain improvements be made on said real property, the scope and purposes as generally outlined in the specifications and plan as described in Exhibit B ("Project");

WHEREAS, Owner has provided to Contractor certain architectural, engineering and construction plans for construction of Project; and said detailed specifications and plans are set forth in Exhibit C; and

WHEREAS, Contractor and Owner desire to set forth in writing the terms and conditions of their Agreement and intend to be legally bound by their Agreement.

NOW, THEREFORE, for and in consideration of the above premises, and of the following terms, conditions and mutual covenants of Contractor and Owner as hereinafter stated, IT IS HEREBY AGREED:

SECTION 1
OWNER'S OBLIGATIONS

1.01 <u>Project</u>.   Owner shall provide Property for Project.

1.02 <u>Design and Engineering</u>.   Owner has furnished Contractor with Owner's design, engineering and detailed construction drawings and specifications as set forth in Exhibit C (to be signed by Owner and Contractor). Construction of Project shall be in accordance with these drawings and specifications and with any subsequent drawings and specifications as approved in writing by Owner and Contractor. The drawings and specifications shall be the property of Owner and are not to be used by Contractor for other projects without the written consent of Owner.

1.03 <u>Owner's Participation</u>.   Owner shall designate in writing a representative who shall have authority to approve Change Orders and to furnish information on a timely basis.

1.04 <u>Funding</u>.   Prior to Contractor commencing construction, Owner shall furnish evidence to Contractor that sufficient funds are available and committed for the entire Guaranteed Maximum Price as set forth in Section 4.02.

3.25   Build-Only Guaranteed Maximum Price (continued)

1.05 <u>Safety</u>.   Owner shall require and cause all of Owner's tenants and all contractors separately hired by Owner to abide by and fully adhere to all applicable federal, state and local safety laws and regulations and to comply with Contractor's request for the elimination or abatement of safety hazards. Owner shall be responsible for the elimination or abatement of safety hazards created at Project by other persons employed by Owner as separate contractors or by Owner's tenants. Owner shall cause such separate contractors and such tenants to coordinate and cooperate with Contractor in all other respects of construction. Owner shall indemnify and hold Contractor harmless from all claims and damages arising from safety hazards caused by Owner's tenants and by separate contractors employed by Owner, including, but not limited to, multiemployer citations issued by the United States Occupational safety and health Administration.

1.06 <u>Subcontractors</u>.   Owner shall not have a contractual relationship with Contractor's subcontractors and Owner shall communicate with such subcontractors through Contractor.

SECTION 2
CONTRACTOR'S OBLIGATIONS

2.01 <u>Requirements</u>.   Contractor shall furnish certified surveys describing the physical characteristics, soil reports, legal restrictions and utility descriptions. Contractor shall obtain at Owner's expense all necessary approvals; easements; assessments; expenses; building, use or occupancy and other governmental permits and licenses required for the construction; use or occupancy of permanent structures of Project; any bonds that may be required; and any legal services that may be required to obtain such items.

2.02 <u>Construction</u>.   Contractor shall be responsible for the construction of Project and shall provide all supervision, labor, materials, tools, machinery, equipment and other items necessary for the completion of Project. Contractor shall use Contractor's best efforts to complete construction and shall at all times furnish sufficient materials and labor to assure an efficient completion of Project. Contractor is experienced and qualified to perform the work provided for herein and shall finance its own operations hereunder. Contractor shall operate as an independent contractor and not as an agent of Owner.

2.03 <u>Completion Date</u>.   The work to be performed under this Agreement shall be completed on or before the _____ day of _____, 20__(Completion Date) as set forth in Paragraph 5.01.

2.04 <u>Accounting</u>.   Contractor shall keep detailed records necessary for financial accounting of Project. Owner shall have access to Contractor's records, drawings, receipts and similar data relating to Project. Contractor shall specifically itemize all changes in Cost of Project and all Change Orders. Contractor shall maintain all records for a period of three years after Final Payment or longer where required by law.

2.05 <u>Safety</u>.   Contractor shall comply with applicable provisions of federal, state and local safety laws for the safety of Contractor's employees and to prevent accidents or injury to persons on Project.

3.25   Build-Only Guaranteed Maximum Price (continued)

2.06 <u>Subcontracts</u>.   All construction that Contractor does not perform shall be performed by subcontractors. The term "Subcontractor" shall not include any separate contractor employed by Owner or such separate contractors' subcontractors. Contractor shall be responsible for the management of subcontractors in the performance of their work. Contractor shall cause all subcontractors to indemnify and hold harmless Owner from all claims for bodily injury and property damage that may arise, other than property damage required to be insured by Owner as set forth in Section 7.02.

2.07 <u>Clean Conditions</u>.   Contractor shall maintain Project free from the accumulation of construction waste and rubbish. Upon completion of Project, Contractor shall deliver Project in a "clean" condition, free from all trash, rubbish, debris, Contractor's tools, construction equipment and machinery, surplus materials and inventory.

2.08 <u>Warranties</u>.   Contractor warrants that all materials and equipment furnished shall be new, unless otherwise specified, and that all construction shall be of good quality, free from improper workmanship and defective materials and in conformance with the drawings and specifications. All workmanship shall conform to the guidelines found in the publication *Residential Construction Performance Guidelines for Professional Builders and Remodelers*. If an item is not covered in that publication, standard industry practice shall govern.

Contractor warrants that title to all work, materials and equipment shall pass to Owner upon delivery to Owner free and clear of all liens, claims, security interests or encumbrances ("Liens"). Contractor shall correct all work performed by Contractor which proves to be defective in material and workmanship within a period of one year from the date of completion. Upon written notice of such defects, Contractor shall, at Contractor's option, either make necessary repairs or request Owner to make such repairs at Contractor's expense. Contractor will secure required certificates of inspection, testing or approval and any and all express warranties from manufacturers, suppliers and subcontractors, and deliver same to Owner.

2.09 <u>Manufactured Equipment</u>.   Contractor shall collect all warranties and equipment manuals and deliver same to Owner. Contractor shall assist Owner's maintenance personnel with the testing and initial start up of such systems and equipment.

2.10 <u>Surety Bond</u>.   Contractor shall furnish an approved Surety Company Bond for the performance of this Agreement. The expense of such Bond shall be that of Contractor.

SECTION 3
MUTUAL REPRESENTATIONS

3.01 <u>Litigation</u>.   Contractor and Owner hereby warrant and represent that neither is a party to or threatened with any litigation proceeding or controversy before any Court or administrative agency nor in default with respect to any judgment, order, writ, injunction, decree, rule, or regulation before any Court or administrative agency which might result in any adverse effect on representations, statements and conditions set forth in this Agreement.

3.25   Build-Only Guaranteed Maximum Price (continued)

3.02 <u>Conflicts</u>.   The execution of this Agreement by Contractor and Owner will not violate or conflict with or result in a breach of or constitute a default under any agreement or instrument which they may be bound. No consent of any third party not a party to this Agreement is required.

3.03 <u>Accuracy of Information</u>.   Contractor and Owner hereby warrant and represent that this Agreement does not contain any false statements and that this Agreement does not omit any material facts.

3.04 <u>Authorization</u>.   Contractor and Owner have the requisite power and authority for execution of this Agreement.

3.05 <u>Legal Responsibilities</u>.   Contractor and Owner shall comply, abide by and fully adhere with all applicable federal, state, local and municipal laws, regulations and ordinances applicable to any responsibilities of Contractor and Owner hereunder.

SECTION 4
FEES AND COSTS

4.01 <u>Contractor's Fee</u>.   Owner shall pay Contractor for the cost of Project as defined in Section 4.03 ("Cost of Project"). Owner shall pay Contractor a fee as compensation for services a fee ("Contractor's Fee") in addition to payments for Cost of Project. Contractor's Fee shall be

_____.

_____.

4.02 <u>Guaranteed Maximum Price</u>.   Contractor guarantees to Owner that the maximum price for (1) Cost of Project and (2) Contractor's Fee ("Guaranteed Maximum Price") shall not exceed _____Dollars ($_____), unless by Change Order per Section 6.01 or Events Beyond Control per section 6.02. In the event that Cost of Project and Contractor's Fee should exceed Guaranteed Maximum Price, then and in that event Contractor shall absorb such excess.

4.03 <u>Cost of Project</u>.   Cost of Project shall include:

(a) Architectural, engineering and consulting fees incurred in design and construction of Project;

(b) Wages for Contractor's employees under (1) applicable collective bargaining agreements, if any, and (2) under salary or wage schedule agreed upon by Owner and Contractor;

(c) Salaries of Contractor's employees when stationed at the field office, and employees from the main office performing functions related to Project;

(d) Cost of all employee benefits and taxes for unemployment compensation and social security (all such cost based on wages or salaries paid to Contractor's employees);

(e) Reasonable transportation, travel, hotel and relocation expenses of Contractor's employees connected with Project;

(f) Cost of all materials, supplies and equipment for Project and cost of transportation and storage;

3.25   Build-Only Guaranteed Maximum Price (continued)

(g) Payments to subcontractors for work performed pursuant to this Agreement;

(h) Cost, including transportation and maintenance, of all temporary facilities and hand tools which are employed or consumed;

(i) Rental charges for machinery and equipment, whether rented from Contractor or others, including installations, repairs, replacements, removal, transportation and delivery costs, at rental rates consistent with those prevailing in the area;

(j) Cost of premiums for all insurance and performance bonds which Contractor is required to obtain or that is deemed necessary by Contractor;

(k) Sales, use, gross receipts or similar taxes related to Project;

(l) Permit fees, licenses, tests, royalties, damages for infringement of patents (and costs of defending suits thereof), and deposits lost for causes other than Contractor's gross negligence;

(m) Losses, expenses or damages to the extent not compensated by insurance or otherwise (including settlements made with the written approval of Owner), and the cost of corrective work;

(n) Expenses such as telegrams, long-distance telephone calls, telephone service at the site and similar minor cash items connected with Project;

(o) Cost of removal of all trash and construction debris;

(p) Cost incurred due to an emergency affecting safety of persons and property;

(q) Cost of accounting services required herein;

(r) Legal fees reasonably and properly resulting from actions taken by Contractor on behalf of Owner or Project; and

(s) Cost of certified surveys describing the physical characteristics, soil reports, legal descriptions and utility locations.

4.04 Non Cost Items.   The following items are specifically excluded from Cost of Project (as set forth in Section 4.03). Such costs are included in Contractor's Fee:

(a) Salaries or other compensation of Contractor's employees at the principal office other than as described in Section 4.03;

(b) General operating expenses of Contractor's principal office other than Project's field office;

(c) Any part of Contractor's capital expenses, including interest on Contractor's capital directly related to Project;

(d) Overhead or general expenses of any kind, except as may be expressly set forth in Section 4.03; and

(e) All Costs of Project in excess of Guaranteed Maximum Price.

3.25   Build-Only Guaranteed Maximum Price (continued)

SECTION 5
PAYMENTS

5.01 <u>Time Schedule</u>.   Construction of Project shall commence not later than the ____ day of ____, 20__ ("Commencement Date"). Completion of Project shall occur on or before the ____ day of _____, 20__ ("Completion Date"). Contractor shall prepare an estimated progress schedule for Project which shall set forth the dates for the commencement and completion of the various stages of construction. The schedule and Completion Date may be revised as provided in Section 6.

5.02 <u>Progress Payments</u>.   On or before the ____ day of each month after Commencement Date, Contractor shall submit to Owner an application for progress payment ("Application for Progress Payment") in such detail required by Owner and based on the construction completed, along with the proportionate amount of Contractor's Fee for such period, such aggregate amount hereinafter referred to as "Progress Payment." Within ten days after receipt of said monthly Application for Progress Payment, Owner shall pay Contractor the appropriate amount for which Application for Progress Payment is made.

5.03 <u>Retainage</u>.   Owner shall retain ten percent (10%) of the amount of each monthly Progress Payment to assure performance of this Agreement.

5.04 <u>Final Payment</u>.   The final payment, ("Final Payment") shall be due and payable when Project is substantially completed, defined as either when the project is delivered to Owner ready for occupancy, or when the Owner occupies the Project, whichever event occurs first.

5.05 <u>Inspection</u>.   Progress Payments to Contractor shall not be construed as an absolute acceptance by Owner of the construction completed to the date of such Progress Payments except as to matters that are open and obvious. Upon Completion Date, Owner shall diligently inspect all work for improper workmanship or defective materials.

5.06 <u>Payments Due and Unpaid</u>.   In the event Owner should fail to pay Contractor at the time that the payment of any amount becomes due under the terms of this Agreement, then and in that event Contractor may, and at any time thereafter, serve written notice that Contractor will stop work within ten days after receipt of the notice by Owner. After the expiration of said ten day period, Contractor shall have the right to stop all work on Project until payment of said unpaid amount has been paid to Contractor.

5.07 <u>Waiver of Claims</u>.   The making of Final Payment shall constitute a waiver of all claims by Owner except those rising from unsettled liens, and latent defects in workmanship and materials appearing within one year after Completion Date, except those previously made in writing and unsettled. The acceptance of Final Payment shall constitute a waiver of all claims by Contractor except those previously made in writing and unsettled.

5.08 <u>Discounts</u>.   All discounts for prompt payment shall accrue to Owner. All trade discounts, rebates and refunds, and all returns from sale of surplus materials and equipment, shall be credited to Cost of Project.

3.25   Build-Only Guaranteed Maximum Price (continued)

5.09 <u>Royalties and Patents</u>.   Contractor shall pay all royalties and license fees for materials, methods and systems. Contractor shall defend all suits or claims for infringement of any patent rights except when a particular design, process or product is specified by Owner.

SECTION 6
CONTINGENCIES

6.01 <u>Change Orders</u>.   All changes to Project shall be authorized by a written change order authorizing such change and signed by Contractor and Owner ("Change Order"). Each Change Order shall be numbered and dated, and shall clearly itemize the amount attributable to (1) Cost of Project, (2) Contractor's Fee and (3) Guaranteed Maximum Price and shall reflect any change in Completion Date. The value of the work added or omitted in a Change Order shall be agreed upon by Owner and Contractor, and the amount thereof added to or deducted from the Guaranteed Maximum Price. A Change Order shall be signed by Contractor and Owner prior to Contractor proceeding with the work set forth in the Change Order.

6.02 <u>Events Beyond Control</u>.   The Guaranteed Maximum Price shall be increased by a reasonable amount and Completion Date shall be extended by a reasonable period upon the occurrence of events beyond Contractor's control as agreed upon by Owner and Contractor. Such additional costs and fee adjustments required by any event beyond Contractor's control shall be evidenced by a written Change Order executed within a thirty day period after such event occurs. Such events shall include, but not be limited to the following: (1) an act or neglect by Owner or by third persons not under the control of Contractor; (2) changes required to comply with new laws, rules or regulations; (3) labor disputes; (4) earthquakes, tornado, windstorms, floods or other actions of the elements; (5) war; (6) fire; (7) concealed and unknown conditions below the surface of the ground or concealed and unknown conditions in an existing structure at variance with the conditions indicated by the drawings and specifications, information furnished by Owner, or of an unusual nature differing materially from those ordinarily encountered and generally recognized as inherent in work of the character provided for in this Agreement; or (8) any cause beyond Contractor's control which Contractor could not have reasonably foreseen.

6.03 <u>Emergencies</u>.   In an emergency affecting the safety of persons or property, Contractor shall act, in Contractor's sole discretion, to prevent threatened damage, injury or loss. Any increase in the Guaranteed Maximum Price or extension of Completion Date on account of emergency work shall be determined as provided in Section 6.02.

3.25   Build-Only Guaranteed Maximum Price (continued)

SECTION 7
INDEMNITY

7.01 <u>Contractor</u>.   Contractor shall purchase and maintain the following insurance:

(a) Workers' Compensation Insurance that shall comply with the state law of the site of the Project relating to compensation of injured workmen; and

(b) Comprehensive General Liability Insurance, for not less than such reasonable limits of liability as may be required by Owner. Such insurance policies shall contain a provision that the policies will not be canceled or not renewed until at least sixty days written notice has been given to Owner and Contractor. Certificates of Insurance showing such coverages to be in force shall be filed with Owner prior to commencement of the work.

(c) Contractor shall purchase and maintain "All Risk" Builder's Risk Insurance.

(d) Contractor will be responsible for any co-insurance penalties or deductibles.

7.02 <u>Owner</u>.   Upon completion of the building, Owner shall purchase and maintain property insurance in a form acceptable to Contractor upon the entire Project for the full cost of replacement. This insurance shall include as named insureds Owner and Contractor and shall insure against loss from the perils of fire, extended coverage, and shall include insurance for physical loss or damage including theft, vandalism, malicious mischief, collapse, flood, earthquake, and damage resulting from defective design, workmanship or material. Owner will increase limits of coverage, if necessary, to reflect estimated replacement cost.

7.03 <u>Waiver of Subrogation</u>.   Owner and Contractor waive all rights against each other, Subcontractors and Sub-subcontractors for damages caused by perils covered by insurance provided by Owner, except such rights as they may have to the proceeds of such insurance. Contractor shall require waivers from all Subcontractors and Sub-subcontractors.

7.04 <u>Indemnity</u>.   Owner hereby indemnifies Contractor against all liabilities, claims and demands for negligent acts or personal injury or property damage arising out of or caused by any act or omission of Owner, Owner's separate contractors and separate sub-subcontractors, Owner's agents and employees arising from the commencement of construction until final completion. Contractor hereby indemnifies Owner against all liabilities, claims and demands for negligent acts or personal injury or property damage arising out of or caused by any act or omission of Contractor, Contractor's separate contractors and separate sub-subcontractors, agents and employees arising from the commencement of construction until final completion. Contractor and Owner agree to use proper care not to cause damage to any adjoining or adjacent property. Contractor shall indemnify and hold Owner harmless from any liabilities, claims or demands for damage to such adjoining or adjacent property caused solely by Contractor.

3.25   Build-Only Guaranteed Maximum Price (continued)

SECTION 8
TERMINATION

8.01 <u>Termination by Owner</u>.   In the event Contractor should at any time fail to perform the work with promptness or diligence, then and in that event Owner shall have the right to terminate this Agreement after ten days notice to Contractor (unless within said ten day period Contractor begins to remedy such failure). In the event of termination by Owner, Owner shall pay Contractor for all work performed and all obligations incurred by Contractor which cannot be canceled, less a reserve for contingencies.

8.02 <u>Termination by Contractor</u>.   In the event (1) the work should be stopped for a period of ten days by Owner, (2) Owner should fail to pay Contractor any sum then payable and due Contractor, or (3) Owner should fail for ten days to perform any other obligation hereunder, then and in that event Contractor may after five days notice to Owner stop work or terminate this Agreement and recover from Owner payment for all work performed, all obligations incurred by Contractor which cannot be canceled, all loss sustained upon Project or material, Contractor's Fee on the Cost of Project incurred, and any other expense, loss or damage which Contractor may sustain.

8.03 <u>Termination Without Cause</u>.   If the work should be stopped for a period of thirty days by any public law, regulation, acts of public officials or other causes not the fault of Owner or Contractor, then Owner shall have the right and option, upon ten days notice to Contractor, to extend this Agreement for a period of one hundred eighty (180) days or to terminate this Agreement, in which event Owner shall pay Contractor for all Cost of Project, all obligations incurred by Contractor which cannot be canceled, all loss sustained upon the Project or materials, and the pro-portionate amount of Contractor's Fee.

SECTION 9
MISCELLANEOUS PROVISIONS

9.01 <u>Arbitration</u>.   Subsequent to the execution of this Agreement by the parties hereto, all claims, disputes, differences, controversies and questions which may arise concerning the matters and obligations set forth in this Agreement, or for the construction or application of this Agreement, or concerning any liabilities created hereunder, or any act or omission of any party hereto, shall be subject to arbitration in accordance with the rules and regulations then in force of the American Arbitration Association. The prevailing party, as determined unequivocally by the Arbitrator, shall be entitled to their costs including reasonable attorney's fees; PROVIDED, HOWEVER, this clause shall not limit the right of any party to seek temporary injunctive relief where an unacceptable interim period may exist between the time the decision to arbitrate is made and the earliest time at which arbitration can be commenced.

9.02 <u>Time of Essence</u>.   Time is of the essence of this Agreement.

3.25   Build-Only Guaranteed Maximum Price (continued)

9.03 <u>Attorney's Fees</u>.   Any party who unreasonably fails to perform any covenant of this Agreement shall pay to the other party the amounts of all attorney's fees and expenses incurred or sustained by such other party in enforcing performance by the other party.

9.04 <u>Notices</u>.   Any notices or other communication to be given under this Agreement to any party hereto shall be mailed certified mail, return receipt requested, addressed to such party as follows:

Owner:_____
_____
_____

Contractor:_____
_____
_____

A change of such mailing address by either party shall be made by giving notice to the other party in accordance with this Section. Such notice or other communication shall be deemed to have been given when so served, or upon the expiration of seventy-two (72) hours after such mailing, as the case may be.

9.05 <u>Entire Agreement</u>.   This Agreement constitutes the entire Agreement between the parties hereto and none of the parties shall be bound by any promises, representations or agreements except as are herein expressly set forth.

9.06 <u>Amendments</u>.   This Agreement can be amended, modified or supplemented only by a written document signed by the parties hereto. Any purported oral amendment, modification or supplement shall be void.

9.07 <u>Filing of Agreement</u>.   This is a confidential Agreement among the parties hereto and this Agreement shall not be filed of record with any city, county, state or federal authority.

9.08 <u>Assignment</u>.   The parties hereto shall not have the power or right to assign their respective duties and obligations hereunder unless such assignment is agreed to in writing by the parties hereto, or is provided otherwise herein.

9.09 <u>Applicable Law</u>.   This Agreement shall be construed according to the laws of the State of_____regardless of where such Agreement is signed or the site of Project.

9.10 <u>Unenforceable Provisions</u>.   If any portion of this Agreement shall be held to be void or unenforceable, the balance thereof shall nevertheless be carried into effect.

9.11 <u>Benefit</u>.   This Agreement shall be binding upon the parties, their heirs, legal representatives, successors and permitted assigns.

9.12 <u>Preamble Clauses</u>.   The preamble clauses hereto are hereby incorporated into this Agreement as though fully rewritten herein at length.

3.25   Build-Only Guaranteed Maximum Price (continued)

9.13 <u>Descriptive Headings</u>.   The descriptive paragraph headings contained herein are for convenience only and are not intended to include or conclusively define all the subject matter in the paragraphs accompanying such headings and, accordingly, such headings should not be resorted to for interpretation of this Agreement.

9.14 <u>Interpretation</u>.   Any words used herein shall be interpreted as singular or plural, and any pronouns used herein shall be interpreted as masculine, feminine or neuter, as the context so requires.

9.15 <u>Exhibits</u>.   All Exhibits attached hereto are made a part hereof by reference and are hereby incorporated into this Agreement as though fully rewritten herein at length.

9.16 <u>Acknowledgments</u>.   Each of the parties to this Agreement hereby acknowledges that such party has received a fully executed copy of this Agreement and further acknowledges that such party has carefully reviewed the representations, terms and conditions contained herein.

IN WITNESS WHEREOF, the parties have entered into this Agreement the day and year first above written.

"Contractor"

_____

By_____

Title_____

"Owner"

_____

By_____

Title_____

3.26   Preliminary Design-Build Agreement

CONSTRUCTION AGREEMENT BETWEEN
GENERAL CONTRACTOR AND OWNER
PRELIMINARY DESIGN BUILD

THIS AGREEMENT, made and entered into this _____ day of _____ , 20_____ , by and between _____ ("Contractor") and ("Owner").

WHEREAS, Owner hereby engages Contractor to provide certain preliminary design work and construction estimates to be made to determine the cost and time required for design and construction of to be located at _____ ("Project").

It is hereby agreed:

1. Owner shall furnish Contractor with full information regarding Owner's requirements for Project and make the necessary decisions for the design and construction estimates to proceed in an orderly manner.

2. Contractor shall prepare preliminary design development documents to illustrate and fix the size and character of Project. Such documents to include as necessary:

    a. Preliminary Drawings consisting of site plan, building plan(s) along with necessary elevations, sections, or sketches visually depicting Project.
    b. Outline Specifications consisting of brief description of the structural, mechanical, and electrical systems, materials, interior and exterior finishes, and other appropriate essential items of Project.
    c. Preliminary Cost Estimate for the completion of the design, including all working drawings and related costs thereof, and construction of Project as described in the preliminary drawings and outline specifications.
    d. Preliminary Construction Schedule showing the estimated time required or planned for completion of the design and construction of Project.

3. Upon Owner's determination of the feasibility of Project as set forth in the preliminary documents, and if Owner elects to proceed with Project as proposed, Contractor and Owner shall enter into a design-build agreement in the form attached hereto and marked Exhibit A.

4. As consideration for preparation of the preliminary design development documents, Owner shall pay to Contractor the sum of ($ _____) which shall be paid _____. Any outside services (engineer, surveyor, component designs, shop drawings) as required shall constitute additional work and shall be fully reimbursed by the owner as the services are billed. Estimated time for the completion of the preliminary design development documents is _____. The preliminary design development documents shall remain the property of Contractor and shall not be used on the Project or other projects without the written consent of Contractor. It is understood that this design fee is not tied to construction costs nor will it be credited to future contracting agreements.

3.26 Preliminary Design-Build Agreement (continued)

5. <u>Arbitration</u>.   Subsequent to the execution of this Agreement by the parties hereto, all claims, disputes, differences, controversies and questions which may arise concerning the matters and obligations set forth in this Agreement, or for the construction or application of this Agreement, or concerning any liabilities created hereunder, or any act or omission of any party hereto, shall be subject to arbitration in accordance with the rules and regulations then in force of the American Arbitration Association. The prevailing party, as specifically determined by the Arbitrator, shall be entitled to their costs including reasonable attorney's fees; The prevailing party shall be entitled to their costs including reasonable attorney's fees; PROVIDED, HOWEVER, this clause shall not limit the right of any party to seek temporary injunctive relief where an unacceptable interim period may exist between the time the decision to arbitrate is made and the earliest time at which arbitration can be commenced.

IN WITNESS WHEREOF, the parties have entered into this Agreement the day and year first above written.

"Contractor"

_____

By_____

Title_____

"Owner"

_____

By_____

Title_____

3.27   Professional Services Agreement

Company Name
Company Logo
Company Affiliations

Professional Services Agreement

1. This AGREEMENT is made this the _____ day of _____, by and between (YOUR COMPANY NAME), and _____, hereinafter referred to as Owners.

2. The Project address is _____, *City, State, Zip Code.*

3. Under the terms of this agreement, (YOUR COMPANY NAME) is authorized by the Owners to provide professional services as follows.

   A. Feasibility analysis on or about _____
   B. Technical construction analysis on or about _____
   C. Budget preparation–scope of work on or about _____
   D. On-site measurements and photos for concept drawings on or about _____.
   E. Concept drawing meeting to choose the best concept on or about _____.
   F. Concept development meeting and initial budget presentation (continue to refine plans) on or about _____.
   G. Construction drawings and final budget meeting on or about _____.

Any monies paid under this agreement are nonrefundable, and separate and apart from amounts paid to (YOUR COMPANY NAME), for actual construction.

4. (YOUR COMPANY NAME) agrees to produce steps as initialed to be billed at the rate of $_____ /hour with a cap of $_____ requiring a maximum of _____ hours of consulting and design services. We will not proceed beyond this cap amount without the owners' approvals written approval. A credit or refund will be issued to the owners if the estimated design time does not equal the actual design time.

5. The design, drawings, and specifications included in this agreement are protected by U.S. copyright laws and may not be copied, reproduced, modified, distributed or used in any other way without the specific written consent of (YOUR COMPANY NAME), the copyright owner.

6. For these services, we are paid ___%, or _____ upon execution of this contract, and the remainder upon presentation of construction drawings and final budget or _____ (fixed price) on or about _____(date due).

Company Address
Phone
Fax
E-mail
Web site

3.27   Professional Services Agreement (continued)

Company Name
Company Logo
Company Affiliations

ACCEPTED:

_____

Owner   Date

_____

Owner   Date

(YOUR COMPANY NAME)

_____

                        Date

Company Address
Phone
Fax
E-mail
Web site

3.28   Predesign Contract

Company Name
Company Logo
Company Affiliations

Predesign Contract

THIS AGREEMENT IS BETWEEN: Job Number:

[Your Company Name]   and   OWNER(S):
[Your Company Address]
[Your Company City, State, Zip Code]

DESIGN PROJECT

PROJECT ADDRESS:

DESCRIPTION OF DESIGN PROJECT. [Your Company Name] will prepare plans and/or schematic drawings and design for work described generally as follows:

Preliminary Design covers the following items or areas:

PRELIMINARY PLANS ARE TO INCLUDE:

*Drawings to scale, illustrating floor and two elevations, with door sweeps and window placements.

*All code and zoning research to insure "buildability" of the project.

*Preliminary notes, cost information, and construction technique.

*Solution of major design problems.

DESIGN FEE

One hundred percent (100%) of the Preliminary Design Fee will be applied towards the Construction Document (Working Drawings) fee if the project is constructed by [Your Company Name].

PRELIMINARY DESIGN FEE: $
DEPOSIT: $
BALANCE: $

Address
Phone–Fax
E-mail–Web site

3.28   Predesign Contract (continued)

Company Name
Company Logo
Company Affiliations

Job Number:_____

TERMS AND CONDITIONS

The Terms and Conditions are expressly incorporated into this agreement. This agreement constitutes the entire understanding of the parties. No other understanding of the representations, collateral or otherwise, shall be binding unless in writing, signed by both parties. This agreement shall not become effective or binding upon <Your Company Name> until signed by an officer of the company. By the signature below, owner(s) acknowledges receipt of a fully completed copy of this agreement.

The design and documents will be developed with the assumption that the project will be built according to <Your Company Name> construction management system and techniques. <Your Company Name> shall not be held responsible for errors or omissions if construction if performed by OTHERS and owner shall indemnify <Your Company Name> against all claims, damages and expenses including reasonable attorney fees, growing out of the unauthorized use. The original drawings and specifications are the property of <Your Company Name>.

1. PAYMENT AND DISBURSEMENTS: Upon signing and agreement, 50% deposit is due. All other payments are due and payable upon receipt of invoice. Overdue payments will bear interest at the maximum legally permissible rate. Failure by owner to pay any invoice within five (5) days after payment is due shall constitute a material breach of this agreement. All checks shall be made payable to <Your Company Name>. <Your Company Name> has the right to <u>stop work</u> if not paid within 20 days of billing.

2. DISCLAIMED WORK: No engineering work is included unless expressly specified. This agreement does not include submission of documents to the building department having local jurisdiction or the acquisition of such parties as may be required for construction of the designed project, unless expressly specified.

3. ADDITIONAL WORK: If the scope or nature of the work is materially changed after the date of this agreement, which necessitates additional work in the preparation of these documents, the amounts payable to <Your Company Name> shall be increased in accordance with the additional work caused by such changes.

Address
Phone–Fax
E-mail–Web site

3.28   Predesign Contract (continued)

Company Name
Company Logo
Company Affiliations

4. PLANS AND SPECIFICATIONS: Measurements, sizes and shapes in plans and specifications are approximate and subject to field verification and structural idiosyncrasies. <Your Company Name> shall not be held responsible for any inaccuracies, errors or omissions of any and all information supplied by owner or agent for owner.

Date: _____

BY: _____

    PROPOSED BY [Your Company Name]   A   BY: _____

                                                                        N   BY: _____

BY: _____   D

Address
Phone–Fax
E-mail–Web site

3.29   Design Contract

Company Name
Company Logo
Company Affiliations

Date

Customer Name
Address
City, State Zip

DESIGN CONTRACT

I (we) agree to compensate *Your Company Name* for the consultation and design of the remodeling project herein described:_____

_____

_____

Furthermore, I understand that this fee of $_____ will be credited against the cost of the remodeling contract should I decide to allow *Your Company Name* to construct the project as stated.*

I also understand that this is the maximum amount of the consultation and design fee, unless the scope of the described project changes. If the scope changes, a new contract will be signed before proceeding. This price includes allowances of two (2) redraws of preliminary drawings based upon the decisions of client and five (5) sets of construction-ready plans.

Payment shall be 25% down upon signing; $_____
50% when first rendering is presented; $_____
Balance upon completion and delivery of the agreed sets of blueprints by _____(date).

_____   _____
Client Signature   Your Company Name

_____   _____
Client Signature   Title

Date _____   Date _____

*   *Should another contractor utilize these plans, <Your Company Name> has no liability for the finished project. As always, the final job is at the discretion of the contractor completing the work. In any event <Your Company Name> shall retain the copyright of the design but the owner is permitted a single use of this design on this home.*

*   *An Arbitration Agreement is attached to this Agreement, and appears as Page 2.*

3.29   Design Contract (continued)

AGREEMENT TO ARBITRATE

We strive to enhance the professionalism of our industry and improve the relations between <company name>, our customers and the public. As a part of that commitment we offer Alternative Dispute Resolution (ADR) beginning with negotiation through the <name of arbitration program>. Should an impasse between the customer and the contractor develop, we will submit to the ADR program to attempt to negotiate a settlement. If this procedure is not deemed satisfactory for either party, the next step is mediation or arbitration by the Better Business Bureau.

As part of this program, the paragraph below is the agreement to settle any differences between the two parties. Careful reading and understanding of this section is necessary to fulfill the goals of the program and to assure you, the customer, of a quality product. You are entering into a contract with the highest level of professionalism possible.

It is agreed between the undersigned member of the Better Business Bureau and the undersigned Customer that, in the event a dispute arises between the parties, the parties will not sue each other in court, but will submit said dispute to binding arbitration by the Better Business Bureau of <Your Company's State> and <Your County> in <Your State> provided, however, that this Agreement to Arbitrate shall not apply to any dispute between the parties involving criminal or statutory violations. This Agreement to Arbitrate also will not apply to and will exclude any claims between the parties for criminal actions, intentional torts, product reliability, personal injury claim, and punitive damages.

In arbitration, an informal hearing will be held in accordance with the BBB's *Rules for Binding Arbitration*. A volunteer BBB arbitrator will render a decision that the arbitrator considers to be a fair resolution of the dispute, and in doing so the arbitrator will not be bound to any legal principles. The arbitrator's decision will be final and binding on both parties, and it is agreed that judgment on the decision may be entered in any court having jurisdiction.

All administrative fees for the arbitration will be paid by the business.

This Agreement to Arbitrate affects important legal rights. By signing it, the parties are agreeing to waive their right to sue in court for disputes that must be submitted to arbitration

THE CUSTOMER DOES NOT HAVE TO SIGN THIS AGREEMENT TO ARBITRATE, AND SHOULD SIGN BELOW ONLY IF THE CUSTOMER AGREES TO RESOLVE DISPUTES THROUGH ARBITRATION AS SET OUT ABOVE.

_____	_____
HOMEOWNER	*YOUR COMPANY NAME*
_____	_____
HOMEOWNER	NAME & TITLE
_____	_____
DATE	DATE

Reply to: Your Company Name, Address
E-mail:
Fax:
Web site:

3.30   Third-Party Financing Addendum

Addendum—3rd Party Financing Addendum

As part of any 3rd party financing arrangements for the Work, Owner hereby accepts responsibility and agrees to reimburse Builder for any and all bank fees relating to wire transfers of funds from Owner's bank account(s) to Builder's bank account for payment of draw requests under the contract.

Owner further accepts responsibility and agrees to reimburse Builder for any and all fees associated with lending institution required inspections.

3.31   Addendum—Concrete Flatwork Disclaimer

Owner acknowledges that the contemplated construction may require access by vehicles and equipment, (excluding cement mixer trucks and other such vehicles exceeding 1 ton capacity) across an existing concrete driveway situated on the Property. Owner further understands that because Builder cannot ascertain the type, amount, or spacing of any reinforcing steel that may or may not be present in an existing driveway, Builder cannot guarantee the performance of such a driveway. **OWNER THEREFORE ACKNOWLEDGES THIS RISK AND AGREES TO RELEASE THE BUILDER FROM ANY CLAIMS FOR DAMAGES TO OR CRACKS IN DRIVEWAYS EXCEPT THOSE ARISING DIRECTLY FROM BUILDER'S CONDUCT THAT IS** WILLFUL, WANTON, RECKLESS OR AMOUNTS TO GROSS NEGLIGENCE.

Estimating and Requesting Proposals

Your primary consideration in estimating is to defend the desired profit margin. By building the job in your head and on paper before beginning work on a jobsite, you will provide better estimates and minimize costly surprises during construction. For estimates to be reliable and protect your profit margin, they must reflect the jobsite conditions and all work to be completed.

A good estimating system has three general characteristics. It is efficient, accurate, and profit-centered. Computers can improve estimating in all three of these areas. They can help you eliminate calculation errors, store data from previous jobs, and create templates to guide cost calculations. Some remodelers have found computerized estimating programs unnecessarily complex for their business models. The estimating forms in this chapter are simple and easily adapted for use with Excel or other basic spreadsheet software.

With only minimal effort, you can create estimates that will positively impact your business's bottom line. Detailed forms prompt you to include all the cost components of a job, thereby minimizing the risk that you will pay for job completion with your profits.

Project Information

In general, estimating comprises the following four steps:

1. Collecting data
2. Assembling and pricing

3. Handing off to production
4. Tracking job progress and completion

Use the Bid Packet Checklist (4.1) for every project. It takes you step-by-step through data collection so you can check off each task as it is completed.

The following forms include space to enter the materials, dimensions, parts, manufacturer names, and other information necessary to develop accurate estimates for various elements of a project. Expand and modify these sheets as necessary:

■ Remodeling Specification Sheet (4.2)
■ Excavation Take-off (4.3)
■ Framing Take-off (4.4)
■ Deck Take-off (4.5)
■ Door and Window Take-off (4.6)
■ Flooring Take-off (4.7)
■ Interior Trim Take-off (4.8)
■ Painting Take-off and Selection (4.9)
■ Roof Materials Take-off (4.10)
■ Window Measuring Sheet (4.11)
■ Electrical Specification Sheet (4.12)

As you examine a kitchen to be remodeled, fill out the Kitchen Checklist (4.13). It includes dimensions, product preferences, and other details useful to the project designer as well as the estimator. Copies of the Save/Reuse Items List (4.14) also go to the estimator and project manager.

Improving Trade Contractor Bids

If trade contractors supply some or all of the work for your remodeling projects, you can use the Request for Proposal (4.15) and Quote Sheet (4.16) to solicit bids. A detailed request for proposal (RFP) has two advantages. First, all trade contractors will calculate prices according to your specifications, so you will be able to make valid comparisons among bids. Second, an RFP describes fully how trade contractors should complete the work.

Employees and trade contractors can help you improve your forms. Some refinements are easy to make and can instantly seal holes in your systems. For example, if you find a jobsite condition that is not addressed in your site visit checklist or other estimating forms, add that item to the list so you remember to look for it on every job. Checking whether the existing walls are drywall or plaster is a simple case in point. Plaster costs more to demo, replace, and repair than drywall, so you should include information about the composition of existing walls.

Often forms can be simplified for efficiency. For example, an electrician recommended that a remodeler structure the RFP as a preprinted list with specifications circled. That format turned out to be so fast and easy to use that the remodeler implemented it for other trades where standardization was possible. Often trade contractors may have their own templates that you can incorporate into your business.

Assembling Estimates

Providing detailed estimates for clients who are just shopping wastes time and money. That's why most professional remodelers will provide ballpark estimates first as part of the sales process to qualify their prospects. This minimizes overhead.

Ballpark

You can use the Short-Form Estimate (4.17) to ascertain the client's willingness to buy at a projected price. If they feel the price is too high, they might be open to reducing the project scope to fit their budget. If the prospective clients have requested a ballpark estimate before entering the design phase of their project, use the Estimate Cover Letter (4.18) to present the estimate. The letter explains the basis for the estimate and the procedure to be followed if they wish to proceed with the design.

When using the short form, base your figures on previous jobs or their components. The Employee Report by Job (*see* chapter 6) and Profit and Loss Report (*see* chapter 7) that are part of your accounting and financial management system are useful references for providing ballpark estimates. However, although information from previous jobs will be accurate enough to provide a ballpark estimate, you should proceed to gather more detailed information for a more comprehensive estimate once customers are qualified.

Detailed

Use the Estimate Form (4.19) to prepare detailed estimates. This worksheet is organized chronologically, from permitting to cleanup, and includes line items for each component of a job. Although many software programs group remodeling work by trade or product category, by consistently building estimates chronologically you will prevent inadvertent omission of a step or detail in the remodeling process. Omission is the most frequent and costly error in estimating. Organizing tasks chronologically in the estimate form makes scheduling a snap too. The scheduler adds days of duration to each task or can paste the entire workflow into Microsoft Project® for manipulation and presentation.

Prices can be calculated, as appropriate, by materials quantity, square footage, or time. To protect the profit margin, apply retail prices to each component, rather than compiling your contractor costs and adding an overhead and profit line at the end. This strategy allows you the flexibility to subcontract any component and still earn your desired profit margin. Moreover, if you choose to handle all of the work yourself or with your employees rather than trade contractors, you may exceed your anticipated profit margin. Some remodelers take an estimating spreadsheet to the project site to prompt thorough information gathering.

Time and Materials

Use the Work Order Invoice (4.20) or Time and Materials Worksheet (4.21) to record the work. Form 4.21 includes workers' compensation cost codes. In addition to enabling you to monitor specific job costs, it can help you generate reports on annual employee hours to help lower your insurance costs. These two forms are also your documentation for time and materials clients; you attach them to invoices for completed work.

Collecting Data

Although many remodelers are comfortable using materials pricing data in off-the-shelf software packages, others prefer to generate their own cost databases. (Because labor costs vary by location and job, remodelers should factor in their own labor costs.) No matter what you base costs on, you should establish a procedural link between actual cost data and your estimating templates, and regularly analyze and adjust your estimating templates for future jobs based on previous experience.

One way to gather a historical record to use in future estimating is to have estimators photograph sites as part of their work. These photographs

- record existing conditions
- are a resource during the design process
- illustrate the "before" picture so you can show the improvement after the completed project

The more photographs the better. Documentation generally costs little compared with the potential problems it can address or alleviate.

Use the Estimate

Once you begin a job, compare the estimate with actual costs as they accrue. Adjust the work pace and production plan if you discover deviations or the scope of work changes, to maintain efficiency and keep spending in check. Use the Estimate-Expense forms that are part of your financial management and accounting system discussed in chapter 7 to verify whether the company's database of costs is current and accurate. Armed with up-to-date numbers, you can improve your estimates.

Chapter 4 Forms

Bids

4.1 Bid Packet Checklist (Word)
4.15 Request for Proposal (Word)

Estimates

4.13 Kitchen Checklist (Word)
4.14 Save/Reuse Items List (Word)
4.16 Quote Sheet (Word)
4.17 Short-Form Estimate (Excel)
4.18 Estimate Cover Letter (Word)
4.19 Estimate Form (Excel)

Specifications

4.2 Remodeling Specification Sheet (Word)
4.11 Window Measuring Sheet (Excel)
4.12 Electrical Specification Sheet (Word)

Take-offs

4.3 Excavation Take-off (Excel)
4.4 Framing Take-off (Excel)
4.5 Deck Take-off (Excel)
4.6 Door and Window Take-off (Excel)
4.7 Flooring Take-off (Excel)
4.8 Interior Trim Take-off (Excel)
4.9 Painting Take-off and Selection (Excel)
4.10 Roof Materials Take-off (Word)

Work Records

4.20 Work Order Invoice (Word)
4.21 Time and Materials Worksheet (Excel)

4.1   Bid Packet Checklist

Company Name

ESTIMATOR'S BID PACKET CHECKLIST

Start Date of Estimate: _____
Due Date of Estimate: _____
Job Name: _____
Job Location: _____

Bid Set Up:

- ☐ Plans received
- ☐ Created scope sheet for each trade and note at category in Tracking Sheet
- ☐ Made job site visit with applicable trades and suppliers
- ☐ Took site photos (if applicable)
- ☐ Compiled list of questions for architect/owner

Bid Packet Completion:

- ☐ Collected minimum of 2 bids for each trade (unless noted otherwise)
- ☐ Cross checked bids for accuracy
- ☐ Cross checked bids for comparability to one another
- ☐ Numbered bids and entered bids into bid sheet with comments
- ☐ Compiled list of items not included in contract
- ☐ Completed calculations for the following (if applicable)

  - ☐ Demolition (number of workers, days, loads)
  - ☐ Volume of dirt to be hauled
  - ☐ Square footage of added or remodeled space
  - ☐ Drywall square footage
  - ☐ Siding or stucco square footage or yardage
  - ☐ Lineal footage of base, case, crown
  - ☐ Lineal footage of cabinets (uppers, lowers, full height)
  - ☐ Number of lavs, WCs, tubs, showers
  - ☐ Flooring square footage for each type of flooring
  - ☐ Lineal footage of railings by type
  - ☐ Insulation square footage

- ☐ Made list of unresolved items
- ☐ Made list of other concerns that need to be addressed

4.2   Remodeling Specification Sheet

Contract data specifications for residence of: _____

Government Unit: _____
Block: _____ Lot: _____

Home Telephone: _____
Work Telephone: _____

Contract Date: _____
Start Date: Upon receipt of building permits

COMPLETION DATE: _____

_____ weeks from date of commencement

Site Preparation

☐ Lot Cleaning
☐ Shrub Removal
☐ Tree Removal
☐ Stump Removal
☐ Removal–All Job Related Debris
☐ Rock Excavation
☐ Soil Hauled Away
☐ Soil Used on Site
☐ Outside Footing Drain
☐ Finish Seeding
☐ Rough Grading

Foundation

☐ 2,500 psi Footing Mix
☐ 8″ × 36″ Footing Trench
☐ 8″ × 16″ Footing
☐ 8″ × 24″ Footing
☐ 8″ Diam. × 36″ Deep Piers
☐ 16″ × 16″ × 8″ Piers
☐ 24″ × 24″ × 12″ Piers
☐ Area + 6″ Proj. Chimney
☐ 1-½″ Cover Slab
☐ 3-½″ Slab
☐ Visqueen and Cover Stone
☐ Visqueen Under Slab
☐ Earth Under
☐ 4″ Stone Under
☐ 6 × 6 #10 Wire Mesh

Block: Foundation   Cinder

☐ 8 × 8 × 16 Solid
☐ 8 × 8 × 16 Hollow
☐ 12 × 8 × 16 Solid
☐ 12 × 8 × 16 Hollow
☐ Parging   ☐ Stucco
☐ Waterproofing
☐ Alum. 8 × 16 Vents   2   3   4
☐ 3″ Steel Pipes

Girders:

☐ Laminated Beam
☐ Light Beam
☐ 1 Beam
☐ WF
☐ Angle
☐ Fitch Plate
☐ Channel

4.2   Remodeling Specification Sheet (continued)

Floor System

Sills:

☐ Single   ☐ 2×4   ☐ 2×6

☐ Termite Proofing

Joists:

☐ Douglas Fir Con. Grade

☐ Southern Pine

1st Floor	2nd Floor	Deck
☐ 2×6	☐ 2×6	☐ 2×6
☐ 2×8	☐ 2×8	☐ 2×8
☐ 2×10	☐ 2×10	☐ 2×10
☐ 2×12	☐ 2×12	☐ 2×12

Spc. 1st Flr.	Spc. 2nd Flr.
☐ 12" o.c.	☐ 12: o.c.
☐ 16" o.c.	☐ 16" o.c.
☐ 24" o.c.	☐ 24" o.c.

☐ Solid Bridging

☐ Cross Bridging

☐ Plyw. Sub-Floor Ext Glue

☐ 1st   ☐ 2nd

Size 1st	Size 2nd
☐ ½"	☐ ½"
☐ ⅝"	☐ ⅝"
☐ ¾"	☐ ¾"

☐ Blocking

☐ Glue to Framing

☐ ⅜" Plyw. Ext. Underlymnt–
   Master Bathroom

☐ ¼" Plywood

☐ Homosote

Location:

Floor System Finish–Wood

☐ Oak

☐ Fir

☐ Pine

Grade:

☐ #1 Select

☐ other

Size:

☐ 1×3   ☐ 1×4

☐ 5/4×6   ☐ Random

Finish:

☐ Prefinished

☐ On site

Floors:

Material, location, and quantity:

☐ Quarry Tile _____ sq. ft.

☐ Tile Ceramic _____ sq. ft.

☐ Composition _____ sq. ft.

☐ Masonry _____ sq. ft. installed

4.2   Remodeling Specification Sheet (continued)

Exterior Enclosure

Framing:

☐ Douglas Fir Cons. Grade

Size - 1st Floor:	Size - 2nd Floor:
☐ 2 × 4	☐ 2 × 4
☐ 2 × 6	☐ 2 × 6

☐ 16" o.c. spacing
☐ 24" o.c. spacing
☐ Plywood Ext. Glue Sheath
☐ Composition Sheathing
☐ Size: ½"   ¾"   1"

Siding:

☐ Plywood
☐ Bevel Select Cedar
☐ Vertical Board
☐ Shakes–Select Cedar
☐ Board and Batten
☐ Shingles–Select Cedar
☐ Asbestos
☐ Aluminum Siding
☐ Size:
    Backer: ☐ Foam   ☐ Composite

Insulation

(R-Values as represented by manufacturer)

☐ Floor: R: _____
☐ Wall: R: _____
☐ Ceiling: R: _____

Windows: Manufacturer _____

☐ Casement
☐ Double Hung
☐ Sliding
☐ Awning
☐ Special
☐ Skylight
☐ Sash Pattern
   6/6 – 2H/2H – 1 Grille
☐ Insulating Glass
☐ Storm Panel   ☐ Screen
☐ Vinyl   ☐ Unfinished
Manufacturer: _____

Doors:

☐ Flush Solid:
☐ Panel:
☐ One Light:
☐ Lights:
☐ Sliding
☐ Vinyl Covered
☐ White
☐ Earth Tone
☐ Aluminum
☐ Factory Finished Prime
☐ Storm   ☐ Screen
☐ Insulating Glass–Double. Pane
☐ Deadbolt
Manufacturer: _____

4.2   Remodeling Specification Sheet (continued)

Fireplace:

- ☐ Prefabricated
- ☐ Masonry   Exterior Facing:
  - ☐ Brick
  - ☐ Block and Stucco
  - ☐ Wood Surround
  - ☐ Siding

  Interior Facing:
  - ☐ Slate   ☐ Marble   ☐ Brick
  - ☐ Wood Surround
  - ☐ Stucco
  - ☐ Opening Size

  Hearth:
  - ☐ Flush   ☐ Raised
  - ☐ Material
  - ☐ Ash Dump
  - ☐ Clean Out

Roof System:

Construction Grade Douglas Fir
Rafters:
  - Size: ☐ 2 x 6   ☐ 2 x 8   ☐ 2 x 10
            ☐ 2 x 12   ☐ Trusses
  - Spacing: ☐ 12″   ☐ 16″   ☐ 24″

Plywood Sheathing,
  - ☐ Exterior Glue - ½″

Shingles: ☐ Asphalt
                ☐ Fiberglass
                ☐ 240#
                ☐ Other
                ☐ Color
                ☐ Match as Available
Exposure   ☐ 5″   ☐ 4″   ☐ 3″
Built up   ☐ _____ Years
            ☐ Roll
Surface   ☐ Slag   ☐ Smooth
Underlayment ☐ 15#   ☐ 30#

Ceiling Joists

Size: ☐ 2 x 4   ☐ 2 x 6
           ☐ 2 x 8   ☐ 2 x 10
Spacing: ☐ 12″   ☐ 16″   ☐ 24″

Vents

- ☐ Continuous Soffit
- ☐ Ridge
- ☐ Gable End

Flashings

- ☐ Alum   ☐ 40#Tin   ☐ Copper

Gutter

- ☐ Aluminum   ☐ Other

Shape:
- ☐ O.G.   ☐ Half Round

Finish:
- ☐ Factory Enamel

Color:
- ☐ White   ☐ Earthtone

Interior Finish

Walls and Ceiling:
- ☐ Sheetrock: Tape and spackle; ready to paint
- ☐ Paneling
- ☐ Special:

Interior Doors

- ☐ Flush
- ☐ Panel
- ☐ Hollow Core
- ☐ Solid Core
- ☐ Special
  - ☐ 1-³⁄₈″   ☐ 1-³⁄₄″
  - ☐ Stain Grd.   ☐ Paint Grd.

Closet Doors

- ☐ Sliding   ☐ Swing
- ☐ Bifold   ☐ Special

4.2   Remodeling Specification Sheet (continued)

Trim

- ☐ Clam Shell   ☐ Colonial
- ☐ Sanitary   ☐ Paint Grd.
- ☐ Match as available
- ☐ Special

Material

- ☐ Wood   ☐ Metal   ☐ Masonry

Stairs

- ☐ Size
- ☐ Material
- ☐ Risers
- ☐ Handrail
- ☐ Balusters

Kitchen Cabinets and Counters

- ☐ Existing
- ☐ New
- ☐ Manufacturer
- ☐ Finish
- ☐ Door Style
- ☐ Hardware
- ☐ Drop Ceiling
- ☐ Material
- ☐ Counter Top
- ☐ Back Splash: ☐ 4   ☐ 6   ☐ Full
- ☐ Formica
- ☐ Corian
- ☐ Tile
- ☐ Other

Bath Cabinets

- ☐ Vanity
- ☐ Finish
- Manufacturer: _____

Bath Accessories

Medicine Cabinet

- ☐ Recessed
- ☐ Surface

Accessories

- ☐ Ceramic
- ☐ Chrome
- ☐ Towel Bar
- ☐ Toilet Paper Holder
- ☐ Grab Bar
- ☐ Shower
- ☐ Shower Door
- ☐ Soap Dish
- ☐ Other

Mechanical/Plumbing

Manufacturer

- ☐ American Standard - A.S.
- ☐ Kohler - K
- ☐ Other

- ☐ Lavatory
  - ☐ Fittings
  - ☐ Color
- ☐ Water Closets
  - ☐ Color
- ☐ Bathtub
  - ☐ Fittings
  - ☐ Color
- ☐ Shower
  - ☐ Fittings

Fans:

- ☐ Attic
- ☐ Bath
- ☐ Kitchen

4.2   Remodeling Specification Sheet (continued)

Appliances and Sinks

- ☐ Kitchen Sink
  - ☐ Fittings
  - ☐ Color
- ☐ Garbage Disposal
- ☐ Ice Maker
- ☐ Bar Sink
- ☐ Range
- ☐ Oven
- ☐ Clothes Washer
- ☐ Dryer

Mechanical/Heating: ☐ Existing   ☐ New

Type of System:
- ☐ Warm Air
- ☐ Hot Water Baseboard
- ☐ Electric Units
- ☐ Radiator

Fuel:
- ☐ Oil
- ☐ Gas
- ☐ Electric

Distribution

- ☐ _____ lin. ft. baseboard
- ☐ _____ # supplies
- ☐ _____ # returns

Air Conditioning

- ☐ Unit
- ☐ Central - existing
  - ☐ Capacity
  - ☐ Model

4.3   Excavation Take-Off

Company Name
Company Logo
Company Affiliations

Job Name: _____   Lot / Block: _____

Job Address: _____   Date of Plans: _____

Underground Markouts		
Shrubbery Removal		
Site Clearing		
Access Drive		
Wheel Cleaning Blanket		
Soil Erosion Control		
Utilities Trenching		
Excavation		
Material Moving		
Backfill		
Finish Grade		
Drainage Piping		
Leader Drains		
Footing Drains		
Seed and Hay		
Crushed Stone		
Misc. Labor		

Address
Phone–Fax
E-mail–Web Site

4.4   Framing Take-Off

Company Name
Company Logo
Company Affiliations

Job Name: _____   Lot / Block: _____

Job Address: _____   Date of Plans: _____

6″ Sill Seal 80′
4″ Sill Seal 40′
$2 \times 4 \times ($) CCA #3
$2 \times 6 \times ($) CCA #3
$\frac{5}{4} \times 3 \times ($) Spruce

	Circle One:			1st Load	2nd Load	3rd Load
$2 \times 4 \times 10$	HF	DF	Utility			
$2 \times 4 \times 12$	HF	DF	Utility			
$2 \times 4 \times 14$	HF	DF	Utility			
$2 \times 4 \times 16$	HF	DF	Utility			
$2 \times 6 \times 8$	HF	DF				
$2 \times 6 \times 10$	HF	DF				
$2 \times 6 \times 12$	HF	DF				
$2 \times 6 \times 14$	HF	DF				
$2 \times 6 \times 16$	HF	DF				
$2 \times 6 \times 18$	HF	DF				
$2 \times 6 \times 20$	HF	DF				
$2 \times 8 \times 8$	HF	DF				
$2 \times 8 \times 10$	HF	DF				
$2 \times 8 \times 12$	HF	DF				
$2 \times 8 \times 14$	HF	DF				
$2 \times 8 \times 16$	HF	DF				
$2 \times 8 \times 18$	HF	DF				
$2 \times 8 \times 20$	HF	DF				
$2 \times 8 \times 22$	HF	DF				
$2 \times 8 \times 24$	HF	DF				

Address
Phone–Fax
E-mail–Web Site

4.4   Framing Take-Off (continued)

Company Name
Company Logo
Company Affiliations

	Circle One:		1st Load	2nd Load	3rd Load
2 × 10 × 8	HF	DF			
2 × 10 × 10	HF	DF			
2 × 10 × 12	HF	DF			
2 × 10 × 14	HF	DF			
2 × 10 × 16	HF	DF			
2 × 10 × 18	HF	DF			
2 × 10 × 20	HF	DF			
2 × 10 × 22	HF	DF			
2 × 10 × 24	HF	DF			
2 × 10 × 26	HF	DF			
2 × 10 × 28	HF	DF			
2 × 12 × 8	HF	DF			
2 × 12 × 10	HF	DF			
2 × 12 × 12	HF	DF			
2 × 12 × 14	HF	DF			
2 × 12 × 16	HF	DF			
2 × 12 × 18	HF	DF			
2 × 12 × 20	HF	DF			
2 × 12 × 22	HF	DF			
2 × 12 × 24	HF	DF			
2 × 12 × 26	HF	DF			
2 × 12 × 28	HF	DF			
2 × 4 pre-cuts 8′ DF					
2 × 4 pre-cuts 9′ DF					
½ CDX plywood					
7⁄16 OSB plywood					
5⁄8 CDX plywood					
¾ T&G plywood					

Address
Phone–Fax
E-mail–Web Site

4.4   Framing Take-Off (continued)

Company Name
Company Logo
Company Affiliations

	1st Load	2nd Load	3rd Load
Glue			
2 × 8 single hangers			
2 × 8 double hangers			
10D common nails #50			
8cc cooler nails #50			
10D cut nails #50			
8′ lolly columns			
9′ lolly columns			
12′ lolly columns			

Other Items:

_____

_____

_____

_____

_____

_____

Address
Phone–Fax
E-mail–Web Site

4.5   Deck Take-Off

Company Name
Company Logo
Company Affiliations

Job Name: _____   Lot / Block: _____

Job Address: _____   Date of Plans: _____

Excavation		
Labor		
Forms		
Concrete		
Labor		
Grading Prep		
Labor		
Posts		
Girders		
Ledger		
Floor Joists		
Box beam		
Blocking		
Decking		
Fasteners		
Railings		
Stairs		
Finishing		
Cleanup		
Debris Removal		
Electrical work		

Address
Phone–Fax
E-mail–Web Site

4.6   Door and Window Take-Off

Company Name
Company Logo
Company Affiliations

Job Name: _____   Lot / Block: _____

Job Address: _____   Date of Plans: _____

Doors	Qty	Spec	Unit Price	Total
Basement				0
Unit				0
Screens				0
Grills				0
Finish				0
First Floor				0
Unit				0
Screens				0
Grills				0
Finish				0
Second Floor				0
Unit				0
Screens				0
Grills				0
Finish				0
Garage				0
Unit				0
Screens				0
Grills				0
Finish				0

Address
Phone–Fax
E-mail–Web Site

4.6   Door and Window Take-Off (continued)

Company Name
Company Logo
Company Affiliations

Windows	Qty	Spec	Unit Price	Total
Basement				0
Unit				0
Screens				0
Grills				0
Finish				0
First Floor				0
Unit				0
Screens				0
Grills				0
Finish				0
Second Floor				0
Unit				0
Screens				0
Grills				0
Finish				0
Garage				0
Unit				0
Screens				0
Grills				0
Finish				0
Total Estimate				0

Address
Phone−Fax
E-mail−Web Site

4.7   Flooring Take-Off

Company Name
Company Logo
Company Affiliations

Flooring Take-Off

Job Name: _____   Lot / Block: _____

Job Address: _____   Date of Plans: _____

Room	Material	Length	Width	Area
				0
				0
				0
				0
				0
				0
				0
				0
				0
				0
				0
				0
SubTotal				0
Prep				
Installation				
Overhead				
Profit				
Total				0

4.7　Flooring Take-Off (continued)

Company Name
Company Logo
Company Affiliations

Sketches

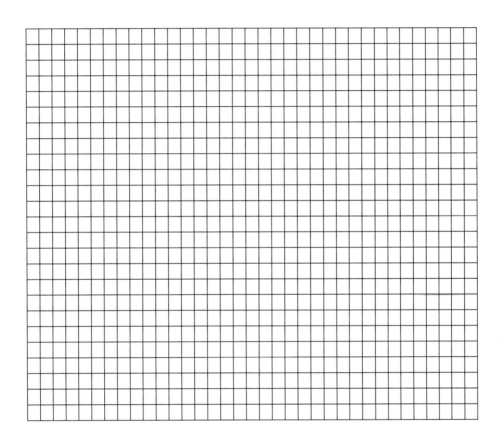

Address
Phone—Fax
E-mail—Web Site

4.8   Interior Trim Take-Off

Company Name
Company Logo
Company Affiliations

Job Name: _____   Lot / Block: _____
Job Address: _____   Date of Plans: _____

Doors	Qty	Type	Unit Price	Total
				0
				0
				0
				0
				0

Base

		Shoe Moulding		0

Window Casing

		Sills		0

Chair Rail

				0

Crown

				0

Trimmed Openings

				0

Wainscoting

				0

Cabinets

				0

Casework

				0

Closets

				0

Shims

				0

Nails

				0
				0

Total Estimate				0

Address
Phone-Fax
E-mail-Web Site

4.9   Painting Take-Off and Selection

Company Name
Company Logo
Company Affiliations

Owner(s): _____   Date: _____

Address: _____   Jobsite: _____

Paint Contractor: _____   Supervisor: _____

Room	#	Surface	Manuf.	Color	Paint #	O = Oil L = Latex	Finish	Coats

Notes: (1) Number of coats includes primer
          (2) All redwood receives oil primer
          (3) Deep colors or gloss finishes may require additional coats

Company Address
Phone
Fax
E-mail
Web site

4.10   Roof Materials Take-Off

Company Name
Address
City, State, Zip
Phone/Fax

Roof Materials

Job Name:		Location:		
SUPPLIERS	**QUANTITY**	**MATERIAL**	**DESCRIPTION**	**COLOR**
		Shingles		
		"D" metal drip edge		
		15-lb felt		
		Ice & water shield		
		90-lb roll roofing		
		Corner flashing		
		Step flashing		
		1-1/4 roof nails		
		1-1/2 roof nails		
		2" ROOF NAILS		
		1-1/2 pipe flashing		
		2 pipe flashing		
		Retro fit		
		3 pipe flashing		
		Roof vents		
		Staples		
		Cap nails		
		Coil stock		
		Drive pins		
		8-d sinkers		
		Sheeting		
		Roof cement		
		NP 1		
		Silicone		

4.11 Window Measuring Sheet

CUSTOMER'S NAME: _____

ADDRESS: _____

CITY: _____

DATE: _____

PHONE: _____

STATE: _____

BUDGET:

BUILDER GRADE	QUALITY	HIGH QUALITY
FULL UNIT	REPLACEMENT UNIT	TILT SASH PACK
WOOD	VINYL	FIBER GLASS	ALUMINUM CLAD
AWNING	DOUBLE HUNG	CASEMENT

QUANTITY	FRAME OPENING		PRODUCT SIZE		PRODUCT DESCRIPTION & COLOR	INTERIOR	EXTERIOR	JAMB WIDTH
	WIDTH	HEIGHT	WIDTH	HEIGHT				

WOOD	PRIMED	PAINTED	CLAD	SINGLE GLASS	⁷/₈ SDL	1⅛ ADL
LOW-E	LOW-E II	LOW-E 4	ARGON	KRYPTON	WOOD STORMS	ALUMINUM STORMS
DECORATIVE GLASS	PRIVACY	TEMPERED GLASS	SPACER BARS	BRICK MOLD	CASINGS	

HARDWARE: BRASS   ANTIGUE BRASS   WHITE   CHROME   POLISHED   POLISHED CHROME   BRONZE

JAMB LINERS: WHITE   OFF WHITE   BROWN   OTHER _____

COLOR: WHITE   OFF WHITE   BEIGE   BROWN   GREEN   RED   OTHER _____   BRONZE

REMOVABLE GRILLES

4.12   Electrical Specification Sheet

Company Name
Company Logo
Company Affiliations

**ALL RECESSED LIGHTING FOR COLD
CEILINGS MUST BE I.C. TYPE FIXTURES**

SWI: Switches
REC: Receptacles
LSURF: Light Surfaces
LREC: Light Recesses

SD: Smoke Detectors
GFCI: Ground-Fault
         Circuit-Interrupters
CATV: Cable Outlet

	SWI	REC	LSURF	LREC	SD	GFI	PHONE	CATV
Entry								
Sun Room								
Living Room								
Dining Room								
Family Room								
Breakfast Room								
Kitchen								
Hall–First Floor								
Powder Room								
Laundry								
Garage								
Outside								
Bedroom, Master								
Bedroom								
Bedroom								
Hall, Second Floor								
Bath, Master								
Bath								
Basement								
Porch								
Deck								
TOTAL:								

4.12   Electrical Specification Sheet (continued)

Company Name
Company Logo
Company Affiliations

MECHANICAL

ELECTRICAL:

Service Capacity—Existing

☐ Equipment Rating
☐ Gen. Pur. Circuit #
☐ Sub-Panel

> *IN ORDER TO PROTECT THE INTEGRITY*
> *OF YOUR SECURITY SYSTEM AND INTER-*
> *CONNECTED FIRE ALARMS, ALL REVISIONS*
> *TO THE SYSTEM MUST BE DONE BY YOUR*
> *ALARM SERVICE CONTRACTOR*

SPECIAL CIRCUITS:

☐ Range   ☐ Furnace
☐ Microwave Oven ☐ Central Air Cond.
☐ Dishwasher   ☐ Water Heater
☐ Refrigerator   ☐ Dryer
☐ Disposal   ☐ Washer
☐ Oven   ☐ Room Air Cond.

Not included in this contract:
Additional:

Outlets	$100.00
Switches	$100.00
Light	$130.00
Telephone	$125.00
Cable	$125.00

Address
Phone—Fax
E-mail—Web Site

4.13   Kitchen Checklist

Customer Name: _____

Address: _____

Phone: _____

Kitchen Checklist

- ☐ Size of kitchen
- ☐ Shape of kitchen
  - ☐ U
  - ☐ Galley
  - ☐ L

☐ Is the floor level?	Yes	No
☐ Are the walls plumb?	Yes	No
☐ Is the ceiling plumb?	Yes	No
☐ Ceiling height	_____	
☐ Bulkheads?	Yes	No

- ☐ Wall covering   tile   wallpaper   paint   plaster   drywall

☐ Window	Yes	No
☐ Height from floor		
☐ Location	Left	Right
☐ Size–outside of casing	_____	
☐ Ceiling cable heat	Yes	No
☐ Type of floor	_____	
☐ Underlayment thickness	_____	
☐ Subfloor thickness	_____	
☐ Is floor higher or lower than adjacent floor?	Yes	No
☐ By how much?	_____	

- ☐ Light layout
  - ☐ Existing
  - ☐ Proposed
- ☐ Electrical layout review (Provide on plan view.)
  - ☐ GFCIs

☐ Space for extra breakers in distribution center	Yes	No

-   ☐ Location of distribution center _____
- ☐ Locations of main water shutoffs
- ☐ Cabinet style
- ☐ Cabinet layout (Provide on plan view.)
- ☐ Countertops

☐ Backsplash height	_____
☐ Thickness of top	_____

4.13   Kitchen Checklist (continued)

☐ Rearrange plumbing?	Yes	No
☐ Sink	Keep	Replace
☐ Style		
☐ Material		
☐ Color		
☐ Faucet	Keep	Replace
☐ Style		
☐ Finish		
☐ Spray		
☐ Soap dispenser		
☐ Hole cover		
☐ Strainer	Keep	Replace
☐ Style		
☐ Material		
☐ Quantity		
☐ Do the drains operate properly?	Yes	No
☐ Water line from	Floor	Wall
☐ Shutoffs	Yes	No
☐ Drain line	Floor	Wall
☐ Shutoffs	Yes	No
☐ Crawl space, basement, or slab?		
☐ Door width & swing		
☐ Jamb thickness	Wood	Steel
☐ Trim Details		
☐ Baseboard _____		
☐ Window _____		
☐ Door _____		
☐ Crown molding _____		
☐ Chair rail _____		
☐ Appliance layout (Provide on plan view.)		
☐ Appliances		
☐ Garbage Disposal	Keep	Replace
Manufacturer		
Model #		
☐ Dishwasher	Keep	Replace
Model #	____	
Color	____	
Size	____	

4.13   Kitchen Checklist (continued)

		Keep	Replace
☐ Refrigerator		Keep	Replace
Model #		____	
Style		____	
Dimensions			
Width		____	
Height including hinge		____	
Depth, less door		____	
Depth with door		____	
Area needed to open doors if side by side		____	
Hinge Type		____	
Icemaker Type		____	
Ice and Water in Door		Yes	No
Color		_____	

		Keep	Replace
☐ Stove		Keep	Replace
		Gas	Electric
Style	Freestanding	Slide in	Drop in
Dimensions			
Width		____	
Height		____	
Depth with handle		____	
Size		____	
Color		____	

		Keep	Replace
☐ Cooktop		Keep	Replace
Style		Gas	Electric
Dimensions			
Width		____	
Depth			
Corners		Radius	Square
Size		____	
Color		____	

	Keep	Replace
☐ Oven	Keep	Replace
Style	Gas	Electric
Cleaning	Self	Manual
Dimensions		
Width	____	____
Height	____	____

	Keep	Replace
☐ Microwave Hood	Keep	Replace
	Vented	Non-Vented
Height	____	____
Color	____	____

4.13   Kitchen Checklist (continued)

		Keep	Replace
☐ Microwave			
Style		‾‾‾	‾‾‾
Width		‾‾‾	‾‾‾
Height		‾‾‾	‾‾‾
Depth		‾‾‾	‾‾‾
Color		‾‾‾	‾‾‾

		Keep	Replace
☐ Hood			
Style		Vented	Non-Vented
Width		‾‾‾	‾‾‾
Height		‾‾‾	‾‾‾
Depth		‾‾‾	‾‾‾
Color		‾‾‾	‾‾‾

			Keep	Replace
☐ Washer				
Style	Top load	Front load	Stack	
Width			‾‾‾	
Height			‾‾‾	
Depth			‾‾‾	
Color			‾‾‾	

			Keep	Replace
☐ Dryer				
Style	Top load	Front load	Stack	
Width			‾‾‾	
Height			‾‾‾	
Depth			‾‾‾	
Color			‾‾‾	

☐ Location of registers (provide on plan view)

☐ Does the current soffit contain mechanicals that need to be relocated ?

☐ Special items _____

☐ Pictures attached ?

☐ Drawing attached ?

4.14   Save/Reuse Items List

Company Name
Company Logo
Company Affiliations

Items To Be Saved or Reused

Items Saved	Description of Item	Existing Area	Relocated Area	Complete
Items Reused	**Description of Item**	**Existing Area**	**Relocated Area**	**Complete**

Address
Phone
Fax
E-mail
Web Site

4.15   Request for Proposal

Company Name
Address
City, State, Zip
Phone/Fax

<Date>

<Subcontractor>
<Address>
<City, St Zip>

Dear < >,

Enclosed are plans for an upcoming renovation project we will be completing. We would like you to participate in this job and would ask you to please compile and forward an estimate/proposal by _____. To access the property please contact our office.

Specifics:

    Job Location:
    Proposed Start Date:
    Special conditions/restrictions:
        • Physical access:
        • Pets
        • Occupancy
        • Work hours
        • Cleanup

Sincerely,

<Your Name>

4.16   Quote Sheet

<YOUR Company>   Date: _____, 20
<Your address>
Phone: Due Date: _____, 20
Fax:

Job Name: _____   Job # _____
Trade Contractor: _____
Contact: _____   Ph (___)____-_____
Fax: _____   E-mail: _____

Materials to be supplied by sub:

_____
_____
_____
_____$_____.00__

Specific work to be completed (labor):

_____
_____
_____
_____$_____.00__

Number of days on work site: _____
Probable date of work or delivery: _____
Delivery available?   Y   N   Included in bid?   Y   N
Lead time for material ordering: _____

4.17   Short-Form Estimate

Company Name
Company Logo
Company Affiliations

JOB NAME	JOB NUMBER	DATE
LOCATION	JOB MANAGER	CHECKED BY
ESTIMATOR		ENTRY BY
JOB DESCRIPTION	*DENOTES FIRM BID	DATE

PHASE	DESCRIPTION	Vendor	Labor	Material	Other	Subcontract	Total
1	PLANS & PERMITS						0
2	DEMOLITION						0
3	SITE WORK						0
4	EXCAVATION						0
5	CONCRETE						0
6	MASONRY						0
7	FRAMING						0
8	ROOFING						0
9	EXT TRIM						0
10	WINDOWS/DOORS						0
11	SIDING & GUTTERS						0
12	PLUMBING						0
13	HVAC						0
14	ELECTRIC						0
15	INSULATION						0
16	DRYWALL						0
17	CEILINGS (DROP, ETC,)						0
18	MILLWORK/TRIM						0
19	CABINETS/TOPS						0
20	FLOORS						0
21	PAINTING						0
22	DEBRIS/CLEAN UP						0
23	LANDSC/PAVING						0
24	MISC.						0
25	SUPERVISION						0
26	DECKS/PATIOS						0
27	ALLOWANCES						0
28							0
	Subtotal	0.00	0.00	0.00	0.00	0.00	0.00
0.10	Overhead	0.00	0.00	0.00	0.00	0.00	0.00
0.15	Profit	0.00	0.00	0.00	0.00	0.00	0.00
	Total Costs	0.00	0.00	0.00	0.00	0.00	0.00

Company Address
Phone
Fax
E-mail
Web site

4.18   Estimate Cover Letter

Company Name
Company Logo
Company Affiliations

<Date>

<Customer Name>
<Address>
<City, St, Zip>

Dear <Customer Name>,

The design process is one of the most important components of a building project. It is at this stage that the groundwork is laid for a successful project. If it is your wish to solicit for competitive bids then it places even more emphasis on the design process. Only with plans and specifications can you get a legitimate comparison from multiple companies. We offer a complete service, from design concept to the completed project. Our goal as a company is to secure your trust and confidence in our abilities and produce the best possible product that we can.

*Based on our brief conversation <insert day>, we are basing a range of costs on<enter job description, size, standard items ie: design, building permit, framing, roofing, insulation, drywall, painting, floor-covering, electrical, heating and cooling registers and guttering>. We are estimating between <insert estimate range>. Please bear in mind that until plans and specifications are drawn, this is just a range of **possible** costs.*

Over the < > years we have been in business, we have built many successful relationships with our clients. I'm confident that you will find our service, attention to detail, and concern for your safety to be one of the best in the industry.

If this estimate range is within your budget for this project, then the next step would be the design phase. Please contact us to schedule an appointment with our design staff.

A list of clients we have worked for in the past is available for your review. Thanks for this opportunity to serve your needs and we hope to hear from you soon.

Sincerely,

<Your Name>
<Your Title>

Company Address
Phone-Fax
E-mail-Web site

4.19   Estimate Form

Company Name
Company Logo
Company Affiliations

		date
Estimate	*Enter your estimated #'s in the "estimate" column.*	phone
client	*Total cost to customer calculates automatically.*	plans
address	*Hide yellow rows/columns before printing for customer.*	architect
city	*Enter Column F subtotals into accounting program to run*	revisions
	Profit & Loss (P&L) by job, actual vs. estimate reports, etc.	

work description	Area #1	Area #2	Area #3
length			
width			
ceiling heights			
perimeter walls			
total area			
total perimeter walls			

Estimate

Class	Item		Description
	Add lines as needed.		
100	**Permits/Fees**		
	Building permits		
	Architectural/Engineering		
	Blueprints		
	Shop drawings		
	Surveys		
	Municipal fees		
200	**Demolition**		
	interior		
	exterior		
	plumbing		
	electrical		
	structural		

Company Address
Phone
Fax
E-mail
Web site

4.19   Estimate Form (continued)

Company Name
Company Logo
Company Affiliations

300   **Site Work**
         Utility connections
         temporary electric
         gas service
         electric service
         telephone service
         other utility connection
         individual wells
         water service
         septic system
         sewer service

400   **Excavation**
         backfill
         move fill
         trucking
         footing drains
         leader drain system

500   **Concrete**
         formwork
         slabs
         structural frame
         stairs
         precast decks and walls
         garage/carport slab
         concrete labor

600   **Footings/ Foundations**
         cement
         concrete blocks
         gravel
         sand

Company Address
Phone
Fax
E-mail
Web site

4.19   Estimate Form (continued)

Company Name
Company Logo
Company Affiliations

rebar and reinforcing steel

other foundation materials

labor footings/foundations

radon

Masonry

Masonry Materials

chimney/fireplace

brick veneer

brick/stone wall

masonry flooring

Waterproofing

Termite Protection

Structural Steel

Stairs

Beams

Posts

700   **Framing**

Framing material

Floor framing

posts

joists

plywood

ledger strips

hardware

cross bracing

Partition and Wall framing

studs

plates

bracing

sheathing

hardware

Company Address
Phone
Fax
E-mail
Web site

4.19   Estimate Form (continued)

Company Name
Company Logo
Company Affiliations

Roof Framing

Trusses

gables

ceiling joists

sheathing

bracing

stairs

hardware

Basement Framing

stairs

studs

plates

bracing

hardware

Framing Labor

floor

partition & wall

roof

basement

800   **Roofing**

roofing materials

metal; roof edgings and
   flashings

roofing labor

900   **Exterior Trim**

cornices/rake trim

soffits: gables flashings

misc trim

Company Address
Phone
Fax
E-mail
Web site

4.19   Estimate Form (continued)

Company Name
Company Logo
Company Affiliations

1000   Windows & Doors
windows
skylights
storm windows/doors
exterior doors
interior/closet doors

sliding glass/French doors
garage doors
hardware
installation

1100   Siding
posts and columns
siding
shutters
gutters and downspouts

1200   Rough Plumbing
Finish Plumbing
tub
shower pan
toilet/bidet
sinks
dishwasher
water heater
laundry tub
fittings
labor

1300   Rough HVAC
Finish HVAC
furnace

Company Address
Phone
Fax
E-mail
Web site

4.19   Estimate Form (continued)

Company Name
Company Logo
Company Affiliations

thermostats
air conditioner
duct work
hardware
labor

1400   **Rough Electrical**

Finish Electrical
fixtures
labor

1500   **Insulation**
foundation/basement
roof and ceiling
wall
floor
weatherstripping and
   vapor barrier
labor

1600   **Drywall**
material
labor

1700   **Ceilings and Coverings**
grid system
ceiling tiles
wall coverings

Ceramic Tile
tile
installation
shower doors

1800   **Interior Trim**
moldings
   base
   chair

Company Address
Phone
Fax
E-mail
Web site

4.19   Estimate Form (continued)

Company Name
Company Logo
Company Affiliations

ceiling
   installation
paneling
   installation
closet
   shelving
   hardware
   installation

1900   Cabinets and vanities
kitchen cabinets
countertops
vanities
hardware
installation

Appliances
range
range hood
disposal
dishwasher
refrigerator
washer/dryer
microwave

2000   Flooring
resilient flooring
carpeting
hardwood
installation

2100   Exterior Painting
paint/stain
labor

Company Address
Phone
Fax
E-mail
Web site

4.19   Estimate Form (continued)

Company Name
Company Logo
Company Affiliations

	Interior Decoration		by owners	
	paint			
	wall covering			
	installation			
2200	**Clean-Up**			
	debris removal			
	dumpsters			
2300	**Landscaping**			
	paving			
	seed / hay			
2400	Miscellaneous Work			
	Exterior Structures			
	patio/deck			
	Punch List			
2500	Supervision			
		hard costs		
		hard costs		
	Overhead			
2600		subtotal		
		profit		
	Total for the above work		$ -	
	Payment schedule			
	on signing	10%	$	
	foundation complete	20%	$ -	
	roof framed	20%	$ -	
	windows set	10%	$ -	
	rough wiring	10%	$ -	
	rough plumbing	10%	$ -	
	drywall installed	10%	$ -	
	completion	10%	$ -	
	Total of payments	100%	$ -	

Company Address
Phone
Fax
E-mail
Web site

4.19   Estimate Form (continued)

Company Name
Company Logo
Company Affiliations

Start Date
within 10 days of issuance of municipal permits

Completion Date
14 weeks thereafter
This proposal is valid for 15 days

_____

for <Customer's Name>

_____

for <Your Company Name>

Company Address
Phone
Fax
E-mail
Web site

4.20   Work Order Invoice

Company Name
Company Logo
Company Affiliations

Work Order/Invoice

Page #   of

Job Name_____   Date _____ Job # _____
Address _____   Associate _____
City _____ State _____ Zip _____ _____ Replacement, Warranty
Telephone (home) _____ (work) _____ _____ Repair, No Warranty
Job Description _____
How did the client learn of this service? _____

TIME AND MATERIAL TERMS

Journeyperson labor @ $ ____ /hour; Apprentice labor @ $ ____ /hour
Material, trade contractors and miscellaneous expenses @ cost plus ____%
The Client understands both the warranty position and the rates stated above.
Payment is due upon completion.

Approved by _____

Description of all work performed:

_____
_____
_____
_____
_____
_____
_____
_____
_____

Company Address
Phone
Fax
E-mail
Web site

4.20   Work Order Invoice (continued)

Company Name
Company Logo
Company Affiliations

LABOR AND MATERIAL BREAKDOWN: Material description, rental tool(s), mileage, etc.	Amounts
Subtotal	
Tax	
Balance Due	
Payment on account / payment in full	

I have the authority to order the work outlined above.

Client's Signature _____   For <Your Company> _____

Company Address
Phone
Fax
E-mail
Web site

4.21   Time and Materials Worksheet

Company Name
Company Logo
Company Affiliations

Employee Name: _____

Job Name: _____

Job Location: _____

Work Activity

02	Demolition	13	HVAC
03	Site Work	14	Electric/Lighting
	03.10 Site Work Demo	15	Insulation
04	Excavation	16	Drywall
05	Concrete	17	Ceiling/Coverings
06	Masonry	18	Millwork/Trim
07	Framing	19	Cabinets/Vanities
08	Roofing/Flashing	20	Floor Cover
09	Exterior Trim	21	Paint
10	Doors/Windows	22	Cleanup
11	Siding	23	Landscaping
12	Plumbing	25	Supervision/Pick up materials

Type of Work Completed:

Time to Complete:

Materials Used:

Others on Job:

Name:
Work Completed:
Hours:

Others on Job:

Name:
Work Completed:
Hours:

Controlling Production

Remodeling company reputations—and profits—are made or lost when jobs are produced. Production tests your company's construction skills, quality standards, and project controls. Disorganization and inefficiency upset clients, harm your company's professional reputation, and bleed profits. In contrast, solid production systems bolstered by practical forms move jobs toward completion efficiently. Sound business systems in production will help you delight clients, make your company stand out from the competition, and increase profits.

Plan, Prepare, and Mobilize

Production planning, like estimating, is best organized chronologically from the first meeting with clients through preconstruction, remodeling, and project completion. Detailed, item-by-item lists, with check boxes for tracking essentials such as materials orders, deliveries, and various project phases, such as the Production Checklist (5.1) assure that you account for each step of a project and organize job steps most efficiently.

Before a project begins, review the Remodel Mobilization Checklist (5.2), which encompasses site preparation, notification of neighbors, gathering "before" photographs, and other essential items.

As soon as a job is sold, start a job folder, placing a list of needed documentation, such as permits and inspections, at the front of the folder and all other paperwork behind the list. This list will help you track the job as it progresses. Put the job name at the top of every page in the job folder. For production managers who juggle several jobs simultaneously, this labeling helps avoid confusing project paperwork.

The folder also should include the following items:

- Product Selection Tracking Form (5.3). Use this form to keep everything in place as the client makes selections. Keep one copy of the form in the project file at the office; put another copy in the jobsite folder so the project manager can monitor deliveries.
- Special Materials Order Form (5.4). This form is an ongoing record of the status of custom or special order materials deliveries. Non-standard materials can create non-standard installation issues and costs. The form includes spaces for key dates, such as when the materials are ordered and when delivery is expected. If there are problems, these dates will be helpful in discussions with suppliers.
- Materials Supplier Contact Information Form (5.5). This comprehensive list doubles as a menu of products to be ordered and a log of requested and received orders. It is kept in the office and the contents can be altered for a specific job by deleting unnecessary tradesmen.
- Long-Lead Item Order List (5.6). This list provides a framework for ensuring timely orders that will protect your production schedule.
- Lead Hazard Procedures Checklist (5.7). Use this checklist to certify that you have followed proper lead abatement and protection procedures.
- Permit and Municipal Inspections Report (5.8). The project manager or lead carpenter uses this form to track permit and inspection status and schedule inspections.

The sales representative should review the job file with the lead carpenter or project supervisor well before the preconstruction meeting with clients. Doing so gives production professionals time to review the specifications, ask questions, and make suggestions. Later, when they sit down at the preconstruction meeting, they already will be familiar with the job specifics, which will reassure your clients that they are in good hands.

Consistent Procedures

Just as checklists regulate production planning, production systems will help you handle tasks consistently, efficiently, and with minimal or no problems. For example, the lead carpenter or project manager should follow the Daily Jobsite To Do List Instructions (5.9) and complete the Jobsite To Do List (5.10).

Involve crews in creating standard production procedures and job-tracking documents, such as the Production Report (5.11). At production meetings, encourage them to recommend changes, improvements, and refinements based on their on-the-job experience. For example, a lead carpenter at one remodeling company requested that finish schedules be prepared room by room so that he could better organize his work flow. In response, the company generated room-specific schedules. The lead carpenter was happy and gratified that his suggestion was implemented, and job efficiency improved.

Production is not a one-time event. It is a system with processes and procedures that are repeated with each project. Using forms that reinforce these processes and procedures increases construction efficiency, builds self confidence among the crew members, and elevates the professionalism of your business and workers, whether they are trade contractors or employees.

Maintain Control

In the press of production, many remodelers are tempted to let the paperwork slide. Don't make this mistake. Those who do so invariably lose control of their projects and suffer profit losses. Instead, design your forms and documents to help, rather than burden, your processes. One remodeler tests production forms to see how quickly they can be completed. For example, if the daily job log can be completed in three minutes or less, she is confident workers will use it.

Daily Job Log

The Daily Job Log (5.12) can inform many components of your system. In fact, this log is one of your company's most important documents. Payroll relies on this record of time an employee has spent on the job, the jobsite attended, and specific worker activities. Data from the log can be transferred into QuickBooks or other payroll software. It also can be used to generate reports for insurers, run job costing reports, and track labor allocation.

The log should detail everything that happened, or was supposed to occur each day, including notes about deliveries, trade contractors, work completed, decisions made, and issues clients raised. The log not only informs the company owner about the progress of jobs, it also highlights inefficiencies. Are there too many or too few workers on a jobsite? Are problems brewing on a project? Entries in the Daily Job Log will tell you. The log can jog memories, help settle disagreements, and suggest whether a remodeler needs to change suppliers or trade contractors.

Crew Assignments

Post the Multi-job Schedule (5.13) and Employee Work Schedule (5.14) in the office so your staff can refer to the schedule of crew assignments.

Quality Control

To enhance efficiency and alleviate changes that cause profit leaks, remodelers should incorporate industry guidelines and standard inspection criteria in their company's performance standards. NAHB's *Residential Construction Performance Guidelines: Contractor's Reference,* available at BuilderBooks.com, offers industry guidelines. The regulatory agencies governing remodeling in your area may also provide minimum performance criteria.

After a trade contractor finishes his or her work, the project manager, foreman, or lead carpenter should do a walk-through using the Trade Contractor Walk-Through form (5.15). The form has space for noting which components are acceptable, which are not, and a deadline for the contractor to correct unacceptable work.

Before the pre-completion walk-through with the clients, your project manager should inspect the jobsite and complete a Quality Control Inspection Report (5.16) to alert the lead carpenter or job foreman of final to-do items.

Change Orders

A remodeling company's change order process—or lack of one—either increases or erodes its profit margins. Use change orders for deviations from the original scope of work that would incur additional production costs. Every requested change can be an opportunity to sell further service, but written documentation of change orders is essential to making the sale worth the extra effort. As soon as clients inquire about a possible change, production personnel should inform the company owner or the supervisor. This allows time to price the potential change and gauge its affect on the schedule. Use the Change Order (5.17) form when clients request a change. It spells out

- what will be done
- price of the change
- effect on the production schedule

The project manager or perhaps the lead carpenter completes the form and copies it. One copy goes to the clients, one to the job file, and one to the billing department. This document provides wide latitude to the contractor to proceed with the work as requested using time and materials billing. Every change order should include an extension of the project completion date.

Even if you are inclined to throw in a small change for free as a goodwill gesture, don't neglect to document the change on a change order form with a "no charge" notation. This reinforces the value added to a project in the client's mind and maintains the integrity of your processes.

Project Completion

Use the Pre-completion Conference Detail List (5.18) at the pre-completion walk-through with clients, detailing punch list items and the date by which they will be completed. When the project is complete, review the company's Project Closure Procedures (5.19) to make sure all jobsite, billing, and marketing steps have been taken.

After a project is completed, clients may contact your company to request warranty repairs. Use a Warranty Work Order (5.20) to collect information about the problem and schedule a crew to follow up on the request.

Safety

Jobsite safety is no accident. It begins with planned safety systems, articulated with written policies and procedures and followed up with regular oversight. Routinely discuss safety issues at production meetings using BuilderBooks' health and safety library of materials listed in the Resources section at the back of this book. Include each safety topic on the Production Meeting Agenda (5.21) and document these discussions. You may be able to garner lower insurance premiums for workers' compensation insurance by demonstrating that your company requires safety procedures and that these procedures are regularly discussed with employees. After discussing them with employees, file safety instructions in your company and employee safety manuals. Complete and clear records of accident prevention measures, safety inspections, and employee accidents—including accident circumstances unrelated to the job and your company—are invaluable when seeking annual bids from general liability and worker's compensation insurance carriers. A line in the daily job log that states, "No accidents on job unless otherwise reported," can reduce a company's vulnerability to later false accident claims.

Chapter 5 Forms

Job Folder

5.3   Product Selection Tracking Form (Excel)
5.4   Special Materials Order Form (Excel)
5.5   Materials Supplier Contact Form (Excel)
5.6   Long-Lead Item Order List (Excel)
5.7   Lead Hazard Procedures Checklist (Word)
5.8   Permit and Municipal Inspections Report (Excel)

Work Crew Management

5.9   Daily Jobsite To Do List Instructions (Word)
5.10   Jobsite To Do List (Excel)
5.14   Employee Work Schedule (Excel)

Project Management

5.1   Production Checklist (Excel)
5.2   Remodel Mobilization Checklist (Word)
5.11   Production Report (Excel)
5.12   Daily Job Log (Excel)
5.13   Multijob Schedule (Excel)
5.17   Change Order (Word)
5.21   Production Meeting Agenda (Word)
(*See* page 261 at the end of Chapter 6 for a list of additional project management forms.)

Quality Control and Project Closure

5.15   Trade Contractor Walk-Through (Word)
5.16   Quality Control Inspection Report (Word)
5.18   Pre-completion Conference Detail List (Word)
5.19   Project Closure Procedures (Word)
5.20   Warranty Work Order (Word)

5.1 Production Checklist

CUSTOMER:
ADDRESS:
SUBDIVISION:

	X	DESCRIPTION	CUST SEL REQ	SALES DEPT	EST DEPT	PROD DEPT	DATE REQ	DATE COMP
1		FIRST SALES MEETING						
2		QUALIFY CUSTOMER						
3		DETERMINE DESIGN CRITERIA INCLUDING LOT COST, # OF						
4		ROOMS, STYLE & DISCUSS DESIGN PROCESS						
5		PRELIMINARY PLANS						
6		PRELIMINARY ESTIMATE						
7		SECOND SALES MEETING						
8		PROFESSIONAL SERVICES AGREEMENT EXECUTED						
9		ORDER SOILS TEST						
10		RETAIN ARCHITECT & ENGINEER						
11		FIRST MEETING ARCHITECT						
12		SITE PLAN / FLOOR PLAN DISCUSSED						
13		PRODUCE SKETCH OF FLOOR PLAN & ELEVATION						
14		CREATE PRELIMINARY SPECIFICATIONS						
15		UPDATE PRELIM COST ESTIMATE BASED ON SKETCH						
16		CUSTOMER TO APPROVE SKETCH (IF APPROVED, MOVE TO						
17		DRAFTED PRELIM)						
18		DISCUSS HOME AUTOMATION						
19		SECOND MEETING ARCHITECT						
20		REVIEW "DRAFTED PRELIM"						
21		FLOOR PLAN FINALIZED / ELEVATIONS REVIEWED / DETAIL						
22		FINISHES, CABINETS, WINDOWS, FLOOR SURFACES, ETC						
23		FINAL BUILDING ENVELOPE APPROVED						
24		PRELIMINARY SITE / PAD DIMENSIONS CHECKED						
25		SURVEYOR TO STAKE IF NECESSARY						
26		THIRD MEETING ARCHITECT						
27		REVIEW & APPROVE "CUSTOMER APPROVAL" SET						
28		IDENTIFY FINAL CLIENT CHANGES						
29		PROVIDE SITE PLAN W/ A/C COMPRESSOR, ELECTRIC						
30		METER, WATER METER, GAS METER & SEWER TAP						
31		LOCATIONS AND FENCES SHOWN						
32		PROVIDE 1/4" ROOF PLAN						
33		PROVIDE SLAB FLOAT PLAN						
34		PROVIDE CABINETS & TRIM DETAILS						
35		PROVIDE STAIR DETAILS						
36		PROVIDE TRANSFERSE & LONGITUDINAL SECTIONS						
37		PROVIDE WALL & ROOF CONSTRUCTION DETAILS						
38		FINAL ARCHITECTURALS APPROVED BY CUSTOMER						
39		SOILS TEST RECEIVED						
40		ORDER STRUCTURAL ENGINEERING						
41		FOUNDATION						
42		FRAMING						
43		PROVIDE HURRICANE STRAPPING DETAILS						
44		FLOOR TRUSS LAYOUT & ENG FROM TRUSS SUPPLIER						
45		STRUCTURAL ENGINEERING RECEIVED						
46		COMPARE ENGINEERED SLAB DIMENSIONS TO						
47		ARCHITECTURAL FLOOR PLAN DIMENSIONS						
48		VERIFY SLAB FLOAT DIMENSIONS						
49		COMPARE TRUSS LAYOUT & W/ ARCHITECTURALS						
50		FINAL ARCHITECTURALS RELEASED - 12 SETS TO BUILDER						
51		UPDATE PRELIMINARY SPECIFICATIONS						
52		CREATE PRELIMINARY SCHEDULE						
53		PRE-CONSTRUCTION SELECTIONS						
54		BRICK, STUCCO, STONE						
55		HEARTH MATERIALS						
56		WINDOWS						
57		GLASS BLOCK						
58		ROOFING						
59		FRONT DOOR & SIDELITES						
60		EXTERIOR DOORS						
61		EXTERIOR HARDWARE						
62		EXTERIOR PAINT COLOR						
63		EXTERIOR WROUGHT IRON						
64		GUTTER COLOR						
65		PLUMBING FIXTURES						
66		SHOWER FIXTURES						
67		MASTER TUB SELECTION						
68		SECONDARY BATHROOM TUBS						
69		TUB FIXTURES						
70		PEDESTALS						
71		LAVATORY BOWLS						
72		LAVATORY FAUCETS						
73		KITCHEN SINK						
74		KITCHEN FAUCET						
75		COMMODES						
76		BIDETS						
77		WET BAR SINK						
78		WET BAR FAUCET						
79		APPLIANCES						
80		KITCHEN CABINETS & BATH VANITIES						
81		FINAL ESTIMATING						
82		CREATE ESTIMATING GRIDS						
83		PLUMBING FIXTURES SCHEDULE						
84		EXTERIOR DOOR SCHEDULE						
85		WINDOW SCHEDULE						
86		APPLIANCE SCHEDULE						
87		FRAME MATERIAL TAKEOFF SCHEDULE						
88		EXTERIOR VENEER SCHEDULE						
89		FLOORING SCHEDULE						
90		HARDWOOD FLOORING						
91		CERAMIC TILE FLOORING						
92		MARBLE / STONE FLOORING						
93		CARPET						
94		INTERIOR TRIM TAKEOFF SCHEDULE						
95		BATH TILE SCHEDULE						
96		COUNTERTOP SCHEDULE						

5.1 Production Checklist (continued)

CUSTOMER:
ADDRESS:
SUBDIVISION:

	X	DESCRIPTION	CUST SEL REQ	SALES DEPT	EST DEPT	PROD DEPT	DATE REQ	DATE COMP
97		**FINAL BIDDING - (TWO BIDS REQUIRED)**						
98		LOT PREP BID *-ENGINEERING REQUIRED*						
99		FOUNDATION PAD BID *-ENGINEERING REQUIRED*						
100		SLAB BID TURNKEY *-ENGINEERING REQUIRED*						
101		PLUMBING BID						
102		PLUMBING FIXTURE BID						
103		ELECTRICAL BID						
104		EXTERIOR DOOR BID						
105		HVAC BID						
106		SECURITY BID						
107		FRAME & CORNICE MATERIAL BID						
108		FRAME LABOR BID						
109		STRUCTURAL STEEL BID *ENGINEERING REQUIRED*						
110		WINDOW BID						
111		ROOF BID						
112		FIREPLACE BID						
113		INSULATION BID						
114		BRICK MATERIAL BID						
115		BRICK LABOR BID						
116		STUCCO TURNKEY BID						
117		STONE TURNKEY BID						
118		SHEETROCK TURNKEY BID						
119		TEXTURE BID						
120		OVERHEAD GARAGE DOOR BID						
121		FLOOR COVERINGS						
122		HARDWOOD FLOOR BID						
123		CERAMIC TILE FLOOR MATERIAL BID						
124		CERAMIC TILE FLOOR LABOR BID						
125		MARBLE / STONE FLOOR MATERIAL BID						
126		MARBLE / STONE FLOOR LABOR BID						
127		CARPET BID						
128		APPLIANCE BID						
129		INTERIOR TRIM MATERIAL BID						
130		INTERIOR TRIM LABOR BID						
131		PAINTING TURNKEY BID						
132		FLATWORK BID						
133		KITCHEN COUNTERS BID						
134		FORMICA BID						
135		BATHROOM VANITY TOP BID						
136		BATH SURROUNDS & SHOWERS BID						
137		CERAMIC TILE BATH MATERIAL BID						
138		CERAMIC TILE BATH LABOR BID						
139		WROUGHT IRON BID						
140		WALLPAPER MATERIAL BID						
141		WALLPAPER LABOR BID						
142		MIRROR & SHOWER DOOR BID						
143		LIGHT FIXTURE BID						
144		HARDWARE BID						
145		LANDSCAPE BID						
146		FENCE BID						
147		PREPARE FINAL BID						
148		**THIRD SALES MEETING**						
149		PRESENT FINAL SPECIFICATIONS						
150		PRESENT FINAL ESTIMATE						
151		PRESENT PRELIMINARY CONSTRUCTION SCHEDULE						
152		**EXECUTE CONTRACT**						
153		CREATE HOMEOWNERS MANUAL						
154		CUSTOMER TO RECEIVE & SIGN FOR HOMEOWNERS MANUAL						
155		**CONSTRUCTION FINANCING**						
156		SUBMIT CONSTRUCTION DOCUMENTS TO LENDER						
157		SIGNED CONTRACT						
158		PLANS & SPECIFICATIONS						
159		LOT SURVEY						
160		APPRAISAL						
161		**CONSTRUCTION LOAN CLOSING**						
162		FILE EPA NOTICE OF INTENT						
163		SUBMIT APPLICATION FOR WATER METER						
164		SUBMIT APPLICATION FOR SEWER TAP						
165		SUBMIT APPLICATION FOR TEMP. POLE METER						
166		SITE INSPECTION						
167		**ACC APPROVAL**						
168		TWO (2) SETS OF PLANS & SPECIFICATIONS						
169		PLOT PLAN						
170		FLATWORK SHOWN						
171		UTILITIES LOCATED						
172		FENCING SHOWN						
173		SETBACKS & EASEMENTS IDENTIFIED						
174		ROOF MANUFACTURER & COLOR						
175		EXTERIOR PAINT COLOR						
176		EXTERIOR MATERIAL & COLOR						
177		LANDSCAPE PLAN APPROVED						
178		FLATWORK MATERIAL & LABOR						
179		EXTERIOR WROUGHT IRON SELECTION						
180		**RECEIVE FINAL APPROVAL**						
181		SUBMIT PLANS & ENGINEERING FOR BUILDING PERMIT						
182		**BUILDING PERMIT RECEIVED**						
183		FAX BUILDING PERMIT NUMBER TO MECHANICAL TRADES						
184		T-POLE ORDERED / SET BY ELECTRICIAN						
185		T-POLE INSPECTION ORDERED BY ELECTRICIAN						
186		ELECTRIC METER ORDERED / SET						
187		WATER METER ORDERED / SET						
188		PLUMBER TO INSTALL HOSE BIB AT METER						
189		**CREATE PRODUCTION CONSTRUCTION PACKAGE - (BINDER)**						
190		CUSTOMER INFORMATION SHEET						
191		PLANS & ENGINEERING						
192		SPECIFICATIONS						
193		CONSTRUCTION BUDGET						

5.1   Production Checklist (continued)

CUSTOMER:
ADDRESS:
SUBDIVISION:

	X	DESCRIPTION	CUST SEL REQ	SALES DEPT	EST DEPT	PROD DEPT	DATE REQ	DATE COMP
194		CONSTRUCTION SCHEDULE						
195		SELECTION SHEET & SCHEDULE						
196		PRODUCTION REVIEW OF CONSTRUCTION PACKAGE						
197		**PRE-CONSTRUCTION MEETING**						
198		PROJECT MANAGER PERSONAL INTRODUCTION						
199		REVIEW PLANS & SPECIFICATIONS						
200		REVIEW THE CHANGE ORDER PROCESS						
201		DETERMINE THE DECISION MAKER						
202		REVIEW THE CONSTRUCTION SCHEDULE						
203		REVIEW PRE-CONSTRUCTION SELECTIONS & REMAINING						
204		SELECTION SCHEDULE						
205		VERIFY FLOOR FINISH SCHEDULE						
206		VERIFY EXTERIOR DOOR SCHEDULE						
207		VERIFY WINDOW SELECTIONS & SCHEDULE						
208		REVIEW BRICK/STUCCO SELECTION						
209		REVIEW ROOFING SELECTION						
210		REVIEW EXTERIOR PAINT COLOR SELECTION						
211		REVIEW GUTTER COLOR SELECTION						
212		REVIEW ANY IN SLAB ELECTRICAL, PLUMBING CONDITIONS,						
213		FLOOR SAFE LOCATIONS AND/OR HEARTH CONSIDERATIONS						
214		REVIEW APPLIANCE SELECTIONS						
215		VERIFY SITE CONDITIONS & UTILITY LOCATIONS						
216		A/C COMPRESSOR, GAS METER, WATER METER, SEWER TAP						
217		IDENTIFY ANY OTHER CUSTOMER CONCERNS						
218		DETERMINE TIME FOR THE WEEKLY MEETINGS						
219		RELEASE WINDOWS						
220		RELEASE BRICK / STONE						
221		RELEASE EXTERIOR DOORS & FRONT DOOR FRAME						
222		RELEASE PLUMBING FIXTURES TO PLUMBER						
223		CONFIRM ORDER DATE W/ PLUMBER						
224		**START ONSITE CONSTRUCTION**						
225		LOT PREP / DEMO / SCRAPE LOT						
226		FOUNDATION PAD STAKED BY SURVEYOR						
227		BUILD FOUNDATION PAD						
228		BUILDING ENVELOPE STAKED BY SURVEYOR						
229		**PHASE MEETING #1**						
230		SLAB ELEVATION SET						
231		PIERS STAKED & DRILLED						
232		PIERS INSPECTED BY ENGINEER						
233		INSPECTION LETTER RECEIVED						
234		PIERS INSPECTED BY MUNICIPALITY						
235		PIERS POURED						
236		FORMS SET						
237		ORDER FORM SURVEY (IF REQUIRED)						
238		FORM SURVEY RECEIVED (IF REQUIRED)						
239		SAND & LEVEL						
240		PLUMBING GROUNDS						
241		PLUMBING INSPECTION BY MUNICIPALITY						
242		SEWER TAP COMPLETED & INSPECTED BY MUNICIPALITY						
243		SLAB MAKEUP						
244		ELECTRICAL CONDUIT / FLOOR PLUGS						
245		MUNICIPAL IN SLAB ELECTRICAL INSPECTION						
246		INSPECTION BY VP OF OPERATIONS						
247		STRUCTURAL INSPECTION BY ENGINEER						
248		SLAB PRE-POUR INSPECTION BY MUNICIPALITY						
249		SLAB POURED						
250		ORDER SLAB SURVEY (IF REQUIRED)						
251		SLAB SURVEY RECEIVED (IF REQUIRED)						
252		PULL FORMS						
253		FORM CLEAN						
254		FORM GRADE						
255		SET COMPANY SIGN IN YARD IF ALLOWED						
256		BUILD WALKWAY FROM STREET TO FRONT DOOR						
257		FRAME 1 DROP						
258		ORDER EXTERIOR MILLWORK						
259		ORDER POCKET DOORS						
260		START FRAME						
261		FRAME 2 DROP						
262		FRAME 3 DROP						
263		FRAME 4 DROP						
264		FRAME 5 DROP						
265		ROOF FRAMED						
266		RELEASE CORNICE MATERIAL						
267		RELEASE ROOF DECKING MATERIAL						
268		BRICK TRAY / FLASHING ORDERED						
269		COMPLETE FIREPLACE CHASE & CAP						
270		SCHEDULE ROOFER						
271		FRAME CLEAN 2						
272		SET EXTERIOR DOORS						
273		SET WINDOWS						
274		INSTALL WINDOW & DOOR FLASHING						
275		FINALIZE FRONT & BACK YARD DESIGNS FOR MECHANICAL REQ						
276		GAS LINES FOR GRILL, LIGHTS, SPA, POOL, ETC.						
277		ELECTRICAL						
278		PLUMBING PRE-WALK						
279		PLUMBING ROUGH IN START						
280		ENTEX GAS LINE ORDERED						
281		HVAC PRE-WALK						
282		**PHASE MEETING #2 - ELECTRICAL PRE-WALK**						
283		HOME AUTOMATION DISCUSSION & COORDINATION						
284		PRIME EXTERIOR WOODWORK						
285		ROOFING / SHINGLES COMPLETE						
286		**THIRTY DAY SELECTIONS**						
287		INTERIOR PAINT & STAIN						
288		WALL TEXTURE SELECTION						
289		WALLPAPER LOCATIONS						
290		WOOD FLOOR & STAIN COLORS						

5.1 Production Checklist (continued)

| CUSTOMER: |
| ADDRESS: |
| SUBDIVISION: |

X	DESCRIPTION	CUST SEL REQ	SALES DEPT	EST DEPT	PROD DEPT	DATE REQ	DATE COMP
291	TILE SELECTIONS						
292	FLOOR TILE						
293	TUB SURROUNDS						
294	SHOWER WALLS & FLOOR						
295	COUNTERTOPS						
296	CULTURED MARBLE						
297	GRANITE						
298	CORIAN						
299	LAMINATE						
300	TILE						
301	FLATWORK DESIGN, LAYOUT & MATERIALS						
302	INTERIOR HARDWARE						
303	LIGHT FIXTURES						
304	CARPET						
305	WALLPAPER						
306	MIRROR TREATMENT / SHOWER DOORS						
307	INTERIOR WROUGHT IRON						
308	LANDSCAPE DESIGN VERIFIED						
309	HOUSE WATER COMPLETE						
310	INSPECTION						
311	FIREPLACE INSTALLED						
312	HVAC ROUGH IN						
313	SHINGLES CLEAN 3						
314	FRAME PUNCH OUT						
316	ELECTRICAL ROUGH IN						
317	MUNICIPAL MECHANICAL INSPECTIONS						
318	PLUMBING COVER INSPECTION						
319	HVAC COVER INSPECTION						
320	ELECTRICAL COVER INSPECTION						
321	SHOWER PAN INSPECTION						
322	MUNICIPALITY STRUCTURAL INSPECTION						
323	ORDER MASONRY SUPPLIES						
324	BRICK / STONE DELIVERED						
325	START BRICK LAYER / STUCCO / STONE						
326	RECEIVE BRICK TIE / STUCCO LATH INSPECTION						
327	SECURITY SYSTEM INSTALLED						
328	INTERCOM / STEREO / CENTRAL VAC ROUGH IN						
329	HOME AUTOMATION ROUGH IN						
330	STOCK SHEETROCK						
331	PHASE MEETING #3 - PRE-COVER VERIFICATION						
332	CHANGE ORDER UPDATE						
333	INSULATION						
334	HANG SHEETROCK						
335	ORDER OVERHEAD GARAGE DOOR(S)						
336	ORDER CONSTRUCTION LOCKS						
337	INTERIOR DOORS & MILLWORK ORDERED						
338	SHEETROCK CLEAN 4						
339	TAPE & FLOAT SHEETROCK						
340	MARK WALLS FOR WALLPAPER						
341	TEXTURE SELECTED & APPLIED						
342	ORDER SUPPLIER TO PROVIDE LIGHT FIXTURE TAKEOFF						
343	WOOD FLOORS INSTALLED						
344	TILE FLOORS FLOATED						
345	MASTER TUB INSTALLED						
346	BRICK / STUCCO COMPLETE						
347	ELECTRICIAN APPLIES FOR TEMPORARY CUT IN PERMIT						
348	ELECTRICAL UNDERGROUND OR OVERHEAD						
349	CUSTOMER TO APPLY FOR ELECTRIC METER						
350	INSPECTION ORDERED FOR ELECTRICAL TEMPORARY CUT IN						
351	ELECTRIC METER INSTALLED						
352	PHASE MEETING #4 - PRE-TRIM						
353	CONFIRM APPLIANCE SELECTIONS FOR CUTOUTS						
354	INSTALL OVERHEAD DOORS						
355	INSTALL CONSTRUCTION LOCKS						
356	INTERIOR DOORS & MILLWORK PACKAGE DELIVERED						
357	START TRIM LABOR						
358	SET INTERIOR DOORS						
359	ORDER CABINETS or BUILD CABINET BODIES						
360	ORDER CABINET DOORS (IF NOT JOB BUILT)						
361	INSTALL CROWN, CLOSETS, BASE & WINDOW TRIM						
362	TRIM STAIRWAY & INSTALL HANDRAILS						
363	HANG CABINET DOORS						
364	PROVIDE INTERIOR PAINT COLOR SAMPLES						
365	BRICK / STUCCO CLEAN 5						
366	ENTEX GAS LINE INSTALLED						
367	DIG SWIMMING POOL IF APPLICABLE						
368	FLATWORK						
369	LAYOUT FLATWORK FOR APPROVAL						
370	ORDER CURB CUT						
371	ROUGH GRADE - CUT / FILL FLATWORK						
372	INSTALL 2" PVC PIPE SLEEVES UNDER FLATWORK						
373	WALLPAPER ORDERED						
374	ORDER COUNTERTOP MATERIAL & RELEASE FOR FIELD MEASURE						
375	TILE & MARBLE ORDERED						
376	ORDER SUPPLIER TO PROVIDE FINISH HARDWARE TAKEOFF						
377	INTERIOR TRIM PUNCH OUT						
378	ORDER FINISH HARDWARE						
379	SHEETROCK PATCHES & TOUCH UP						
380	TRIM CLEAN 6						
381	TRIM MATERIAL CREDIT						
382	PLUMB MASTER TUB						
383	COMPLETE ATTIC INSULATION						
384	INTERIOR PAINT & STAIN						
385	INSTALL SHOWERS & TUB SURROUNDS						
386	WINDOW CLEAN						
387	INSTALL GUTTERS						
388	ORDER LIGHT FIXTURES						

5.1   Production Checklist (continued)

CUSTOMER:							
ADDRESS:							
SUBDIVISION:							

X	DESCRIPTION	CUST SEL REQ	SALES DEPT	EST DEPT	PROD DEPT	DATE REQ	DATE COMP
389	INSTALL CORIAN / FORMICA						
390	INSTALL GRANITE COUNTERS						
391	INSTALL VANITY TOPS						
392	INSTALL A/C REGISTERS						
393	TILE FLOORS INSTALLED						
394	ORDER WEATHERSTRIPPING & THRESHOLDS						
395	WALLPAPER INSTALLED						
396	MIRRORS & SHOWER DOORS						
397	DELIVER EXTERIOR & INTERIOR HARDWARE						
398	INSTALL FRONT DOOR(S)						
399	INSTALL EXTERIOR DOOR HARDWARE						
400	INSTALL INTERIOR HARDWARE & BATH ACCESSORIES						
401	WEATHER-STRIP DOORS & INSTALL THRESHOLDS						
402	LIGHT FIXTURES DELIVERED						
403	APPLIANCES DELIVERED						
404	APPLIANCES INSTALLED						
405	ELECTRICAL TRIM / FIXTURES INSTALLED						
406	SECURITY TRIM						
407	INTERCOM / STEREO / CENTRAL VAC TRIM						
408	APPLICATION TO GAS Co. FOR METER						
409	PLUMBING TRIM / FIXTURES INSTALLED						
410	PLUMBER TO APPLY FOR GAS METER TEMPORARY CUT IN						
411	ORDER INSPECTION FOR GAS METER						
412	INSTALL GAS METER						
413	WATER SERVICE TRANSFERRED TO OWNER'S NAME BY OWNER						
415	CONDENSERS SET & STARTED						
417	**CREATE PUNCH LIST BY TRADE**						
418	FINAL INSPECTIONS FROM MUNICIPALITY						
419	PLUMBING FINAL						
420	ELECTRICAL FINAL						
421	HVAC FINAL						
422	COMPLETE HOME AUTOMATION						
423	INSTALL FENCES						
424	COMPLETE POOLS, SPAS, DECKS & WOOD DECKS DECKS						
425	FINAL GRADE						
426	INSTALL SPRINKLERS						
427	INSTALL LANDSCAPING						
428	ORDER FINAL SURVEY						
429	FINAL MUNICIPAL BUILDING INSPECTION ORDERED						
430	FINAL MUNICIPAL BUILDING INSPECTION RECEIVED						
431	CERTIFICATE OF OCCUPANCY RECEIVED						
432	PRE-CLOSING CHANGE ORDER UPDATE						
433	INSTALL GARAGE DOOR OPENER'S)						
435	FINISH HARDWOOD FLOORS						
436	PRE FINAL CLEAN						
437	**PHASE MEETING #5 - PRE-CARPET**						
438	CARPET						
439	FINAL CLEAN #1						
440	FINAL PAINT TOUCH UP						
441	FINAL COAT HARDWOOD FLOORS						
442	FINAL CLEAN #2						
443	CUSTOMER PRE-CLOSE WALK						
444	PUNCH LIST COMPLETE						
445	WARRANTY BINDER PACKAGE						
446	FINAL SURVEY RECEIVED						
447	FINAL SITE & SEWER INSPECTION						
448	FINAL CLEAN #3						
449	**PHASE MEETING #6 - CUSTOMER ORIENTATION**						
450	EVENT INCLUDES CUSTOMER, PROJECT MANAGER						
451	Customer walk-through sign-off						
452	COMPLETE ANY ITEMS DISCUSSED AT ORIENTATION						
453	PRESENT FINAL ACCOUNTING TO CUSTOMER						
454	CLOSING & FUNDING						
455	CUSTOMER MOVE IN						
456	DELIVER COMPLIMENTARY LUNCH & DRINKS FOR MOVE IN						
457	FOLLOW UP SURVEY						
458	THIRTY DAY LIST						
459	SALES FOLLOW UP "THANK YOU" LETTER						
460	PRODUCTION FOLLOW UP PHONE CALL						
461	Job Close down						
462	change furnace filter						
463	remove job sign						
464	remove portable sanitation						
465	remove all excess materials						
466	remove lockbox						

5.2   Remodel Mobilization Checklist

Company Name
Company Logo
Company Affiliations

Remodel Mobilization Checklist

☐ Post policies & procedures.
☐ Notify neighbors with the appropriate letter.
☐ Turn off gas if structure is not occupied.
☐ Locate water cutoff and test it.
☐ Heeding lighting conditions and angles, take *before* pictures as follows:
    ☐ exterior front and all other elevations
    ☐ all areas that will change
    ☐ exterior pictures of where an addition will go
    ☐ exterior pictures of where an elevation change will go
    ☐ at least one horizontal photo for each location (a requirement for most contests) and a vertical if appropriate
☐ Give film, camera, or memory card (as appropriate) to office manager to save pictures in office files.
☐ Locate main breaker panel and kill power to areas being demolished. Mark the breakers for the areas to receive work.
☐ Set up portable restroom or determine what bathroom the trades will use; mark it accordingly.
☐ Check the policy for signage restrictions in the neighborhood. If permitted, post a sign as soon as possible.

Company Address
Phone/Fax
E-mail
Web site

5.3 Product Selection Tracking Form

Item	Type; Model #; Details	Supplier; Contact Name; Phone #	Date Ordered	Date Needed	Date Delivered	Comments
Exterior Selections						
Entry Door						
Entry Door Hardware						
Garage Entry Door						
Garage Entry Door Hardware						
Master Bedroom Exterior Door						
Master Bedroom Exterior Door Hardware						
Great Room French Doors						
Great Room French Door Hardware						
Windows						
Window Trim						
Roofing						
Gable Vents						
Shutters						
Gutters						
Gutter Color						
Exterior Color						
Exterior Trim Color						
Masonry						
Stair Railing						
Exterior Lighting						
Exterior Siding						
Interior Selections						
Interior doors						
Interior door Hardware						
Interior Lighting						
Baseboard & Window Trim						
Fireplace						
Fireplace Hearth						

5.3   Product Selection Tracking Form (continued)

Item	Type; Model #; Details	Supplier; Contact Name; Phone #	Date Ordered	Date Needed	Date Delivered	Comments
Fireplace Mantel						
Fans						
Stairs						
Kitchen						
Cabinets						
Countertop						
Sink						
Sink Plumbing Fixtures						
Disposer						
Microwave						
Dishwasher						
Oven						
Range						
Flooring						
Floor Trim						
Master Bathroom						
Tile						
Tile Edge Pieces						
Grout Color						
Cabinets						
Counter Tops						
Flooring						
Nu Heat						
Tub						
Tub Enclosure						
Tub Deck Configuration						
Shower						
Sink						
Plumbing Fixtures						
Towel Bars						
Toilet						
Mirrors, Tub Enclosures						
Bath #1						
Tile						
Tile Edge Pieces						
Grout Color						
Cabinets						

5.3   Product Selection Tracking Form (continued)

Item	Type; Model #; Details	Supplier; Contact Name; Phone #	Date Ordered	Date Needed	Date Delivered	Comments
Counter Tops						
Flooring						
Floor Trim						
Radiant Heat						
Tub						
Tub Enclosure						
Shower						
Sink						
Plumbing Fixtures						
Towel Bars						
Toilet						
Mirrors, Tub Enclosures						
Bath #2						
Tile						
Tile Edge Pieces						
Grout Color						
Cabinets						
Counter Tops						
Flooring						
Floor Trim						
Radiant heat						
Tub						
Tub Enclosure						
Shower						
Sink						
Plumbing Fixtures						
Towel Bars						
Toilet						
Mirrors, Tub Enclosures						
Laundry Room						
Washer						
Dryer						
Cabinets						
Countertop						
Sink						
Flooring						
Floor Trim						
Plumbing Fixtures						

5.4   Special Materials Order Form

Company Name
Company Logo
Company Affiliations

Materials Special Orders

Ordered From: _____

Sales Person: _____   Date Ordered: _____

Date Expected: _____   Job # _____   P.O. # _____

Ordered By: _____   Supplier to call: Yes_____   No ____

Rec.	B.O.	# Ordered	Description	Amount

Dates Checked On: _____   _____

Order In: _____   Information Taken By: _____
            (date)

Picked Up: _____   By: _____
            (date)

Company Address
Phone
Fax
E-mail
Web site

5.5   Materials Supplier Contact Information

Company Name
Company Logo
Company Affiliations

| ADDRESS: | | | | DATE | | | |
ITEM	TRADE/SUPPLIER	CONTACT	PHONE #	ACCEPT	INTERVIEW	COMMENTS	
Demolition							
Foundation Pad							
Testing							
Foundation Labor							
TermiteTreatment							
Framing Labor							
Framing Material							
Plumbing							
A/C Heating							
Electrical							
Windows							
Exterior Doors							
Roofing Labor & Materials							
Flashing/Waterproofing							
Brick Labor							
Brick Material							
Stucco							
Fireplaces							
Shutters/Millowork Exterior							
Glass Block							
Security/Burglar Alarm							
Sound System							
Insulation							
Sheetrock							
Central Vacuum System							
Plumbing Fixtures							
Elevator							
Columns							
Cabinets							
Appliances							
Trim Labor							
Trim Material							
Interior Doors							
Paint Labor & Material							
Tile Labor							
Tile Material							
Wood Floors							
Countertops-Corian							
Countertops-Laminate							
Countertops-Stone							
Cultured Marble							
Carpet							
Standard Finish Concrete							
Garage Door & Opener							
Gutters							
Hardware							
Landscaping							
Sprinkler System							
Lighting Fixtures							
Mirrors & Shower Door							
Wallpaper							
Interior Cleanup							
Grading							
Yard Drainage							
Water Filtration System							
Decks							
Fences							
Trusses							

Company Address
Phone - Fax
E-mail - Web site

5.6   Long-Lead Item Order List

Company Name
Company Logo
Company Affiliations

Date_____

Job Name_____   Job #_____

Sub/Supplier	Description of Item	Date Order Placed	Date Required	Complete

_____   _____
Customer   Contractor

Company Address
Phone
Fax
E-mail
Web site

5.7   Lead Hazard Procedures Checklist

[Note: Internal Use only by the renovator to demonstrate compliance to EPA OECA]

Name of Firm:_____

Date and Location of Renovation:_____

Brief Description of Renovation: _____
_____

Name of Assigned Certified Renovator:_____

Name(s) of Trained Workers, if used:_____
_____

Name of Dust Sampling Technician, Inspector, or Risk Assessor, if used:_____
_____

☐ Copies of renovator and dust sampling technician qualifications (training certificates, certifications) on file.

☐ Certified renovator provided training to workers on (check all that apply):

    ☐ Posting warning signs   ☐ Setting up plastic containment barriers

    ☐ Maintaining containment   ☐ Avoiding spread of dust to adjacent areas

    ☐ Waste handling   ☐ Post-renovation cleaning

☐ Test kits used by certified renovator to determine whether lead was present on components affected by renovation (identify kits used and describe sampling locations and results):_____
_____
_____

☐ Test kit results and information provided to the person who contracted for the renovation within 30 days of completion of the renovation.

☐ If emergency renovation, describe the nature of the emergency and the sections of the LRRP Rule not employed.

☐ Warning signs posted at entrance to work area.

☐ Work area contained to prevent spread of dust and debris.

Interiors:

    ☐ All objects in the work area removed or covered

    ☐ HVAC ducts in the work area closed and covered

    ☐ Windows in the work area closed

    ☐ Doors in the work area closed and sealed

    ☐ Floors in the work area covered with taped-down plastic 6 feet beyond the perimeter of surfaces undergoing renovation, or at a distance sufficient to collect falling debris, whichever is greater

    ☐ Doors that must be used in the work area covered to allow passage but prevent spread of dust

5.7   Lead Hazard Procedures Checklist (continued)

Exteriors:

- [ ] Windows in and within 20 feet of the work area closed
- [ ] Doors in and within 20 feet of the work area closed and sealed
- [ ] Doors that must be used in the work area covered to allow passage but prevent spread of dust
- [ ] Ground covered by plastic extending 10 feet from work area, or at a distance sufficient to collect falling debris, whichever is greater, unless prevented by location of property line; plastic anchored to building and weighted down by heavy objects
- [ ] If necessary, vertical containment installed to prevent migration of dust and debris to adjacent property

- [ ] Waste contained on-site and while being transported off-site
- [ ] Work site properly cleaned after renovation
  - [ ] All chips and debris picked up, protective sheeting misted, folded dirty side inward, and taped for removal
  - [ ] Work area surfaces and objects cleaned using HEPA vacuum and/or wet cloths or mops (interiors)
- [ ] Certified renovator performed post-renovation cleaning verification (describe results, including the number of wet and dry cloths used):_____

  _____

- [ ] If dust clearance testing was performed instead, attach a copy of report and provide a copy to the person who contracted for the renovation within 30 days following the completion of the renovation.
- [ ] I certify under penalty of law that the above information is true and complete.

_____   _____

Name and Title   Date

5.8   Permit & Municipal Inspections Report

Company Name
Company Logo
Company Affiliations

Owner's Name:	

Job Location:	

Block & Lot #s:	

Permit #:	

Municipality's Phone #:	

Contact Name:	Follow-up Date submitted Date issued

Permit list
Site plan
Soils disturbance
Health department
Electrical
Plumbing
Construction
Fire permit
Road access
Other

Inspection Type	Date Called In	Scheduled Inspection Date	Scheduled Inspection Time	Passed/ Failed

Company Address
Phone—Fax
E-mail—Web site

5.9   Daily Jobsite To Do List Instructions

The purpose of this form is to create lists of things to be done by the crew. In the event that current leadership cannot be on-site, a substitute leader can take the list and get going. The list also helps in projecting labor and material needs, improving efficiency, organizing the workflow and establishing short term goals.

Step-by-step instructions for completing the Job To Do List & Instructions

1. Fill in the name of the person who will do the work.
2. State the date when work is to be performed.
3. Fill in the project name.
4. Describe in detail the work to be completed.
5. Review all of the descriptions of work to be done, assigning a priority number to each.
6. Post the completed forms on your desk/notice board for the relevant employee.

Explain to the person who gets the To Do List that they should report back when the list is complete. After all work is completed, use the list as a quality checklist. By initialing the box next to each description of work performed, job leadership indicates that the work is complete and meets standards. Collect all of the completed To Do Lists and submit them to the Project Manager as soon as possible.

Task

Name	Expected Completion date	duration	Sign off– supervisor	Sign off– Home owner

5.10   Jobsite To Do List

Daily Personnel To Do List

Name: _____   Date: _____

Job Name: _____

Priority:	Work Description:	Initials

5.11   Production Report

Company Name
Company Logo
Company Affiliations

Dates

Start:	Finish:
Baseline Start:	Baseline Finish:
Actual Start:	Actual Finish:
Start Variance:	Finish Variance:

Duration

Scheduled:	Remaining:
Baseline:	Actual:
Variance:	Percent Complete:

Work

Scheduled:	Remaining:
Baseline:	Actual:
Variance:	Percent Complete:

Costs

Scheduled:	Remaining:
Baseline:	Actual:
Variance:	

Task Status   ## Resource Status

Tasks not yet started:	Work Resources:
Tasks in progress:	Overallocated Work Resources:
Tasks completed: _____	Material Resources: _____
Total Tasks:	Total Resources:

Address
Phone—Fax
E-mail—Web site

5.12   Daily Job Log

Company Name
Company Logo
Company Affiliations

Employee Name: _____   Day & Date: _____
                                          Weather: _____
Job Name: _____   Temperature: _____
Job Location: _____

	02 Demolition
Work Activity	03 Site Work
Start of work:	03.1 Site Work Demo
8	04 Excavation
9	05 Concrete
10	06 Masonry
11	07 Framing
12	08 Roofing/Flashing
1	09 Exterior Trim
2	10 Doors/Windows
3	11 Siding
4	12 Plumbing
	13 HVAC
Completion of work:	14 Electric/Lighting
	15 Insulation
Others on Job:	16 Drywall

Name:	
Work Completed:	
Hours:	

17 Ceiling/Coverings
18 Millwork/Trim
19 Cabinets/Vanities
20 Floor Cover

Name:	
Work Completed:	
Hours:	

21 Paint
22 Cleanup
23 Landscaping
25 Supervision/Pick up materials

5.12   Daily Job Log (continued)

Phone Calls:		Nature of Call:	
Phone Calls:		Nature of Call:	
Phone Calls:		Nature of Call:	

Materials Ordered:		Quantity:	

Remarks:

I hereby certify that the above time is true and accurate to the best of my knowledge. By signing this Daily Job Log, I am verifying that I was NOT injured on the job and did NOT have an accident on this job resulting in injury to myself.

Employee's Signature _____   Supervisor's Approval _____

5.13   Multi-job Schedule

Company Name
Company Logo
Company Affiliations

Project	date Monday	date Tuesday	date Wednesday	date Thursday	date Friday	date Saturday	date Sunday
Project 1							
Project 2							
Project 3							
Project 4							
Project 5							
Project 6							
Project 7							
Project 8							
Project 9							
Project 10							

*Displayed on dry erase board

Company Address
Phone
Fax
E-mail
Web site

5.14   Employee Work Schedule

Company Name
Company Logo
Company Affiliations

		JOB A	Job B	Job C	Maintenance tasks
Monday	<Employee #1>				
	<Employee #2>				
	<Employee #3>				
	<Employee #4>				
	Trade contractors				
	Trade contractors				
Tuesday	<Employee #1>				
	<Employee #2>				
	<Employee #3>				
	<Employee #4>				
	Trade contractors				
	Trade contractors				
Wednesday	<Employee #1>				
	<Employee #2>				
	<Employee #3>				
	<Employee #4>				
	Trade contractors				
	Trade contractors				
Thursday	<Employee #1>				
	<Employee #2>				
	<Employee #3>				
	<Employee #4>				
	Trade contractors				
	Trade contractors				

Company Address
Phone
Fax
E-mail
Web site

5.14   Employee Work Schedule (continued)

Company Name
Company Logo
Company Affiliations

		JOB A	Job B	Job C	Maintenance tasks
Friday	‹Employee #1›				
	‹Employee #2›				
	‹Employee #3›				
	‹Employee #4›				
	Trade contractors				
	Trade contractors				
Saturday	‹Employee #1›				
	‹Employee #2›				
	‹Employee #3›				
	‹Employee #4›				
	Trade contractors				
	Trade contractors				

Company Address
Phone
Fax
E-mail
Web site

5.15   Trade Contractor Walk-Through

Company Name
Company Logo
Company Affiliations

Trade Contractor Walk-Through

DATE _____

Contractor: _____

Job Name: _____

Item	Quality Acceptable	Not Acceptable	Comments
_____	_____	_____	_____
_____	_____	_____	_____
_____	_____	_____	_____
_____	_____	_____	_____
_____	_____	_____	_____
_____	_____	_____	_____
_____	_____	_____	_____
_____	_____	_____	_____
_____	_____	_____	_____
_____	_____	_____	_____
_____	_____	_____	_____
_____	_____	_____	_____
_____	_____	_____	_____
_____	_____	_____	_____
_____	_____	_____	_____
_____	_____	_____	_____
_____	_____	_____	_____
_____	_____	_____	_____

All rough-in work needs to be acceptable by _____.

All final items need to completed by _____.

<Your Company>   <Contractor>

_____   _____
REPRESENTATIVE   REPRESENTATIVE

Company Address
Phone/Fax
E-mail
Web Site

5.16   Quality Control Inspection Report

Company Name
Company Logo
Company Affiliations

Quality Control Inspection Report*

Date:

TO: Lead Carpenter/Foreman

FROM: Project Manager

JOB:

PROJECT #:

THE PROJECT LOOKS GREAT! HERE ARE A FEW MINOR THINGS I NOTICED ON MY LAST SITE VISIT.

- Items to be changed
- Items to be cleaned/maintained
- Items trade must do to keep on schedule
- Actual progress versus progress per proposal
- Other notes

---

*Refer to *Residential Construction Performance Guidelines* or your own published standards.

Company Address
Phone
Fax
E-mail
Web site

5.17   Change Order

Company Name
Company Logo
Company Affiliations

Change Order

Name:_____   Date work began: _____

Address:_____

City:_____   Date work completed:_____

Additional Work Description:

Additional Materials: _____

_____

_____

_____

Additional time required for work, which will extend contract completion: _____days

Completion Date: $_____

Additional Cost: $_____

You are hereby authorized to make the above change(s) in your work on the original Agreement and it is understood that this additional work will be executed under the terms of and the conditions embodied in our contract and is subject to final approval and acceptance by ‹your company name›. All guarantees and warranties shall be consistent with the terms in the contract. Payment for any and all additional Change Order(s) are due and payable prior to commencement of such extra work and upon signing of this Change Order Form. All Change Orders have a minimum fee of $50.00 for overhead and processing. In the absence of a fixed price, work will be billed on a time and materials basis.

_____

Owner (signature)   Date:

_____

Production Supervisor (signature)   Date:

Address
Phone–Fax
E-mail–Web site

5.18 Pre-completion Conference Detail List

Company Name
Company Logo
Company Affiliations

Pre-completion Conference Detail List

Job Name: _____   Conference Date: _____   Time: _____

_____
_____
_____
_____
_____
_____
_____
_____
_____
_____
_____
_____
_____
_____
_____
_____
_____
_____
_____
_____
_____

The above detail list represents all of the remaining items that need attention prior to project completion. These items will be completed on or before: _____. At project completion the Project warranty card will be delivered and the final payment will be due.

APPROVED BY:

_____   _____
Owner   Consultant

_____   _____
Owner   Project Manager

Company Address
Phone
Fax
E-mail
Web site

5.19   Project Closure Procedures

Company Name
Company Logo
Company Affiliations

Project Closure Procedures

Project Name: _____

Project Address: _____

PRODUCTION

- Have all finish-up items been completed?   YES/NO
- Has the production manager or coordinator visited
  the project on completion and done a quality
  control inspection?   YES/NO
- Have we verbally communicated with the owner to
  confirm that all items have been taken care of?   YES/NO
- Has a list of sub-contractors/suppliers been
  submitted to the office for billing purposes?   YES/NO
- Have we taken finish pictures?   YES/NO

ALL ITEMS COMPLETED _____   DATE _____

OFFICE

- Have we sent a thank you or gift if appropriate?   YES/NO
- Has bill contacted the owners to thank them for
  a successful project?   YES/NO
- Have we gone over the project with the lead
  carpenter And production manager to make sure
  that all invoices Have been accounted for?   YES/NO

ALL ITEMS COMPLETED _____   DATE _____

Address
Phone–Fax
E-mail–Web site

5.20 Warranty Work Order

Company Name
Company Logo
Company Affiliations

Warranty Work Order

Date: _____   Time: _____

NAME: _____   HOME # _____

ADDRESS: _____   WORK # _____

CITY: _____   MOBILE #_____

ZIP: _____   JOB #: _____   BEEPER #_____

Whom did the caller ask to speak with? _____

Nature of call back: _____
_____
_____

Date job was closed: _____

Workers on the jobsite: _____

Total cost of job: _____

Additional comments/inspection report: _____
_____
_____
_____

Set up job number: Y _____ N _____   If yes, new job #: _____

Cost to repair: $_____

*‹Your Name›*_____

Reply to: Your Company Address
Phone:
Fax:
E-mail:
Web site:

5.21 Production Meeting Agenda

Company Name
Company Logo
Company Affiliations

Production Meeting Agenda

Project Manager: Address: Date:

Attendees:

I. Introduction
II. Previous Meeting Minutes
III. Status Report
   A. Current Status
   B. Schedule
   C. Selections
   D. Budget
   E. Change Orders
   F. Orders
   G. Subcontractors
IV. Old Business
V. New Business
VI. Priority Action
VI. Closing
   Next meeting date

Company Address
Phone/Fax
E-mail
Web site

6

Making Business Operations Work

Sound business management keeps you on course as you navigate toward reaching your company's profit goals. Like a pilot sitting at a control yoke, you have a multitude of systems to monitor and regulate that include both people and projects. Well-ordered business systems make these complex responsibilities manageable. They allow a remodeler to read every indicator on the control panel systematically to gauge company health and adjust the operation as needed. Because every business owner is naturally better at some aspects of management than others, a good business management system will allow you to delegate certain tasks to others, even as you stay fully informed and constantly in control. The backing of a good system will help you use your time and talent productively.

Planning and Monitoring

Effective business management begins with a plan, as discussed in chapter 1. The next steps are to carry out the plan and then measure its effectiveness. As the saying goes, "Anything worth doing is worth measuring." Each focal area of your business planning and operations should have measurable goals. Measuring progress against the goals requires tools for collecting data and analyzing results.

Business management includes short- and long-term planning, controlling daily operations, and managing human resources, projects, and equipment. (Financial management, an essential component to running a business effectively, is specifically addressed in chapter 7.)

You can routinely collect information on employee productivity, using the Employee Report by Job (6.1); customer service, using the Performance Evaluation–Customer (2.31); and other areas essential to business success. You can compile this data and generate reports periodically to analyze performance. Build time into your schedule to review performance reports weekly, monthly, and quarterly. The larger your company and the more removed you are from daily activities, the more critical it is for you to study company progress reports often.

Building the Company Team

Nothing is more important to the success and profitability of your business than having employees and trade contractors who work productively and well, who maintain your work quality standards, and who are trustworthy ambassadors for your company. Having clear expectations, and then selecting, training, supporting, and evaluating workers according to these expectations, are essential business management functions.

Hiring and Beyond

Before your company can hire employees, each position should have a detailed job description. Applicants should review it and hiring managers should refer to it when reviewing applications and preparing performance evaluations. The following sample job descriptions are included in this book:

- Office Manager Job Description 1 (6.2)
- Office Manager Job Description 2 (6.3)
- Carpenter Job Description (6.4)
- Sales Associate Job Description (6.5)

When interviewing field personnel for potential hire, you can use Telephone Interview Questions (6.6). Applicants whom you are considering hiring should complete a Job Application (6.7). The Hiring Evaluation Rating Sheet (6.8) can be used to evaluate job applicants.

Other essential human resource management tools include the following:

- Employee Compensation Record (6.9), Separation Form (6.10) and Employee Exit Statement (6.11).
- Vacation Request Form (6.12). Employees requesting leave for vacation should complete this approval form. Their supervisor or manager will review the request, accept or reject it, and return a copy of the signed form to the employee.
- Vacation Hand-off (6.13). In preparation for a smooth transition before field personnel leave for vacation, they should complete this form and give it to their managers.

Employee Handbook

Once you hire employees and trade contractors, provide them with documents to give them the information they need to meet your expectations. Every worker should receive an employee handbook. Use the Employee Handbook Template (6.14) to generate a handbook for your company. You can bind it in a loose-leaf notebook so you can easily update it and customize it to an employee's position. As you develop new policies or adopt new regulations, discuss them at company meetings, then distribute new pages for employees to add to their handbooks.

Review the handbook with each new employee to be sure he or she understands and accepts the information. Consider having the employee sign and date each section he or she has read, indicating that acceptance.

The handbook consolidates company information and employee policies in one organized reference. It includes a profile of your company, such as years in business, ownership, remodeling specialties, business philosophy, mission, and goals. Sections of the handbook explain administrative procedures regarding hiring and performance evaluation, payment, leave, use of company vehicles and equipment, expense reimbursement, and other employee-related programs such as educational assistance. Each section contains samples of relevant forms the company uses to implement the procedures, along with instructions for using the forms.

It also contains written rules and standards that employees must follow—for example, policies on moonlighting, attire on the job, and smoking—as well as more specific requirements regarding jobsite behavior and interaction with customers. It is important to include safety and health procedures in the handbook, both for the employees' well being and to establish for insurance purposes that you have communicated the information to your employees as required.

Communicating with Employees

Employees, especially those working in the field, need written guidance, including established policies and procedures. Company Rules (6.15) guide workers to be vital contributors to your business vision and how it is carried forth. Employees carry your vision to the customer. Therefore, communicate clearly and concisely their role, your expectations, acceptable business practices, and guidelines for on-the-job behavior. A manager often sends a message more effectively with 30 words than with 300. Be brief and direct.

Managing Trade Contractors

When trade contractors are working on your jobs, they are your team members. Trade contractors should know your policies and procedures. To ensure they conform to your company's standards and systems, have them read and sign company policy statements including the following:

- Trade Contractor Agreement (6.16). This legal document states the documentation a contractor must have and policies he or she must honor in order to do business with your company.
- Jobsite Policies and Procedures (6.17). Review these jointly with trade contractors to be confident the trade contractor understands them and agrees to conform to your expectations.

Scope of work is everything in a construction contract. The scope of work states not just what work the company expects will be performed but also how the work will be done. For example, one plumber's scope of work might specify using PEX piping and crimp fittings tested to 100 lbs of pressure while another may use copper or not test his work prior to final connections. Specify details such as materials to be used and the work to be completed. For example, one remodeler's tile installer often neglected to apply sealant. Because use of a sealant is standard practice for the remodeler, he now lists it on all tile installation agreements. Form 6.18 is a scope of work for cabinets. Be vigilant in clearly explaining and documenting your expectations. In addition, since trade contractor team members are experts in their fields, listen to their input. Ideally they are bringing more to the project than their work time.

Send trade contractors the Notice of Schedule (6.19) with a project schedule attached, as needed. Also maintain a record of trade contractors' liability and workers' compensation insurance coverage. Use the Certificate of Insurance Request (6.20) to request certificates of insurance when policies are nearing expiration.

Evaluating Performance

A good business management system continually seeks opportunities to improve company performance by evaluating everything, including employee, trade contractor, and supplier performance. By assessing worker performance, you may uncover training needs or discover employee attitude problems. Both performance and attitude problems require prompt corrective measures and further decisive action if problems are not resolved.

Regular performance evaluations help companies to acknowledge achievements, identify areas for improvement, and set performance goals. Therefore, managers should evaluate their employees, employees should evaluate themselves and the company, companies should evaluate trade contractors (and vice versa), and clients should be asked for feedback on their experience with your company, as discussed in chapter 2. In addition to the performance evaluation tools in chapter 2, the following tools will help you create, or improve upon, your performance evaluation system:

- Employee Self-Evaluation (6.21)
- Company Evaluation of Trade Contractor or Supplier (6.22)
- Trade or Supplier Evaluation of Company (6.23) and Evaluation Cover Letter (6.24)
- Employee Evaluation (6.25)

Always welcome and encourage feedback about your company, whether it is positive or negative, by acknowledging and thanking the person who offers it. All feedback is valuable because it tells you what your company is doing well and even more important, where it is off track. If appropriate, share this business intelligence with appropriate members of your team so they can help you improve performance and share in the company's success. Establish an atmosphere that welcomes constructive criticism and forges productive changes, rather than fear. Over time, your company will become smarter, stronger, and more profitable.

Project Management

Systematic project management entails regular written communication with suppliers, trades, architects, and clients. You can use the Transmittal Cover Sheet (6.26) for e-mailing or faxing information to them. The sheet also provides you with a dated record of the transmittal and the action requested of the recipient.

Another essential component of project communication is regular meetings with staff and with clients. The Management and Production Meeting Agenda (6.27) lists important agenda items to routinely discuss during these meetings. In addition, maintain meeting records using Weekly Meeting Notes (6.28). This form provides cues for identifying open items before a meeting and providing status reports. Give a copy of these notes to clients.

The following three forms are designed to help remodeling companies maintain accurate records of injuries and accidents that may occur in the course of a project. Keep the first two forms in your workers' compensation insurance file and maintain a supply of blank vehicle accident reports in the glove compartments of company vehicles.

- Accident Report Form (6.29)
- Report of Illness or Injury (6.30)
- Vehicle Accident Report (6.31)

Managing Equipment

Your business has invested capital in equipment. To ensure that your company has the right equipment in good working order when needed, your system should include a periodic inventory and procedures for borrowing tools and other company property. The following forms will help you manage company equipment:

- Equipment Inventory (6.32). Use this log to record the date and condition of each piece of equipment that is examined. This form can be tied into your asset class accounts that your bookkeeper uses to depreciate equipment. Smaller items are expensed for tax purposes but should remain in inventory for good management.
- Tool Inventory (6.33). Periodically complete a tool inventory to manage the company's property and monitor breakage and loss.
- Supply Checkout Log (6.34). Use this sign-out sheet for company property that employees borrow as needed.
- Roof Equipment List (6.35). Use specialized equipment lists such as this one to manage company property in conjunction with setting up a job.

Many remodelers buy and remodel properties for resale or to hold and lease, creating passive income. These business opportunities can be lucrative for the savvy remodeler but are a very different business than retail remodeling. *The Paper Trail* includes a Real Estate Contract (6.36) for this purpose. However, if you want to hold real estate in your name, include this as part of your business plan and stay focused on the profitability of the enterprise.

Success is a team sport in which players visualize a game plan, mobilize, follow the playbook, and monitor results to complete projects successfully, increase project wins, and minimize or eliminate profit losses. You can correct problem-inducing deviations from the playbook if you monitor them. Neither success nor failure should be a surprise.

Chapter 6 Forms

Planning and Monitoring

6.1   Employee Report by Job (Excel)

Human Resources

6.2   Office Manager Job Description 1 (Word)
6.3   Office Manager Job Description 2 (Word)
6.4   Carpenter Job Description (Word)
6.5   Sales Associate Job Description (Word)
6.6   Telephone Interview Questions (Word)
6.7   Job Application (Word)
6.8   Hiring Evaluation Rating Sheet (Excel)

<u>6.1   Employee Report by Job</u>

Company Name
Company Logo
Company Affiliations

Jan-Dec xxxx

Name		
Job Name	**Hours Worked**	
Employee Name #1		
Clerical	1,603.50	
Total Employee Name #1		1,603.50
Employee Name #2		
Job Name #1	16.00	
Job Name #3	40.00	
Job Name #8	80.00	
Job Name #12	56.00	
Job Name #14	40.00	
Total Employee Name #2		232.00
Employee Name #3		
Job Name #2	8.00	
Job Name #4	45.00	
Job Name #8	33.00	
Job Name #9	11.50	
Job Name #12	4.00	
Job Name #14	16.00	
Total Employee #3		117.50
Employee Name #4		
Job Name #3	8.00	
Job Name #7	29.50	
Job Name #11	2.50	
Total Employee #4		40.00
Employee Name #5		
Job Name #10	4.00	
Job Name #12	4.50	
Job Name #13	17.75	
Total Employee Name #5		26.25
TOTAL		2,019.25

Company Address
Phone
Fax
E-mail
Web site

6.2   Office Manager Job Description 1

Company Name
Company Logo
Company Affiliations

Office Manager Job Description

Financials

- Set up chart of accounts.
- Post all journal entries.
- Produce all financial reports (see list).
- Keep current and past year's files.
- Prepare all reports for accountant for year end per CEO.
- Work with CEO to ensure accuracy of financials.
- Solicit and track certificates of insurance.

General Ledger

- Post all cash disbursements.
- Post all cash receipts.
- Reconcile bank statement.
- Run all reports.
- Track and distribute petty cash.

Sales/Accounts Receivable

- Receive all signed contracts, supplements & work orders.
- Post all sales and set up for job cost report.
- Meet with production manager to determine progress of jobs for invoicing.
- Prepare invoicing for typing.
- Produce all receivable reports (aging, open orders & sales).
- Record, post and deposit all receipts.
- Send gift to client upon request by salesperson.
- Notify assistant to start closing procedures.
- Give reports to CEO.
- Give each employee a copy of customer evaluation for his jobs.

Accounts Payable

- Receive all invoices.
- Have invoices approved.
- Post all invoices and hold in file to compare with statements.

Address
Phone–Fax
E-mail Web Site

6.2   Office Manager Job Description 1 (continued)

Company Name
Company Logo
Company Affiliations

- Produce aging reports for CEO and Product Manager.
- Produce checks for payment upon approval by CEO & Product Manager.
- Prepare invoices for mailing.
- Keep current and past years' files.
- Direct paid invoices for filing.
- Produce all 1099s and 1096s.

Payroll

- Post all payroll.
- Print checks.
- File all time sheets.
- Make Federal 941 deposit at bank as required.
- Run all reports at end of month.
- Check the reports for accuracy with deposits.
- Prepare withholding report and copy and pay at end of each month.
- File copy of withholding report for year end.
- Run all reports at end of each quarter.
- Prepare and send quarterly federal 941.
- Prepare, pay and send FUTA and SUTA.
- File all copies in current year's file.
- Prepare annual federal and state reports (941, 940, W-2, W-3).
- File all of these reports.
- Keep current and past years' files
- Track all vacation and absenteeism.
- Update employee records, increases in wages, new W-4, etc., annually.
- Notify employee of changes in insurance coverage or rate increases.

Job Cost

- Post all entries to Job Cost Update with supplements.
- Give Job Cost reports to CEO, Production Manager and Sales monthly.

Communications

- Contact or direct for contact all business pertaining to telephones, radios, computers, and pagers.

Address
Phone-Fax
E-mail-Web Site

6.2   Office Manager Job Description 1 (continued)

Company Name
Company Logo
Company Affiliations

Office Supplies

- Purchase or direct purchase of all office supplies, including stamps.
- Meet with suppliers for purchases.

Office Equipment

- Update records at each purchase.
- Contact or direct for contact for service.

Vehicles

- Post and code all expenses.
- Direct for license purchase.

Insurance

- Obtain approvals from CEO.
- Prepare reports as needed.

Business Meetings/Seminars

- Make all reservations.
- Make arrangements for transportation and accommodations.
- Maintain files for all.

Company Meetings

- Provide agenda and minutes.

Trade shows

- Provide assistance with exhibit as may be assigned per CEO.

Remembrances

- Direct sending of cards for:
  - ☐ employee birthday
  - ☐ employee anniversary with company
  - ☐ sympathy
  - ☐ congratulations

Address
Phone–Fax
E-mail–Web Site

6.2   Office Manager Job Description 1 (continued)

Company Name
Company Logo
Company Affiliations

Misc.: Office/Building

- Watch/maintain reception area, conference room, hall, copier and fax area, lunchroom and file and supply area for order.
- Purchase coffee, sugar, creamer, soda.
- Have cups, spoons, etc. available as needed.
- Purchase/maintain activity books, games, puzzles, etc. for the clients' children to use while client is in the office meeting with the salesperson.
- Watch for need of paper and soap products for restrooms.
- Arrange for the photos, pictures, or reprints to be hung.

FINANCIALS

A—Chart of Accounts/Budgets

Set up and/or keep current.

B—Journal Entries

Set up and add as needed.

C—Recurring Journal Entries

Set up all that are the same each month.

D—General Journal

Can view all journal entries.
Run the end of each month.

E—Trial Balance

Run at end of each month.
Check to be sure it is in balance.

F—Financials

Run end of each month.

G—Comparative Accounts

Set up at the end of each fiscal year.

Address
Phone-Fax
E-mail-Web Site

6.2   Office Manager Job Description 1 (continued)

Company Name
Company Logo
Company Affiliations

H—Quick Stat Report
Run each week for CEO.

G—Payment Types
Set up cash account types.

H—Bank Deposits
Make daily if necessary.

Address
Phone—Fax
E-mail—Web Site

6.3   Office Manager Job Description 2

Company Name

Office Manager Job Description

Administrative Duties

General
- Runs the office on a day-to-day basis
- Handles all administrative details for the company

Specific
- Type, photocopy, fax, and file all general correspondence, forms and memos.
- Operate computer system, input data, generate reports, perform backups and restores.
- Answer the phone, control communications network, including beeper system, coordinate/ liaise with jobsite personnel, and handle calls from clients, trade contractors, and/or property managers.
- Act as personal secretary to the Company President, including typing letters and memos.
- Screen, record, and track incoming job leads.
- Set up office system standards and procedures, maintain all record-keeping systems, files, and filing systems.
- Maintain all trade contractor insurance records.
- Maintain office and office equipment.
- Perform miscellaneous duties.

Other
- All above work relates to <Your Company Name>.

Accounting Duties

General
- Handle all bookkeeping and organization of accounting information for outside accountant.

Specific
- Institute computer tracking systems for accounts payable and accounts receivable.
- Maintain accounts payable and accounts receivable, enter deposits, handle invoicing and bill payments.
- Track all state and federal tax responsibilities.
- Make all required state and federal tax deposits and payments.
- Generate payroll and follow up on job log compliance.
- Organize tax and accounting information for year-end tax filing to be sent to accountant.
- Generate P&L reports on jobs and properties and financial reports.
- Set up current-year operating budget and maintain annual budgets.

Other
- Above work relates to <Your Company Name> where applicable.

6.3   Office Manager Job Description 2 (continued)

Designer/Draftsman

General
- Responsible for the development of designs and plans if required by job.

Specific
- Observe job conditions, consult with client, as required, regarding job parameters, interpret Company President's outline of job parameters.
- Take jobsite measurements, note jobsite details.
- Call building departments regarding permit/code information.
- File permits.
- Prepare design drawings and construction plans.
- Investigate material and product specifications/availability.
- Update product literature files.

Other
- Above responsibilities pertain to <Your Company Name>.

Estimator

General
- Learn costing for preparation of accurate, detailed cost estimates.

Specific
- Create take-off of job materials and labor from architectural plans or Company President's notes.
- Create materials lists.
- Obtain materials quotes and review for best cost advantage.
- Order and review confirmation of order for accuracy.
- Prepare initial estimate sheet with costing for review and completion by President.
- Coordinate delivery and/or pick up of materials for job scheduling.

Other
- Above descriptions pertain to <Your Company Name>

Future Responsibilities

General
- Increase sales, estimating and project management responsibilities to provide relief for Company President.

Specific
- Increase client interaction from initial lead through completion of project.
- Increase estimating responsibilities to include complete job costing.
- Increase coordination of job management.
- Take on more responsibilities of Company President.
- Assist in more fieldwork to increase general construction knowledge.

6.3   Office Manager Job Description 2 (continued)

Organizational Relationship

Reports to

- President and Partner

Cooperates with

- All employees of company
- Trade contractors
- Clients
- Accountant
- Attorneys
- Engineers
- Architects
- Suppliers
- Property managers
- Tenants
- Builders' Association members

6.4   Carpenter Job Description

Company Letterhead

Carpenter's Job Description Guidelines

To be complete, a job description should contain most if not all of the elements listed below.

Position Objective: A brief description of the purpose of the position and why it exists in the company or organization

Key Duties and Responsibilities: The essential functions of the job (usually 5 or 6 items)

Nature of the Work: Examples of routine tasks and of complicated ones

Working Relationships: Lists the regular communications the person must maintain both internally and externally to succeed in the job. Some job descriptions include the reporting relationships under this heading; others include it in a separate section. Some just say "Reports to" and the name of the supervisory position.

Resources: Describes the company resources for which the person in the position is responsible (tools or a vehicle, for example)

Experience, Skills, and/or Knowledge Required: Also includes diplomas, certificates, degrees, or courses essential to obtain the knowledge. These items might be treated as three different topics or lumped together as was done here. Because of the technical nature of a carpenter's work and the skills required, some remodelers also use a skills list with the job description.

These items don't have to be in this order, nor do they need to bear these exact names. Typically, entries under the categories begin with action verbs. For some jobs you might not need all categories. For example, not all job descriptions would include resources.

6.4   Carpenter Job Description (continued)

Company Letterhead

Carpenter's Skills

You are expected to meet all the requirements of the apprentice carpenter in addition to having the skills to do the following:

1. Understand and implement blueprint drawings and written specifications.
2. Use a transit level to establish grades and elevations.
3. Be proficient in all phases of nonstructural demolition.
4. Set flatwork forms, strike concrete level, and rough finish concrete flatwork.
5. Establish grades for proper drainage of flatwork and simple structures.
6. Know and identify masonry units by size, shape, and specification.
7. Lay out and install metal stud-wall framing.
8. Lay out framing members for walls, floors, ceilings, roofs, and decks.
9. Lay out and install a simple set of stairs for a basement or deck using a framing square.
10. Use fasteners properly, depending on length needed and material being used.
11. Be proficient in use of tools for wood framing and millwork.
12. Be proficient in layout and installation of all asphalt/cedar roofing products, including valleys, flashings, and roof penetrations.
13. Be proficient in installing prehung door units and windows furnished with nailing fins or masonry clips.
14. Be proficient in drywall sheathing installation and in properly taping drywall sheathing.
15. Lay out and install a standard metal suspended-ceiling system.
16. Install cultured marble wall panels and tub/shower surrounds.
17. Install standard wall-hung cabinetry and accessories.
18. Properly install kitchen and bathroom cabinetry and countertops.
19. Be proficient in installing wood casing, base trim, crown mold, and simple wood moldings.
20. Properly install prefabricated fireplaces and flues.
21. Do simple repairs in painting/staining, HVAC, plumbing, electrical, and flooring.

6.5 Sales Associate Job Description

Company Name
Company Logo
Company Affiliations

Job Description for Remodeling Salesperson

Overall responsibility of the remodeling salesperson is to sell remodeling projects to customers that meet the needs of the customer, represent value to the customer, and generate a profit for the company. Priority should be given at all times to providing the best customer service possible.

1. Attire

   The salesperson will present a neat appearance at all times. The salesperson will dress as a professional when interacting with customers. Men shall wear dress slacks and dress shirt. A tie and sport coat are optional. Women shall wear dress slacks, skirts, or suits with blouses or sweaters.

2. Equipment
   A. A late-model vehicle in good condition is required. The vehicle will be kept clean and neat at all times.
   B. The salesperson must carry with him/her to sales appointments the following materials:
      1. Note pad and pencil or pen
      2. Business cards
      3. Camera
      4. Measuring tape
      5. Cell phone/GPS/PDA/Laptop

3. Hours

   The salesperson is expected to work a minimum of 40 hours per week making sales calls, prospecting for customers, and ensuring that jobs under construction are running smoothly. Because of the necessity for evening calls, the hours are flexible.

4. Responsibilities

   The salesperson will be responsible for the following:

   A. Developing sales skills through attendance in work groups
   B. Maintaining working knowledge of new products and industry trends by regularly reading the following magazines:
      a. *Professional Remodeler*
      b. *Professional Builder*

Company Address
Phone/Fax
E-mail—Web site

6.5   Sales Associate Job Description (continued)

Company Name
Company Logo
Company Affiliations

     c. Qualified Remodeler

     d. Remodeling

     e. Sales and Marketing Ideas

  C. Becoming involved in a minimum of one community or business organization approved by the Sales Manager

  D. Becoming involved in a professional organization, such as the NAHB Remodelers or the NAHB Sales and Marketing Council

  E. Maintaining a basic knowledge of the cost and health consequences that hazardous issues such as lead, asbestos and radon will have on current and future projects

  F. Completing all estimates and accompanying paperwork necessary for production to perform all duties as written in contract

  G. Maintaining knowledge of current financing opportunities and rates in order to assist clients

5. Specific Duties

  A. **Lead Receipt.** When the company receives a lead, either the sales assistant or administrative assistant may set an appointment. The salesperson must arrive at the appointment on time and determine the customer' needs and desires. After that, the salesperson determines whether the client will be better served in signing a pre-design agreement or a complete design agreement.

  B. **Predesign.** Upon signing of agreement, the salesperson will acquire information from the residence (photos, measurements, site plan) necessary to start concept drawings. Before leaving the home, the salesperson will set an appointment for a second meeting at <Your Company's> office with both parties. The second meeting should include a presentation of the concept design and carefully listening to home owners' questions and comments. After answering their questions, suggest the next step in the process of completing a design agreement.

  C. **Complete Design Agreement.** If during the initial appointment a complete design agreement would better serve their needs, the salesperson should attempt to secure a signed contract and deposit or, prior to leaving the client's home, set a second appointment to gather the information necessary to start the design process. The salesperson will then revisit the site to take measurements and photos and to analyze the conditions in detail. If the project will require an architect or designer, that professional will need a basic layout of the proposed renovations and accurate dimensions. <Your Company Name's> policy is for the salesperson to obtain all pertinent information from the client that the architect or designer will need to prepare permit-ready drawings. All product selection decisions are then made prior to ren-

Company Address
Phone/Fax
E-mail—Web site

6.5   Sales Associate Job Description (continued)

Company Name
Company Logo
Company Affiliations

dering the final design. Upon completion of the final drawing, a final cost estimate and contract language can be prepared. If the home was built before 1978, and lead cleanup costs will be incurred, sales should work with the estimator to determine costs and include them in the owner's proposal.

D. **Lead Counseling:** Under federal law, remodelers must notify clients living in homes built before 1978 of possible exposure to lead in interior trim, hardwood floors, doors, exterior siding, and other materials. The salesperson will describe–and make the home owner aware of–the potential problems with and procedures for dealing with this hazard. Furthermore, either before the contract is signed or before construction has started, the salesperson will give the client a U.S. Environmental Protection Agency brochure titled *Protect Your Family from Lead in Your Home* and obtain the client's signature on the lead pamphlet receipt form. The salesperson will counsel the client about the potential additional costs of protection, cleanup, and blood testing. The salesperson will obtain either the client's signature on the lead blood test release form or a copy of the client's blood test results. **These procedures are mandatory.**

E. **Contract Signing.** The following procedures are required to package contract paperwork:
  1. Submit a cost breakdown, sales checklist, original copy of signed contract, lead pamphlet receipt form, lead blood test release form (or test results), client's deposit check, all phone quotes, special orders, and subcontractor quotes to the sales assistant for distribution. Please note that all contracts, supplements, working drawings, etc., are to be signed by both parties.
  2. Acquire written proposals, with estimator assistance, from all major subcontractors, along with special orders. Above items should include complete descriptions of products, including special details or circumstances.
  3. Submit a list of all decisions the customer must make prior to starting the job. Finalize allowance figures and selections, including paint color, flooring, tile, etc. The salesperson is responsible for obtaining these selections from the customer prior to project start. The customer is responsible for supplying samples to the salesperson.
  4. Secure all permits necessary to complete the project, except those that the subcontractor must obtain.
  5. Prior to start of project, handle changes, including drafting and securing signatures on supplementary agreements, estimates, product selection sheets, and signatures. After the project is under way, the Production Department becomes responsible for additional changes.

Company Address
Phone/Fax
E-mail–Web site

6.5   Sales Associate Job Description (continued)

Company Name
Company Logo
Company Affiliations

F. **Maintaining Customer Contact.** The project superintendent initiates a preconstruction conference prior to the start of work. At the meeting, he or she will review specifications for the last time and address potential problems. After the preconstruction conference, the production department assumes responsibility for completing the project. However, the salesperson will still be involved by periodically contacting the customer to ensure they are satisfied with how the job is running. The salesperson will be the liaison between Production and the customer as follows:

1. If problems arise during a job because specifications were interpreted in more than one way, work with the customer and production department to resolve issues to everyone's satisfaction.

2. Attend the preclose meeting between production and the customer. This meeting is intended to check for missed items on the contract or changes to be made prior to drywall.

3. Participate in the final walkthrough of the client's project, arranged by the administrative assistant. The project manager prepares a punch list, if necessary, which details work to be completed. All parties initial this punch list. The salesperson shall complete a final walkthrough with the production manager and client to get final approval and sign-off of the work by the client.

6. **Customer Service**

The salesperson is responsible for sending out handwritten thank-you cards to his/her customers 30 to 40 days after final payment is received. Administrative staff will give sales a blank card upon final payment.

7. **Sales Meetings**

The salesperson attends all monthly sales meetings.

8. **Record Keeping Requirements**

The salesperson will submit to the sales assistant a copy of the lead form or give necessary information so the administrative assistant can enter the lead on the sales reports. This must be done when the lead is received.

9. **Commission Policy**

   See Sales Compensation Plan.

Company Address
Phone/Fax
E-mail—Web site

6.6 Telephone Interview Questions

Company Name
Company Logo
Company Affiliations

Phone Interview Form

Date _____   Interview Date/Time _____

Ad Date _____   Ad Placement _____

Candidate Name _____   Phone # _____

Address _____

_____

Person Conducting Interview _____

1. How did you hear of our company?

2. If an ad, which one?

3. What is your current work situation?

4. If currently employed, how long have you been working for the company?

5. Why are you looking for a new position?

6. How long have you been a <trade>? Other construction experience?

7. Who were your previous two employees and how long were you with each?

Company Address
Phone/Fax
E-mail
Web site

6.6   Telephone Interview Questions (continued)

Company Name
Company Logo
Company Affiliations

8. How were you compensated in your last three positions?

	Position	Compensation	Benefits
1st			
2nd			
3rd			

9. Is your experience in remodeling or new construction? Commercial or Residential?

10. Why are you interested in remodeling?

11. Why are you interested in our company?

12. What is your income expectation for this position?

13. I am scheduling interviews between _____ & _____ on:

Mon.   Tues.   Wed.   Thurs.   Fri.

When would be convenient for you? *(Fill in date/time at top of form.)*

Ask candidate to bring

a list of references
a resume
tools (if there are tool requirements for the position)

Company Address
Phone/Fax
E-mail
Web site

6.7   Job Application

Company Logo
Company Name

Job Application

PERSONAL INFORMATION:

Name: _____
(Last)   (First)   (Middle)

Social Security Number: _____

Address: _____
(Number)   (Street)   (Apt./Unit No.)

_____
(City)   (State)   (Zip Code)

Telephone: _____   _____   _____
(Daytime)   (Evening)   (Mobile)

Recruitment Information:

Position Desired: _____

Work Preference: ☐ Full-time or ☐ Part-time

How did you learn about this company and position?

☐ Job advertisement
(Name of publication or other media) _____

☐ Employee referral
(Name of employee) _____

☐ Other
(Agency, job fair, college recruitment office, etc.) _____

Education:

For each level of schooling listed below, please give the school name, the city and state where it is located, your major and minor subjects, and the degree or diploma received.

High School _____   _____
(Name of School)   (City)   (State)

_____
(Degree or Diploma Received)

College 1 _____   _____
(Name of School)   (City)   (State)

_____   _____   _____
(Major)   (Minor)   (Degree or Diploma Received)

College 2 _____   _____
(Name of School)   (City)   (State)

_____   _____   _____
(Major)   (Minor)   (Degree or Diploma Received)

6.7   Job Application (continued)

Graduate School _____   _____
                            (Name of School)   (City)   (State)

_____   _____   _____
      (Major)   (Minor)   (Degree or Diploma Received)

Business, Trade, Other _____   _____
                                      (Name of School)   (City)   (State)

_____   _____   _____
      (Major)   (Minor)   (Degree or Diploma Received)

WORK HISTORY:

Please list the following information regarding the last three companies for which you have worked:

(Current or Most Recent)

Employer's name _____

Employer's address _____
                                            (Number)   (Street)   (Suite/Unit No.)

_____
                 (City)   (State)   (Zip Code)

Position and dates of employment

_____   _____
                          (Position)   (Date Started)–(Date Ended)

Your salary level (or hourly rate) when you left the company

$ _____ (annual salary) or $_____ (hourly rate)

Job responsibilities: _____

_____

Name of immediate supervisor(s) _____

Employer's phone (__)_____   Employer's fax (__)_____

(Prior Employment)

Employer's name _____

Employer's address _____
                                            (Number)   (Street)   (Suite/Unit No.)

_____
                 (City)   (State)   (Zip Code)

Position and dates of employment

_____   _____
                          (Position)   (Date Started)–(Date Ended)

Your salary (or hourly rate) when you left the company

$ _____ (annual salary) or $_____ (hourly rate)

Job responsibilities _____

_____

Name of immediate supervisor(s) _____

Employer's phone (__)_____   Employer's fax (__)_____

(Prior Employment)

Employer's name _____

Employer's address _____
                                            (Number)   (Street)   (Suite/Unit No.)

_____
                 (City)   (State)   (Zip Code)

6.7   Job Application (continued)

Position and dates of employment

_____   _____
(Position)   (Date Started)–(Date Ended)

Your salary (or hourly rate) when you left the company

$ _____ (annual salary) or $_____ (hourly rate)

Job responsibilities _____
_____

Name of immediate supervisor(s) _____
Employer's phone (__) _____   **Employer's fax (__)** _____

PERSONAL REFERENCES:

Please provide three (3) personal references, only one (1) of which should be a co-worker or a relative.

Personal Reference 1

Name _____   **Relationship** _____
Address _____
              (Number)   (Street)   (Suite/Unit No.)

_____
              (City)   (State)   (Zip Code)
Telephone (__) _____   **Fax (__)** _____

Personal Reference 2

Name _____   **Relationship** _____
Address _____
              (Number)   (Street)   (Suite/Unit No.)

_____
              (City)   (State)   (Zip Code)
Telephone (__) _____   **Fax (__)** _____

Personal Reference 3

Name _____   **Relationship** _____
Address _____
              (Number)   (Street)   (Suite/Unit No.)

_____
              (City)   (State)   (Zip Code)
Telephone (__) _____   **Fax (__)** _____

Please answer the following questions regarding information pertaining to the applicant:

1. Have you ever been convicted of a felony or misdemeanor offense including any traffic violations?   ☐ Yes   ☐ No

   If yes, please explain, including date of offense and the outcome.

   _____
   _____
   _____
   _____

6.7   Job Application (continued)

2. Have you ever been terminated from employment?   ☐ Yes   ☐ No

   If yes, please explain, including date and reason for dismissal:

   _____

   _____

   _____

   _____

3. What is your best trait or characteristic?

   _____

   _____

4. Describe an event where teamwork was required and how you successfully encouraged teamwork.

   _____

   _____

   _____

   _____

5. Describe a weakness that you have and how you have worked to overcome the weakness.

   _____

   _____

   _____

   _____

6. Do you have a valid driver's license?   ☐ Yes   ☐ No

APPLICANT CONSENT:

Please read each of the following statements and place your initials by each one to indicate that you understand and agree to the terms stated, and then sign this form in the space indicated below.

___ I certify that all information I have supplied on this form is correct to the best of my knowledge. I understand that omissions or deliberate misinformation will disqualify my application or, if hired, would serve as grounds for dismissal.

___ I consent to have <Your Company Name> contact the people listed on this form for references and authorize these individuals to provide truthful information regarding my qualifications for employment and previous work. I also agree to waive liability against persons named as references, provided the information they supply is honest, factual, and given without malice.

Signature: _____   **Date:** _____

6.8 Hiring Evaluation Rating Sheet

Company Name
Company Logo
Company Affiliations

Date: _____

Candidate   **Name:** _____

Address: _____

_____

Phone: _____

1	Inadequate
2	Marginal
3	Adequate
4	Impressive
5	Outstanding
NA	Not Applicable

FACTORS	1	2	3	4	5	NA
TELEPHONE						
Expression						
Patience/Composure						
Courtesy						
RESUME						
Appearance						
Realistic Attitude						
Continuity of Work History						
Quality of Experience						
1ST/2ND INTERVIEW						
Appearance						
Promptness						
Experience						
Composure						
Courtesy						
Inquisitiveness						
Math Skills						
Blueprint Skills						
Long Range Goals						
Reasons for Changing Job						
Educational Background						

6.8   Hiring Evaluation Rating Sheet (continued)

FACTORS	1	2	3	4	5	NA
Quality of Questions						
Energy Level						
Integrity/Honesty						
REFERENCE CHECK						
Credibility						
Relevance to Job						

Company Address
Phone/Fax
E-mail
Web site

6.9   Employee Compensation Record

Company Name
for office use only

Employee Compensation Record

☐ New Position   ☐ Replacement   ☐ Temporary Help

☐ Permanent Hire   ☐ Part Time

I.   Employee Name

Hire Date

Position Title

Rate of Pay $_____ per hour   Full Time ☐
                                                    Part Time ☐

Reason for Position

Rate Change   Effective Date % _____ Increase _____

II. Present Salary Rate $_____ per hour

New Salary Rate $_____ per hour

Reason for Change

III. Approval/Date

6.10   Separation Form

Separation Form

Employee Name

Effective Date

Status: ☐ Voluntary   Amount of Notice _____ Reason: _____
         ☐ Involuntary   Amount of Notice _____ Reason: _____
         ☐ Layoff   Amount of Notice _____ Reason: _____

COMPENSATION: Payroll Hours Due: _____

OTHER: ☐ Eligible for Rehire
       ☐ Loans/Advances Repaid
       ☐ Separation Checklist Completed
       ☐ Other _____

My signature below indicates my agreement with the above-stated facts.

Signed: _____   Date: _____

Signed: _____   Date: _____

6.11   Employee Exit Statement

Company Name
Company Logo
Company Affiliations

Employee Exit Statement

At termination of employment with <Your Company Name>, before receiving their final compensation and/or transfer of any other company-generated benefits, employees must sign an exit statement similar to the following:

1. All printed forms and materials produced by <Your Company Name> are the property of <Your Company Name> or its owners. Should the exiting employee remove any of these from the premises, it is hereby understood that these forms and materials must be returned before final day of employment. Failure to do so could result in criminal prosecution.

2. Exiting employee must return their <Your Company> Procedure Manual. Marketing materials, signs, cards, notebooks, etc. must be returned at the same time.

3. The disclosure of any of the management decisions to other parties is also a violation of Company Policy.

4. The exiting employee hereby agrees that they are leaving <Your Company Name> of their own free will, to pursue other interests.

5. Employee further acknowledges that they are entering into employment with:

   New Employer's: *Name:* _____

   Address: _____
   Street # and Suite #

   Phone #: _____
   Area Code

   This information is necessary should any questions pertaining to the previous employee's incomplete projects result in the need to contact the previous employee.

6. If Employee uses <Your Company Name> Health Insurance Plan, Employee must sign insurance forms to be eligible to continue coverage under COBRA.

   Employee's Signature: _____

   Date: _____

6.12   Vacation Request Form

Company Name
Company Logo
Company Affiliations

TO: Personnel Department
RE: Vacation Request

Employee Name: _____   Date: _____   Time: _____

Please approve my vacation request for

My vacation will begin on   Date _____   Time _____

I will be returning from vacation on: Date _____   Time _____

Notes_____

_____

_____

For management to complete

Vacation request has been: (Circle one)   Accepted   Denied

Date _____

Notes_____

_____

_____

Approved

_____   _____

_____   _____

Date   Date

Company Address
Phone/Fax
E-mail
Web site

6.13 Vacation Hand-off

Project: _____ (complete a form for each project)

Vacation Dates: _____

This form must be <u>completed and turned in</u> to your manager and the general manager <u>before</u> your vacation.

- _____ Project Manager (P.M.) to manage project while you are gone
- Meeting with relief P.M. to discuss job specific information
    - Date: _____   Time: _____
- Will there be any **draws due** while you are gone? If yes, please note: _____
- List **trade contractors** that will be working on the job while you are gone and days they will be working:

    _____ / _____   _____ / _____

    _____ / _____   _____ / _____

    _____ / _____   _____ / _____

- Do any **inspections** need to be scheduled? What type? _____
  What day? _____ Who will stand? _____
- Schedules have been given to office, crew and relief P.M. noting where *individual field employees on schedule will be working.*
- P.M. Plans and Permit given to relief P.M.
- Tools given to relief P.M.
- Crew and office notified of vacation
- **Cell phone voice mail changed** to state you are on vacation and who to call (office/P.M.)
- **E-mail:** Auto-responder added to e-mail (or notified office that your e-mail needs to be checked)
- _____ P.M. to develop the next week's Weekly Schedule
- **Updated your meeting note "to-do" items with Administrative Assistant**
- Update office on any last minute details:

    _____

    _____

    _____

- Client notified of your vacation and who to call if needed (relief P.M./office)
- Client weekly meeting will be:
    - Handled by _____(Client has been notified.)
    - Cancelled (Client has been notified.)
    - Held on the usual day and time (Not affected by vacation)

Company Name
Employee Handbook

6.14 Employee Handbook Template (continued)

Table of Contents

Section 1   *Purpose*
About Our Company

Section 2   Employee Records
                    Attachment #1   *Employment Application*
                    Attachment #2   *IRS Form W-4*
                    Attachment #3   *Employment Consent Form*
                    Attachment #4   *Employee Status Form*

Section 3   Employment Status & Evaluations
           Probation
           Evaluation
           Termination
                    Attachment #5   *Separation Form*

Section 4   Payment Policy
                    Attachment #6   *Daily Job Log*

Section 5   Office Procedures
           Check Request
           Expense Reimbursement
           Company Credit Cards
                    Attachment #7   *Check Request Form*
                    Attachment #8   *Expense Reimbursement Form*

Section 6   Holidays, Vacations & Leave

Section 7   Company Standards & Regulations
           Call-In Time
           Smoking
           Moonlighting
           Travel
           Attire
           Employment of Relatives

Section 8   Company Vehicles, Tools, and Equipment

Section 9   Jobsite and Customer Relations

Section 10   Employee Safety
                    Attachment #9   *Safety and Health Program*
                    Attachment #10   *Fall Protection Program*
                    Attachment #11   *Report of Illness or Injury*

Section 11   Educational Assistance

6.14   Employee Handbook Template (continued)

Purpose

This handbook is provided to you for informational purposes. Employees will receive an employee handbook upon hire. We urge you to consult this handbook for answers to questions about your employment. If you do not find the answer here, please contact the office. Employee concerns are given the highest priority. Only the owner or <his or her> designee is authorized to interpret the contents of this handbook.

Absent a separate written employment contract, employment at <Your Company Name> is at will and may be terminated at any time for any reason. Nothing in the employee handbook is intended to create a contract or obligation of any sort on the part of <Your Company Name> or any of its employees, officers, directors, or agents. <Your Company Name> reserves the right at any time to amend, discontinue, modify, or take action contrary to any of the policies or practices described in this handbook.

About Our Company

<Enter brief description and history about your company here>

6.14   Employee Handbook Template (continued)

Employee Records

Information recorded in your personnel record is extremely important to you and to <Your Company Name>. If you move, marry, change your phone number, or change your number of dependents, be sure your file is updated. The information contained within the file is company property and may not be removed by an employee. It is your responsibility to ensure that all information is correct and up to date.

Be sure to notify the office if there are changes in any of the following areas:

- Name
- Home address
- Home telephone number
- Marital status
- Number of dependents
- Military status
- Educational status
- Correction to your Social Security number

Enclosed with this manual you will find forms that we need to keep for our files (Attachments #1, #2, #3). Please complete them and return them to the office manager within the first week of employment.

Attachment #1   Employment Application
Attachment #2   Internal Revenue Service Form W-4
Attachment #3   Employment Consent Form
Attachment #4   Employee Status Form

6.14   Employee Handbook Template (continued)

Employment Status and Evaluations

PROBATION

New employees automatically enter a 90-day trial period, during which time their responsibility, ability, and work attitude are evaluated. During this trial period there will be no promotions or advancements in pay.

You will be evaluated after this 3-month period by owner or designee. Evaluations will be discussed with you and a copy will go into your personnel file. This probation period can be extended another 6 weeks if your performance deems this necessary. If at the end of this 90-day trial period your relationship with our company is mutually agreeable to us and to you, and you are a full-time employee, you will be considered a permanent employee and will be entitled to all benefits and privileges outlined in this handbook.

If for some reason your work is unsatisfactory during this period, your employment may be terminated. You will receive a complete, clear explanation if this occurs.

Evaluation

Each employee's job performance is formally evaluated twice annually. You will receive a copy of this evaluation. Various means of evaluation are used, which may include a written test of skills, job performance, procedure compliance, punctuality, etc.

Termination

An employee will be terminated for the reasons listed below.

- Lack of necessary skills to accomplish work assigned
- Failure to have necessary hand tools, general skills, motivation, loyalty, honesty, reliability, and integrity
- Failure to comply with safety regulations
- Refusing assignment
- Drinking alcohol or using illegal drugs while driving a company vehicle or while on assigned job site
- A total of three (3) accidents that have been determined negligent on your part
- As determined by owner or designee to be in the best interests of the company

Upon termination, you will fill out forms to be filed with your records, including an employee separation form (Attachment #5). These forms will confirm any pay due to you, and return of any company tools, credit cards, vehicles, etc.

Attachment #5   Separation Form

6.14   Employee Handbook Template (continued)

Payment Policy

The basic work week schedule for regular full-time employees consists of 40 hours per week, 8 hours per day, 5 days per week. You are asked to be on the jobsite by 8 a.m. until 4:30 p.m., with one-half (1/2) hour for lunch.

<Your Company Name> employees working an hourly schedule are paid each Friday for work performed the preceding Friday through Thursday. These employees are not required to punch a time card, but there are job log sheets (Attachment #6) that each employee must complete. A job log sheet has 4 basic functions:

- It is a basis for computing your pay.
- It provides valuable cost information for our accounting records.
- It provides a record of others on the site.
- It is used for recording additional work or materials.

It is important that an accurate job log be submitted weekly. Regular hours, overtime hours, sick leave, and holidays are to be indicated, as well as job identification information. Your supervisor will explain the procedures to be followed.

If you are out sick or on vacation on a payday, your check will be held in the office until your return.

Deductions from paychecks include the following:

- Federal income tax determined by number of exemptions claimed
- State income tax
- Federal Insurance Corporation Act (FICA)
- Disability and Workers' Compensation

Office Procedures

It is important that you turn in any and all receipts for purchases, either on account, by credit card, by check or by cash. All receipts must be turned in to the office manager no later than Thursday of the week in which they occur.

Check Request

The check request form (Attachment #7) should be filled out when you need a company check to pay for COD supplies or as-needed materials. It is important that you complete it as fully as possible to help us in tracking job costs. The check request form should be submitted to the office manager.

Expense Reimbursement

Occasionally an employee incurs an out-of-pocket expense. This should not occur often if careful planning is implemented. However, if you need reimbursement for a company expense, you should fill out an expense reimbursement request form (Attachment #8). Again, we ask that you fill it out completely and deliver it to the office manager. These reimbursement checks will normally be delivered with the next week's paychecks, depending upon current financial standing.

Company Credit Cards

Company credit cards are issued on an as-needed basis. The possession of these cards should be considered a privilege and should be used with as much discretion as if they were your own. The authorization for obtaining or revoking credit card privileges rests with owner or designee.

- Company credit cards may never be used for personal items.
- Whenever practical, an attempt should be made to purchase all items "on account." Use of a credit card instead of an open account would be expected for items for which time is a critical factor, or when an item can be purchased for a lower cost from a firm with which we do not have an account.
- All receipts must be turned in to the office no later than Thursday of the week in which they occur.

Attachment #7   Check Request Form
Attachment #8   Expense Reimbursement Request Form

6.14   Employee Handbook Template (continued)

Holidays, Vacations, and Leave

<Your Company Name> observes six (6) paid holidays:

1. New Year's Day
2. Memorial Day
3. Independence Day
4. Labor Day
5. Thanksgiving Day
6. Christmas Day

When a holiday falls on a Sunday, it will normally be observed on the following Monday. When a holiday falls on a Saturday, it will normally be observed on the preceding Friday.

Any change from this procedure will be announced well in advance. An employee is eligible for holiday pay after one (1) year of consistent, full-time employment, and must have worked his last scheduled work day before the holiday and his first scheduled work day after the holiday.

In addition to the holidays listed above, each full-time employee may be allowed unpaid personal days. These days must be approved in advance by owner or designee.

Military Field Training Leave

Any employee who is a member of a United States Armed Services Active Reserve or National Guard unit will be granted a leave of absence to join his or her unit for temporary field duty upon presentation of written orders.

Company Standards & Regulations

Call-in Time

Call-in time is on the jobsite, equipped and ready to start at 8:00 AM.

Smoking

Employees are not allowed to smoke in homes or on jobsites. Butt cans are to be used at all outside jobsites.

Moonlighting

<Your Company Name> employees are not permitted to work for our customers on a moonlighting job during the time you are in our employ without express permission from owner or designee. Also, small jobs received as a result of working on a jobsite are not permitted without express permission from owner or designee.

Travel

All employees are required to provide their own transportation to and from assigned jobs unless instructed otherwise.

Attire

Employees are allowed great freedom in selecting their dress; therefore, it is very important that the appropriate attire is chosen for specific jobs and is consistent with good taste. Work boots are mandatory. Sleeveless shirts or obscene language or logos on clothing are not permitted.

Employment of Relatives

<Your Company Name> feels the employment of relatives is not objectionable and so we will welcome the opportunity to discuss employment with your relatives. In the placement of qualified relatives, every effort will be made to avoid situations in which a question of favoritism may arise.

6.14   Employee Handbook Template (continued)

Company Vehicles, Tools and Equipment

Vehicles

Only drivers authorized by owner or designee shall be allowed to drive company vehicles.

Company vehicles are to be properly maintained by authorized drivers. Fluid levels, tire changes and general engine problems must be checked regularly and reported to the office.

Any drivers or occupants of company vehicles who drink alcoholic beverages while driving or riding in company vehicles will be fired.

Tools and Equipment

Employees shall provide their own basic hand tools and any other tools listed below which may be required on their particular job assignment. This shall be necessary before any consideration for a pay raise is given.

Basic Tools Required for Employment

hard hat	nippers	tool pouch
safety glasses	utility knife	framing hammer
goggles	pointed trowel	square
steel-toed boots/shoes	screwdrivers	
tape measure	flat chisel	

Other

M-1 shears	toolbox with lock	$^3/_8$" drill
straight shears	trammel points	hacksaw
flat file	level–24" minimum	circular saw
flat trowel	framing square–24"	
adjustable wrench	pop rivet gun	

It is also the responsibility of employees to care for and to perform normal maintenance on company tools and equipment in their possession. Clean, oil, and grease tools such as table saw, chop saws, drills, compressors, etc. Report and deliver to the office any company tools that are broken, not working properly, or are missing parts.

Jobsite and Customer Relations

- Customer relations should be friendly and non-threatening.
- All openings to the house should be protected from dust with tarps.
- All debris should be collected and put into a dumpster or can daily.
- All jobsites should be broom cleaned at the end of each day and when the job is completed.
- The jobsite should be as clean or cleaner than when the work began.

6.14   Employee Handbook Template (continued)

Employee Safety

It is the policy of <Your Company Name> to strive for the safest possible performance on each jobsite. The following safety and loss control guidelines represent a wealth of practical experience tested in the safety-conscious environment of many successful projects. Implementing these procedures will protect the well-being of our employees and company resources from any harm or financial loss caused by accidents. Therefore, as a condition of employment by <Your Company Name>, each employee is required to understand and abide by these procedures.

Because each construction project is unique, some of these procedures may need to be refined or expanded to meet the site-specific safety and loss control needs of a particular project. The job supervisor may refine or expand these procedures as needed, with the approval of owner or designee. For more information on complying with specific safety policies and procedures, please contact the job supervisor or owner/designee. Safety is as critical to operations as planning, scheduling, or billing: it is an integral part of our routine operations. Further, <Your Company Name> believes that accidents are preventable, and that it is up to each of us to ensure that we practice safety as a routine part of our daily work.

<Your Company Name> is committed to maintaining safe and healthful workplaces and to protecting the public against any potential hazards caused by our operations.

Attachment #9   Safety and Health Program
Attachment #10   Fall Protection Program
Attachment #11   Report of Illness or Injury

6.14　Employee Handbook Template (continued)

Educational Assistance

The company provides educational assistance to salaried employees for the purpose of improving their job performance or improving their potential for advancement within our company.

1) If an employee is furthering his/her education at the specific request of the company, the entire cost will be paid by the company. This benefit also includes the cost of seminars.

2) If the course of study requested by the employee is degree oriented and/or job related, up to one-half of the educational cost <u>may</u> be reimbursed by the company, provided the following criteria are met:

   • An employee must submit an application for assistance in advance of registration for the chosen course and prior approval by owner or designee must be obtained.
   • Courses must be started after completion of the 90-day probationary period of employment.
   • Courses must be applicable to your position or be oriented toward a professional degree in a field related to <Your Company Name>'s activities.
   • Courses must be taken at an accredited college or university.
   • Evidence of a passing grade must be submitted for reimbursement.

6.15   Company Rules

Company Name
Company Logo
Company Affiliations

Company Rules

Our mission is to provide excellent service on schedule, within budget, and with honesty and a team approach. Our purpose is to establish quality relationships and to promote personal growth within the <Your Company Name> team. Clients refer contractors who they like and who produce a great product. Therefore

1. No alcohol is allowed on a jobsite or immediately preceding work.
2. No employee pets of any kind are allowed on the jobsite.
3. No tobacco use of any kind (smoking, chewing, etc.) is allowed during working hours. Smoking is not allowed at the office, shop, on the jobsite, or in company vehicles.
4. Employees are expected to begin the workday in clean clothes and to be neatly groomed. Repeated tardiness will not be tolerated.
5. Keep the jobsite clean. Use drop cloths, tarps, and/or plastic sheeting to control dust, paint splatter, etc. Broom clean the jobsite daily. Vacuum as necessary.
6. Do not use profanity, play music, or argue with fellow workmen. Keep a low profile. Focus on the work.
7. At the beginning of a project, locate the nearest available restroom facility, or ascertain which restroom in the client's home is available for your use.
8. Do not leave trash lying around. Keep the jobsite neat! A garbage can should be placed on every jobsite for common debris.
9. Do not use the client's phone or personal property.
10. Unplug and secure all tools at the end of each day.
11. Do not leave doors and windows open when you leave for the day. Do not leave any ladders up.
12. Always be polite! No boots or dirty shoes are permitting in a client's home: protective paper booties are available from the supervisor.
13. Do not ask for food or drink on the jobsite. If it is offered, politely refuse.
14. Moonlighting for a client after hours is not permitted.
15. Do not borrow a client's tools or appliances.
16. Do not perform tasks other than those you have been assigned, even if the client requests it, without an authorized additional work request.

Company Address
Phone-Fax
E-mail-Web site

6.15   Company Rules (continued)

Company Name
Company Logo
Company Affiliations

17. SUPPLIES: materials picked up from any vendor or supplier must have a job number and name marked on the ticket.
18. CELLULAR PHONES: field personnel will be assigned cellular phones. It is their responsibility to maintain the phones and keep the batteries charged for use during working hours. Personal calls are not permitted on these company phones!
19. COMPLETION OF TASKS: timely completion of assigned tasks is expected of all employees. If a problem or question arises that may cause delay, inform the foreman or supervisor immediately.

The items above are necessary and crucial when working in clients' homes. This is nothing less than being considerate, polite and understanding the clients and respecting them, as well as maintaining our image as a professional contractor in this community. Always refer questions about a project to your supervisor.

Company Address
Phone-Fax
E-mail-Web site

6.16   Trade Contractor Agreement

Company Name
Company Logo
Company Affiliations

Subcontractor Agreement
and
Insurance Requirements and Payment Policies
Revised _____

Our Mission Statement:
To provide excellent service, on schedule, within budget,
through honesty and a team approach.

Our requirements for insurance coverage, invoice submittals and payments, and scheduling respon-sibilities are explained below. Should you have any questions concerning these requirements and policies, please contact the company prior to signing the attached agreement and prior to perform-ing any work.

INSURANCE CERTIFICATION REQUIREMENTS

Under State Law, any and all payments to Uninsured Subcontractors (that is, subcontractors who are not covered under a <u>current</u> Worker's Compensation policy) must be reported with the General Contractor's payroll report to determine the premium amount due. Since this premium is a substan-tial cost to the General Contractor, we require that all subcontractors have a <u>current</u> Worker's Compensation Policy in force.

State Law ( ) also requires that we have a Certificate of Coverage on file for insured subcontractors. We <u>must</u> have this certificate on file before you can be paid for any work performed. Otherwise, you will be considered uninsured and the applicable premium will be deducted from your next payment.

Due to the continuing problems being encountered in the insurance industry, we are now required to keep on file copies of Certificates of Liability insurance on all Subcontractors. The procedure for getting these certificates to us is the same as that for Worker's Compensation. Please note that no payments will be made until we have <u>current</u> certificates on file in the office.

TAX IDENTIFICATION NUMBERS

The Internal Revenue Service requires that we have your Tax I.D. number (either a Federal Tax I.D. number or your Social Security number) on file for inclusion with your Form 1099-MISC that you will receive at the end of the year. If we do not have this tax number, we are required to do Backup Withholding at a rate of 31% of the gross payments. Unfortunately, there are no exceptions to this regulation.

6.16   Trade Contractor Agreement (continued)

Company Name
Company Logo
Company Affiliations

INVOICE SUBMITTALS AND PAYMENTS

All invoices submitted for payment <u>must</u> have a <u>JOB NUMBER, CLIENT NAME AND ADDRESS,</u> in order to be identified and paid. ADDRESSES AND/OR NAMES WILL NOT BE ACCEPTED IN LIEU OF A JOB NUMBER. Obtain this number from the company before you send in an invoice for payment. We also need a brief description of the work performed and the date on which it was done. If work was done outside the scope of your bid, please list that work separately and label it as "Extras" (see Additional Work Policy below). Subcontractor checks are processed and mailed on the 15th and 30th of each month. If the 15th or 30th falls on a weekend or legal holiday, the checks will be processed the next regular business day. <u>Invoices must be received a minimum of five working days prior to the check processing day.</u> This means that to be paid on the 15th, your invoice MUST be received by the 10th, and by the 25th to be paid on the 30th. We are unable to make exceptions to this policy due to the time required to process the payments.

ADDITIONAL WORK POLICY

Although we strive to package our work to prevent change orders, changes may occur during the course of the project. We must inform the client of the additional charges involved prior to the work being done. If we are unable to do so then we must offer them a not-to-exceed price agreeing that a fixed-price will be provided no later than 30 days after the work is completed. We request from all subcontractors a <u>written price change order either fixed or not-to-exceed prior to the work being performed.</u> Without this written change order, we cannot guarantee payment of the change order.

SCHEDULING

Due to the size, complexity, and large number of projects we are involved in, scheduling is critical. If you are unable to maintain your agreed-upon schedule, it is your responsibility to notify the company (office or Production Manager) a minimum of 48 hours in advance. Our aim is to increase profit—yours and ours—and, to increase our clients' equity. This cannot be accomplished without accurate, prompt communication, i.e. scheduling.

Company Address
Phone
Fax
E-mail
Web site

6.16   Trade Contractor Agreement (continued)

Company Name
Company Logo
Company Affiliations

SUBCONTRACTOR AGREEMENT

I have read the attached Policy Statement and understand my responsibilities.

I hereby agree to furnish ‹*Your Company*› with the following:
1. Current certificate of Worker's Compensation Insurance.
2. Current certificate of Liability Insurance.
3. Federal Tax Identification number.
4. Signed copy of this Subcontractor Agreement.
5. Signed copy of Site Requirements Agreement

I agree to provide ‹*Your Company*› with:
1. signed written change orders for authorized additional work performed.
2. to notify the office or Production Coordinator of any schedule changes.

I hereby agree to all of the conditions stated on this contract:

Signed:

Company:

Date:

Company Address
Phone
Fax
E-mail
Web site

6.17   Jobsite Policies and Procedures

Company Name
Company Logo
Company Affiliations

Jobsite Policies and Procedures

WORK HOURS

Work hours are 8:00 a.m.-4:30 p.m. Monday through Saturday. Please park in front of the house on our side of the street. Absolutely no work can be performed on Sundays. If it is necessary to work late inside a home, please contact the owner to request permission.

NO SMOKING

Under no circumstances will there be any smoking in the house or any interiors. Please deposit all cigarette butts in the receptacle provided. As always, no drugs, alcohol use, or possession of the aforementioned will be tolerated.

FLAMMABLE MATERIAL

All solvents and/or flammable material must be stored in a well-ventilated area or off site. Under no conditions shall they be left inside overnight.

LUNCHES

Please eat lunch off site or inside the garage. Do not sit out in the front yard or loiter out front at anytime. All lunch trash shall be bagged and removed from the project daily.

CLEAN UP

All loose construction debris shall be secured at the end of each day to prevent windblown distribution. Broom-clean/vacuum the project at the end of every work day.

RADIOS

No radios on the project.

UTILITIES

Do not use the telephone. All workers will use a designated restroom.

ANY BREECH OR VIOLATION OF ANY OF THESE POLICIES IS GROUNDS FOR IMMEDIATE TERMINATION.

IN CASE OF EMERGENCY CONTACT:

_____

Agreed by trade contractor: _____

Date:

Company Address
Phone-Fax
E-mail-Web site

6.18   Scope of Work

Standards and Description of Work Performance

CABINETS

The Company's **Terms and Conditions** are by reference a part of all **Scope of Work** requirements.

Construction Requirements:

Generally speaking the work of Trade Contractors and their employees is expected to be performed in a good and workmanlike manner. Workmanlike quality is defined as workmanship that meets or betters those criteria indicated in applicable building codes, using materials and installation methods identified in the construction plans and this Scope of Work.

Code Requirements:

All jobs shall conform to those standards stipulated in the building code, mechanical code, plumbing code, and electrical code applicable in the local jurisdiction. All construction on The Company's jobsites shall meet or exceed NAHB Performance and Building Standards.

General Comments:

The Company considers our Trade Contractors to be experts at producing a high-quality job. But everyone on our construction team—staff, Trade Contractors, and suppliers—must recognize the importance of providing quality in both the product and service areas while on our jobsites and in the homes of our purchasers.

Since we work as a team, poor quality or service from any of us reflects unfavorably on all of us. An exceptional level of product quality and highly effective service can help us all to increase our business and grow.

The Company's definition of quality construction also requires that every job be completed correctly the first time. When this does not occur it costs both of us additional money, imposes on the purchaser, and hurts our reputations as quality builders. That is why, in situations where construction was not completed in a quality manner, prompt corrective action is required to remedy specific deficiencies.

In the following information the term Site Superintendent shall refer to any <The Company> representative with authority to perform the specified task. The term Trade Contractor shall mean the Trade Contractor's organization or any representative that is assigned the authority to perform the specified task.

General: For most buyers, the look of finished carpentry, millwork, and cabinetry defines quality construction. The look, feel, and number of cabinets are the major selling points of most homes. The first impression created by the kitchen and baths must be a pleasant one and when looked at closely must continue to be pleasant. Lack of quality workmanship in these areas "turns-off" homebuyers.

Care should be taken in the storage and handling of finish materials to avoid damage and soiling. Installed materials should be protected when necessary.

_____ Company Rep's Initials
_____ Trade Contractor's Initials

6.18   Scope of Work (continued)

Materials: All cabinet materials, construction, type, etc., is determined by the model of the home, the location of the subdivision, and whether the cabinets are standard or upgrades.

Installation: All installations are to be performed by the Trade Contractor. All work is to be done by trained, experienced individuals. Cabinets should be installed with sufficient care to avoid damage. Cabinets should be attached with screws, not nails, to studs and other framing members. As it is attached, each cabinet should be checked front to back and across the front for level. Cabinet units may not exceed a ⅜-inch differential in 10 feet in surface alignment. A gap between the cabinet and wall that is greater than ¼ inch is unacceptable.

Countertops should be fastened to cabinets with screws, front and back, at least every 4 feet. Care should be taken not to penetrate the countertop surface with the fasteners. Countertops should be installed within ¼ inch of level in 8 feet and ¼ inch of level front to back. Deck area countertop joints may not exceed a 1/16-inch gap and a maximum of 1/16-inch differential in surface alignment.

Cabinet faces more than ⅛ inch out of line, and cabinet corners more than 3/16 inch out of line are unacceptable.

Cabinet doors and drawers shall open and close with reasonable ease.

Warped cabinet faces or drawer faces shall not be installed.

Prior to the manufacture of cabinets for the house, the Trade Contractor is responsible for field measuring all cabinet areas to ensure the correct fit of the cabinets.

Warranty: The Company believes that all work done and all materials installed, in connection with one of our homes should be of high quality and that all Trade Contractors should stand behind the quality of their work and materials. Therefore we require all Trade Contractors to warrant the quality of their work for a period of one (1) year from date of closing of the house. Please refer to our printed Limited Warranty booklet for specific items that are covered under Warranty as they apply to cabinets.

The Trade Contractor shall have seven (7) days in which to correct any Warranty problem. If the problem is not corrected within seven (7) days then The Company shall correct the problem and will backcharge the Trade Contractor at the rate of $25.00 per hour, with a minimum charge of $100.00 plus the cost of any materials.

Inspection Reports: The Trade Contractor and the Site Superintendent shall walk the job together and complete each section of the inspection report(s). The Trade Contractor must correct any deficiencies found during the inspection and the job must be 100-percent complete before payment will be made. The Trade Contractor and the Site Superintendent must sign-off on all sections of the inspection report(s) attesting that the job is 100-percent complete and is correct per the job requirements found in this Scope of Work.

____ Company Rep's Initials
____ Trade Contractor's Initials

6.18   Scope of Work (continued)

Detailed Job Requirements:

1. A new set of plans is required for each house. Plans are subject to changes and modifications. It is the responsibility of the Trade Contractor to have the new plans before beginning work. Plans should be picked up at the job trailer from the Site Superintendent. The Trade Contractor at no cost to The Company will correct any errors that occur from using an incorrect set of plans.

2. Purchase orders will be mailed to the Trade Contractor from the office.

3. Color selection sheets that detail cabinet and countertop colors may be picked up from the Site Superintendent or will be mailed from the office at least three (3) weeks prior to installation.

4. The Trade Contractor and the Site Superintendent must walk the job together and complete the pre-work section of the inspection report(s) before work may begin. The pre-work section of the inspection report(s) must be signed-off on by both parties.

5. The Trade Contractor is responsible for field measuring all cabinet areas to ensure proper sizing.

6. If plans call for marble countertops, the Trade Contractor and the marble company should compare cabinet dimensions to ensure the proper fit of cabinets and countertops.

7. Cabinets are to be built and installed to plan, with necessary cutouts for range, sinks, dishwasher, vent-a-hood, built-in microwave, etc.

8. The HVAC vent in the kick plate of the cabinet should be cut high enough to allow the HVAC grill to be above the shoe molding when the shoe molding is installed.

9. Cabinets are to be installed per the manufacturer's installation instructions, but not with less quality than is stated herein.

10. The Trade Contractor is responsible for the cabinets being level, plumb, and securely attached. A differential of more than $3/8$ inch in 10 feet is unacceptable.

11. All cabinet doors and drawer fronts shall be level, plumb, and undamaged. A differential of more than $1/8$ inch out of line and cabinet corners that are more than $3/16$ inch out of line are unacceptable.

12. Cabinet shelves shall be level and undamaged.

13. Adjustable shelves shall rest securely on shelf holders and no shelf holder shall be missing.

14. If the cabinets have knobs, handles, or other hardware attached, the screws that attach the hardware shall be set smooth and should not damage the inside of the drawers or doors.

15. In all cabinets that include rollout shelves the roller tracks shall be attached tightly and correctly. The shelf shall roll smoothly and not tilt when fully extended. The shelf should be easy to remove for cleaning.

16. In all cabinets that contain a lazy susan, the lazy susan shall work smoothly, not tilt, and be securely anchored top and bottom.

____ Company Rep's Initials

____ Trade Contractor's Initials

6.18   Scope of Work (continued)

17. All end/backsplashes must be properly fitted, snug, and secure.
18. If colored countertops are selected, colored caulking, matched as closely as possible to the color of the countertops, should be used if at all possible.
19. After cabinets are installed, all countertops should be protected with cardboard that is taped securely. Tape shall be of a type that will not damage cabinets or countertops.
20. All construction debris must be removed to the dumpster or to an area designated by the Site Superintendent. The job will not be considered complete and payment will not be issued until all trash and debris are removed from the house and/or site.
21. House is to be left clean and broom-swept.
22. The Trade Contractor and Site Superintendent must walk the job together and perform a final inspection of the job. The final section of the inspection report(s) must be completed and signed-off on by both parties. The inspection report(s) must be attached to the office's copy of the purchase order and the Trade Contractor's invoice or payment will not be issued.
23. Any items found during the final inspection that need correction shall be corrected before payment will be made.

I _____ agent for _____

_____ have read and fully understand the above **Scope of Work** and I hereby agree to perform all work in accordance with the above.

Date: _____

_____
Signed: Trade Contractor (or agent)

Date: _____

_____
For The Company

6.19 Notice of Schedule

Company Name
Company Logo
Company Affiliations

Notice of Schedule

<Date>

<Subcontractor's Name>
<Address>
<City, State, Zip>

Dear <Subcontractor>,

Production on _____ will begin _____. We will be ready for you to begin your portion of the work on _____.

Should your scope involve multiple phases (removals, rough-ins, and finish) of work, kindly see the attached overall project schedule for additional dates.

We will call the week prior with a reminder.

If there are any conflicts with this schedule, please contact us immediately.

Thank you.

<Your Company>

Attached: project schedule

Company Address
Phone
Fax
E-mail
Web site

6.20   Certificate of Insurance Request

Company Name
Company Logo
Company Affiliations

<Date>

<Contractor's Name>
<Address>
<City, State, Zip>

Dear <Contractor>,

Our records indicate that your liability and/or worker's compensation insurance policy expires _____.

Payments for work completed will not be released without our first receiving a current Certificate of Insurance. To avoid any delay in your receiving payments due, please have your insurance agent send us a current certificate showing both liability and worker's comp insurance at their earliest convenience. Our phone, fax and e-mail contact information is shown below.

Sincerely,

<Your Name>
<Your Title>

Company Address
Phone/Fax
E-mail
Web Site

6.21   Employee Self Evaluation

Name: Position:

This report covers: Date of hire:

Goals:

- A candid and respectful conversation about performance and personal goals
- To use this form as a foundation for dialogue about the dynamic balance in your working relationship with (Your company name)

Part One:

This is a chance to assess your work performance in relation to your current job requirements. Here are some numbers to assign to each quality. There is also room to further elaborate on your thoughts.

> 5 = Outstanding. Your performance consistently exceeds expectation.
> 4 = Very Good. Your performance is of high quality and exceeds most position expectations.
> 3 = Good. Your performance meets position requirements in an acceptable manner.
> 2 = Improvement needed. Your performance is deficient. Improvement is necessary.
> 1 = Unsatisfactory. Your performance is below satisfaction; requires immediate improvement.

Part Two:

This is a chance for you to think more broadly about who you are as a person. How can our company best support your goals?

Part Three:

This is a chance for you to evaluate our company. Where can we improve?

Name & Date: By:
PART ONE: Performance

___   **Leadership:**
      Your ability to elicit trust and confidence from others and to coordinate, advise and direct others effectively toward objectives; to be an important part of your community. Elaborate a statement regarding the extent to which you see yourself as a leader.

___   **Trust:**
      Elaborate a statement regarding the extent to which you elicit and nurture trust with your team and in your client relations.

6.21   Employee Self Evaluation (continued)

___   **Collaboration:**
The extent to which you go to make your team work; be it architects, trade partners, clients, suppliers, designers, co-workers . . .

___   **Creativity:**
Elaborate a statement regarding the extent to which you propose ideas, and find new and better ways to do things.

___   **Contribution:**
Elaborate a statement regarding your willingness and ability to grow and develop the company into something better than it is now.

___   **Communication:**
Your ability to speak, write, and listen in a way that nurtures trust, sets expectations, and provides leadership.

___   **Quality:**
The accuracy and thoroughness of your own work and of the work you are responsible for.

___   **Financial Acumen:**
The extent to which you feel comfortable working with and presenting numbers and understanding profitability models.

___   **Being a part of the company's future:**
The extent to which you are able to see yourself as a part of the company's plan for growth and development.

___   **Self:**
The extent to which you strive to be better than you are now.

___   **Work/Life Balance:**
The extent to which you are able to live a balanced and whole life. The extent to which you seek opportunities to learn and engage outside of work.

Name & Date:
PART TWO: More about you

1. What things have been going well for you?

2. What things have been challenging for you?

3. Why does our company need you on our team?

6.21 Employee Self Evaluation (continued)

4. What's over the horizon for you?

5. What makes you come to work everyday? To what extent are you able to bring your heart to work?

6. List your three professional goals (long or short term)

7. List your three personal goals (long or short term)

Name & Date:

PART THREE, The Company

1. I feel our company has a well-organized, successful approach to business
   Strongly disagree   1   2   3   4   5   Strongly agree
   Comments:

2. I understand the direction our company is headed and feel well informed about how I can contribute to our success:
   Strongly disagree   1   2   3   4   5   Strongly agree
   Comments:

3. I believe the top two goals of our company are:

4. Our company follows through on its commitments to me:
   Strongly disagree   1   2   3   4   5   Strongly agree
   Comments:

5. My skills, talents, and personality are valued at our company:
   Strongly disagree   1   2   3   4   5   Strongly agree
   Comments:

6. My ideas and suggestions are requested and often utilized:
   Strongly disagree   1   2   3   4   5   Strongly agree
   Comments:

7. I am fairly paid for what I do:
   Strongly disagree   1   2   3   4   5   Strongly agree
   Comments:

8. I could perform my job more effectively if . . .

6.21   Employee Self Evaluation (continued)

9. I understand why our company needs to be profitable and exactly what has to happen for our company to be profitable. I understand my role in making our company profitable.
   Strongly disagree   1   2   3   4   5   Strongly agree
   Comments:

10. The leadership's worst weakness is:

11. The leadership's biggest strength is:

12. I would like our company to start doing:

13. I would like our company to stop doing:

14. I'd like to still be associated with our company in five years:
    Strongly disagree   1   2   3   4   5   Strongly agree
    Comments:

15. Overall, here's how I feel about our company:

6.22   Company Evaluation of Trade Contractor/Supplier

Company Name
Company Logo
Company Affiliations

Company Evaluation of Trade Contractor/Supplier

Trade/supplier name _____   Date _____

Services performed by trade/supplier _____

Rating:	Excellent	Good	Average	Fair	Poor
Overall work quality of trade/supplier	☐	☐	☐	☐	☐
Completes projects within ‹your company name›'s schedule	☐	☐	☐	☐	☐
Punctuality of trade/supplier's employees for scheduled meetings	☐	☐	☐	☐	☐
Customer evaluation of trade/supplier (based on ‹your company name› questionnaire)	☐	☐	☐	☐	☐
Jobsites are left clean and organized	☐	☐	☐	☐	☐
Response time to submit bid	☐	☐	☐	☐	☐
Trade/supplier begins work on scheduled date	☐	☐	☐	☐	☐
Thoroughness of trade/supplier's proposal	☐	☐	☐	☐	☐
Trade/supplier's response time to return calls	☐	☐	☐	☐	☐
Trade/supplier's responsiveness in handling call-backs	☐	☐	☐	☐	☐
Trade/supplier's willingness to help in material handling, etc.	☐	☐	☐	☐	☐
Professionalism of trade/supplier's staff	☐	☐	☐	☐	☐
Trade/supplier's handling of extras	☐	☐	☐	☐	☐
Trade/supplier's fairness of price/ value on extras	☐	☐	☐	☐	☐
Trade/supplier's history of actual costs matching estimate	☐	☐	☐	☐	☐

Total volume last year _____
Recommendations/conclusions _____

_____

Evaluation completed by _____

Company Address
Phone/Fax
E-mail-Web site

6.23   Trade or Supplier Evaluation of Company

Company Name
Company Logo
Company Affiliations

Trade/Supplier Evaluation of Company Name

Name of Trade/Supplier _____   Date _____

Rating:	Excellent	Good	Fair	Poor
‹Your Company›'s overall work quality	☐	☐	☐	☐
‹Your Company›'s ability to keep it's job schedules	☐	☐	☐	☐
Ability to have jobs ready when you show up to begin work	☐	☐	☐	☐
‹Your Company›'s notification of your schedule	☐	☐	☐	☐
Cleanliness of ‹Your Company›'s jobsites	☐	☐	☐	☐
‹Your Company›'s response time to approve your job	☐	☐	☐	☐
‹Your Company›'s payment policy	☐	☐	☐	☐
Thoroughness of specs/drawings provided by ‹Your Company›	☐	☐	☐	☐
‹Your Company›'s response time to return calls	☐	☐	☐	☐
‹Your Company›'s ability to develop loyalty with trades/suppliers	☐	☐	☐	☐
‹Your Company›'s employees' willingness to help with material handling, etc.	☐	☐	☐	☐
‹Your Company›'s Professionalism of staff	☐	☐	☐	☐
How would you rate ‹Your Company›'s handling of extras?	☐	☐	☐	☐
How well does ‹Your Company› perform in explaining trade/supplier expectations?	☐	☐	☐	☐

Recommendations/conclusions:

_____

_____

_____

Evaluator's name (You do not have to provide your name if you wish to remain anonymous.)

_____

Company Address
Phone
Fax
E-mail
Web site

6.24   Evaluation Cover Letter

Company Name
Company Logo
Company Affiliations

<Date>

<Trade Contractor Name>
<Address>
<City, State, Zip>

Dear <Trade Contractor>,

When we do work for our clients, we depend on you a great deal as part of the overall construction team. We are trying very hard to improve our working relationship with our "Team Players." Your suggestions on how we have performed, how we are performing now, and how we can improve are very important to us. Please take a few minutes to give us your thoughts.

The attached mission statement reflects our philosophy and what we are trying to communicate to our clients and our community.

You don't have to sign your name, but feel free to identify yourself if you would like to.

Thanks for your help in making us a better company.

Sincerely,

<Your Name and Title>
<Your Company Name>

Company Address
Phone/Fax
E-mail
Web site

6.25   Employee Evaluation

Employee Name	Evaluator Name	Date
Name:	Position:	
This report covers:	Date of hire:	

Goals:
- To have a candid and respectful conversation about performance and personal goals
- To use this form as a foundation for dialogue about the dynamic balance in your working relationship with <Your Company>.

Part One:

This is a chance to assess your work performance in relation to your current job requirements. Please assign one of the following numbers to each quality listed. You may elaborate using the space provided beneath the description of each quality.

> 5 = Outstanding. Your performance consistently exceeds expectation.
> 4 = Very Good. Your performance is of high quality and exceeds most position expectations.
> 3 = Good. Your performance meets position requirements in an acceptable manner.
> 2 = Improvement needed. Your performance is deficient. Improvement is necessary.
> 1 = Unsatisfactory. Your performance is below satisfaction; requires immediate improvement.

Part Two:

This is a chance for you to think more broadly about your personal and professional goals. How can <Your Company> best support your goals?

Part Three:

This is a chance for you to evaluate our company. How can we improve?

Part I: Performance

___   **Leadership.** Leadership is the ability to elicit trust and confidence from others and to coordinate, advise, and direct others effectively toward objectives. Leadership encompasses community, as well as professional leadership. Discuss the extent to which you see yourself as a leader.

___   **Trust.** Discuss the extent to which you elicit and nurture trust with your team and with clients.

___   **Collaboration.** Discuss how you collaborate to make your team work, whether that team includes architects, trade partners, clients, suppliers, designers, or coworkers.

6.25   Employee Evaluation (continued)

___ **Creativity.** Discuss the extent to which you propose ideas and find new and better ways to do things.

___ **Contribution.** Discuss your willingness and ability to grow and develop the company to be even better.

___ **Communication.** Discuss your ability to speak, write, and listen in a way that nurtures trust, sets expectations, and provides leadership.

___ **Quality.** Discuss the accuracy and thoroughness of your own work and of other work you are responsible for.

___ **Financial Acumen.** Discuss the extent to which you feel comfortable working with and presenting numbers and understanding profitability models.

___ **Being a part of the company's future.** Discuss the extent to which you are able to see yourself as a part of the company's plan for growth and development.

___ **Self Evaluation.** Discuss the extent to which you strive to be better than you are now.

___ **Work/Life Balance.** Discuss the extent to which you are able to live a balanced and whole life, the extent to which you seek opportunities to learn, and the extent to which you engage in activities outside of work.

Part II: More about You

1. What things have been going well for you?

2. What things have been challenging for you?

3. Why does our company need you on our team?

4. What's over the horizon for you?

5. What makes you come to work everyday? To what extent are you able to bring your heart to work?

6. List your three professional goals (long- or short-term).

7. List your three personal goals (long- or short-term).

6.25   Employee Evaluation (continued)

Part III: The Company

Please circle a response to the following, adding comments as desired.

1. I feel our company has a well-organized, successful approach to business.
   Strongly disagree   1   2   3   4   5   Strongly agree
   Comments:

2. I understand the direction our company is headed and feel well informed about how I can contribute to our success.
   Strongly disagree   1   2   3   4   5   Strongly agree
   Comments:

3. Our company follows through on its commitments to me.
   Strongly disagree   1   2   3   4   5   Strongly agree
   Comments:

4. My skills, talents, and personality are valued at our company.
   Strongly disagree   1   2   3   4   5   Strongly agree
   Comments:

5. My ideas and suggestions are requested and often utilized.
   Strongly disagree   1   2   3   4   5   Strongly agree
   Comments:

6. I am fairly paid for what I do.
   Strongly disagree   1   2   3   4   5   Strongly agree
   Comments:

7. I understand why our company needs to be profitable and exactly what has to happen for our company to be profitable. I understand my role in making our company profitable.
   Strongly disagree   1   2   3   4   5   Strongly agree
   Comments:

8. I'd like to still be associated with our company in five years.
   Strongly disagree   1   2   3   4   5   Strongly agree
   Comments:

6.25 Employee Evaluation (continued)

Please complete the following statements:

9. I believe the top two goals of our company are

10. The leadership's worst weakness is

11. The leadership's biggest strength is

12. I would like our company to start

13. I would like our company to stop

14. My overall feelings about our company are

6.26   Transmittal Cover Sheet

Company Name
Company Logo
Company Affiliations

Letter of Transmittal

TO:

DATE:

JOB:

RE:

WE ARE SENDING YOU   ATTACHED   UNDER SEPARATE COVER THE FOLLOWING ITEMS:

SHOP DRAWINGS   PRINTS   PLANS   SAMPLES
SPECIFICATIONS   COPY OF LETTER   CHANGE ORDER

OTHER:

COPIES	DATE	DESCRIPTION

THESE ARE TRANSMITTED AS CHECKED BELOW:

FOR APPROVAL   APPROVED AS SUBMITTED   RESUBMIT   COPIES FOR APPROVAL
FOR YOUR USE   APPROVED AS NOTED   SUBMIT   COPIES FOR DISTRIBUTION
AS REQUESTED   RETURNED FOR CORRECTIONS   RETURN   CORRECTED PRINTS
FOR BIDS DUE   FOR REVIEW AND COMMENT   PRINTS RETURNED AFTER LOAN TO US

REMARKS:

COPY TO:

SIGNED_____

Company Address
Phone–Fax
E-mail–Web site

6.27 Management And Production Meeting Agenda

Date

Agenda

I.   Weekly Plan Discussion
   • Review signed contracts for month
   • Leads
     Remodeling
     Design
II. Old Business
III. New Business
   • Marketing
   • Production
   • Open House
   • Pictures Needed
   • Web Page Update
   • Thank You Notes & Surveys
IV. Job Cost Reports
V.   Safety Issues
   • Broken Tools
VI. Production Tips
VII. Open Discussion
VIII. Conclusion

6.28   Weekly Meeting Notes

Company Name
Company Logo
Company Affiliations

Date: _____

Attendees: _____

_____

_____

_____

RE: Weekly Progress Meeting   **Job** _____

Open Items from Last Week: _____

_____

_____

_____

_____

_____

_____

_____

_____

_____

_____

_____

Work in Progress

Ordering Status _____

_____

Trade Contractor Status _____

_____

Budget Status _____

_____

Schedule Status _____

_____

_____

_____

Other Items Discussed _____

_____

_____

_____

_____

6.28   Weekly Meeting Notes (continued)

Company Name
Company Logo
Company Affiliations

On Site Change Orders This Week _____

_____

_____

_____

_____

_____

_____

Next Meeting Will Be On _____

cc: _____

6.29   Accident Report Form

Insured _____   Insurance company _____

Address _____   Policy number _____

_____   Policy period _____

Employee's full name _____   DOB _____   SSN _____

Employee's address _____   Phone _____

Occupation or job title _____

Hourly wage _____   Number of work days per week _____

Will employee miss any time from work?   ☐ yes   ☐ no   If yes, approximately how long? _____

Day & date of accident: _____   Time _____ a.m. _____ p.m.

Did accident occur on employer's premises?   ☐ yes   ☐ no   If yes, where? _____

How did accident happen? _____

_____

_____

_____

What parts of the body were injured? _____

_____

_____

Name and address of treating doctor _____

_____

Name and address of hospital _____

_____

Additional Comments _____

_____

_____

6.30   Report of Illness or Injury

Company Name
Company Logo
Company Affiliations

1 Name _____

2 Date of Accident _____

3 Time of Accident: _____
   Street _____
   City/State/Zip _____

4 Time work began for employee on injury date: _____

5 How did the accident occur? _____
   _____
   _____

6 What was employee doing when injured? _____
   _____
   _____

7 Name of the object or substance that directly injured the employee: _____
   _____
   _____

8 Describe the injury/illness in detail (include part of body affected): _____
   _____
   _____
   _____

9 List of Witnesses: _____
   _____
   _____
   _____
   _____

10 Medical attention performed by: _____
    _____

*If additional space is needed, please use back of sheet.
**Submit this report to the office on the day of the injury.

Company Address
Phone
Fax
E-mail
Web site

6.31   Vehicle Accident Report

Company Name
Company Logo
Company Affiliations

Case driver information:

Employee Name_____   Employee #_____

Driver's License #_____   Division_____

Phone # _____   Truck # _____

Tag #_____   VIN #_____

Year/Make/Model_____

Other driver information:

Name _____   Driver's License #_____

Address_____

City/State/Zip_____

Home Phone #_____   Work Phone #_____

VIN #_____   Tag #_____

Year/Make/Model_____

Insurance Company_____   Policy #_____

Insurance Phone #_____

Witness Information:

Name _____   Contact #_____

Name _____   Contact #_____

Police Information:

Officer Name_____   Contact #_____

Accident Report #_____   Court Date_____

Was a ticket issued?   Y   N   To whom_____

What was the charge?_____

Company Address
Phone–Fax
E-mail–Web site

Company Name
Company Logo
Company Affiliations

EQUIPMENT	Model #	Date of Purchase	Supplier	Cost	Depreciable Life (mark if direct expense)	Warranty	Scheduled maintenance	Repairs (date, nature)	Disposition					
ADD ITEMS AS NEEDED														
1–18' ALUMINUM EXT. LADDER														
1–32' ALUMINUM EXT. LADDER														
1–28' FIBERGLASS EXT. LADDER														
3–24' ALUM. WALK BOARDS														
18–16' WOOD WALK BOARDS														
18–SCAFFOLD BUCKS														
9–SCAFFOLD BRACES														
4–SCAFFOLD LEVELING JACKS														
4–SCAFFOLD ROLLERS														
4–LADDER JACKS														
7–PUMP JACKS														
4–ROOF JACKS														
–HAMMER DRILL														
1–DEWALT GRINDER														

	1–BOSCH JACK HAMMER	1–BOSCH CHIPPING HAMMER	1–CHAIN SAW	2–TABLE SAWS	2–DELTA SAW BUCS	1–SEARS BAND SAW	1–PORTER/MORTISING KIT	1–TOLMAN REBAR CUTTER	1–BLOWER	1–GENERATOR	1–AIR COMPRESSOR	1–20 TON JACK	1–12 TON JACK	2–SHOP VACS	1–TORPEDO HEATER	2–SUMP PUMPS	1–TRANSIT/TRIPOD/GAGE STICK	3–SUCTION CUPS	1–CARPET KICKER	1–TORCH	2–TANKS	2–PUMP-UP SPRAYER	1–HAND TRUCK	3–LINE SPRAYERS	2–DROP CLOTH RUNNERS

6.33   Tool Inventory

Company Name
Company Logo
Company Affiliations

Tool Inventory

Date:	

Qty	Item
2	JUMPER CABLES
3	RAINCOATS
2	PUSH BROOMS
7	WHEELBARROWS
1	WOOD CLAW HAMMER
3	FLOOR SCRAPERS
2	BOLT CUTTERS
2	HARD RAKES
3	AXE
1	SCRUB BRUSHES
1	CAR WASH BRUSH
1	16# SLEDGE HAMMER
1	8# SLEDGE HAMMER
1	BULL FLOAT
1	25' MEASURING TAPE
4	BRICK TONGS
3	JACKHAMMER BITS
1	FIRST AID KIT
2	RUBBING STONES
1	FIBERGLASS HAMMER
2	50' RUBBER HOSE
1	CONCRETE RAKE
2	MOPS
1	DUST MOP

Company Address
Phone
Fax
E-mail
Web site

6.33   Tool Inventory (continued)

Company Name
Company Logo
Company Affiliations

Qty	Item
1	UTILITY KNIFE
119	FORM PINS
2	STEEL BRUSHES
3	BRICK HAMMERS
4	SQUARE SHOVELS
2	POST-HOLE DIGGER
5	ROUND SHOVEL
4	MATTOCKS
4	PICKS
2	SHARP SHOOTER
2	PITCH FORKS
1	POTATO DIGGER
1	HEDGE CLIPPERS
4 pr	LADDER MITTS
1	HOE
1	SWING BLADE
5	COLD CHISELS
1	LEAF RAKE
1	HACKSAW
2	HANDSAWS
4	CROW BARS
2	FILE w/WOOD HANDLE
1	MALL
1	FLAT BAR
1	FLASHLIGHT
1	PAIR PLIERS

Company Address
Phone
Fax
E-mail
Web site

6.34   Supply Checkout Log

Company Name
Company Logo
Company Affiliations

Supply Checkout Log

EMPLOYEE NAME   DATE

ITEM	ISSUED/ INITIALS	MANAGER'S INITIALS	RETURNED/ INTIALS	MANAGER'S INITIALS
First Aid Kit				
Safety Book				
Hard Hat				
Radio				
Radio Charger				
Radio Battery				
Clipboard				
Office Keys				
Shop Keys				
Lockbox Keys				
Business Cards				
Company Credit Card				

Company Address
Phone/Fax
E-mail
Web site

6.35   Roof Equipment List

Roof Equipment List

Job _____

ROOF EQUIPMENT				
			JOB #	
NEEDED	EQUIPMENT	QUANTITY	NOTES	
	LONG EXTENSION LADDER			
	SHORT EXTENSION LADDER			
	SHINGLE RIPPERS			
	STAPLE GUNS			
	TRASH CANS			
	WHEEL BARRELS			
	MAGNETS			
	YARD RAKES			
	ROOF JACKS			
	TOE BOARDS			
	12' WALKBOARD			
	24' WALKBOARD			
	LADDER JACKS			
	OLD PLYWOOD			
	LADDER LIFT AND GAS			
	ALUMINUM BRAKE			
	HAND BRAKE			
	OLD TARPS			
	NEW TARPS TO COVER ROOF			
	VISQUEEN			
	BUNDELS OF LATH			
	SCAFFOLDING			

Company Address
Phone/Fax
e-mail
Web Site

6.36   Real Estate Contract

Consult your Lawyer before signing this contract—it has important legal consequences.

Contract for Sale of Real Estate

This contract is made and dated

Between the Seller: **And the Buyer:**

Seller's Info:

Buyer's Info:

(from now on called "the Buyer")

The words "Seller" and "Buyer" include all sellers and all buyers under this Contract.

The Seller and the Buyer agree as follows:

Sale and Purchase:

    1. The Seller shall sell and the Buyer shall buy the Property under the terms of this Contract.

Property:

    2. The word "Property" in this Contract includes (a) through (d) below:

        (a) all of the land located in the   Town of   County of   and State of, specifically described as follows:

        Street Address:

        Municipal tax map designation: Lot No.   Block No.

Building and other Improvements

        (b) All buildings, driveways and other improvements on the land.

All Other Rights

        (c) All other rights of the Seller with regard to the land.

Fixtures and Personal Property

        (d) All equipment, fixtures, and personal property attached to or otherwise used with the land, buildings, and improvements when present at the time of the signing of this Contract, unless specifically excluded below. These are fully paid for and owned by the Seller. They include the following: plumbing, heating, electric, and cooking fixtures, electric dishwasher, hot water heater, water conditioner, lighting fixtures, TV antenna, wall-to-wall carpeting, fireplace equipment, smoke and burglar alarms, wall shelves, bookshelves, attached mirrors, window shades and blinds, rods and valances, storm windows and doors, windows and door screens, awnings, pool equipment, garage door openers, and gas barbeque grill.

        The following are excluded from this sale: furniture, household furnishings, refrigerator, freezer, clothes washer, clothes dryer, window air-conditioners, snow blower, lawn mower, and tools.

(Delete items above not included)

6.36   Real Estate Contract (continued)

Purchase Price and Payment:

3. (A) The purchase price is   Dollars ($)
and is payable by the Buyer to the Seller as follows:

Preliminary Deposit

❑   (a) Deposit previously paid . . . . $

Deposit

❑   (b) Deposit paid on the signing of this Contract,
by check subject to collection . . . .$

Escrow is the delivery of the deposit to a third party to be held in trust
until certain conditions are met. The deposit shall be held in escrow by the
Seller's attorney until (1) the closing of the title, at which time the deposit shall
be made to the Seller or (2) the exercise of a permitted right of cancellation
under this Contract in which event the deposit shall be returned to the Buyer.

Mortgage Money

❑   (c) Money borrowed from an established lender as a first mortgage loan
on the Property in the principal amount of . . . .$. This amount
shall be paid to the Seller at closing. The Buyer shall promptly apply
for this loan and make a good faith effort to obtain it. The written
commitment of the lender must be received by the Buyer by
20   . The terms of the commitment must be at least as
favorable to the Buyer as following:

- Type of mortgage (❑ conventional, ❑ FHA, ❑ VA,
  ❑ other . . .)
- Annual interest rate   8.75   %
- Length of mortgage: 15   years with monthly payments based
  on year payment schedule.
- "Points" if any to be paid: by Buyer   by Seller

The Seller and the Buyer may later agree to extend the date for obtaining the
commitment. The Buyer may accept a commitment on less favorable terms or
agree to buy the Property without this mortgage loan. If none of these events
occurs and the Buyer does not receive the written commitment by the above
date, either party may cancel this Contract.

Assumption of Mortgage

❑   (d) By the Buyer assuming the payment at the closing of the mortgage
now on the property which is held by   and has an approximate unpaid balance of . . . .$. This mortgage shall be in good
standing at the closing. It is payable with interest at the yearly rate
of   % in   monthly installments of $
The entire unpaid amount of the principal on   20
Either party may cancel this Contract if the holder of the mortgage does
not permit the buyer to assume the mortgage.

6.36   Real Estate Contract (continued)

Note and Mortgage to Seller

❏   (e) By a note and mortgage from the Buyer to the Seller in the principal amount of . . . .$ This amount shall be payable with interest at the yearly rate of   % by monthly installments of $. It shall be due in full in   years with full prepayment rights and day default period.

The Note, Mortgage, and Mortgagor's Affidavit of Title to be signed by the Buyer at the closing shall be prepared on standard law forms generally available in New Jersey. They shall be prepared by the Seller's attorney at the cost to the Buyer of   plus recording costs, cost of credit report on Buyer, and cost of a mortgagee policy of title insurance to be furnished by the Buyer.

Remainder of Purchase Price

❏   (f) Remainder of purchase price at closing, subject to adjustments provided for in this Contract . . . .$_____

Total Purchase Price . . . .$_____

Acceptable Funds

(B) All moneys to be paid by the Buyer to the Seller at the closing (both the Buyer's funds and the lender's funds) shall be in the form of any one or more of the following: (a) cash (but not over 2% of the purchase price), (b) bank check, (c) cashier's check, and (d) certified check. All checks must be payable to the order of the Seller or to the order of the Buyer. If payable to the order of the Buyer, the check must be endorsed by the Buyer to the order of the Seller in the presence of the Seller or the Seller's attorney.

Closing of Title

4. The closing of title (also called the "closing") is the meeting at which the Seller transfers ownership of the Property by deed to the Buyer and the Buyer pays the balance of the purchase price to the Seller. The closing of title shall take place at the office of   .M. on   20   . This is the estimated date. Either party may set a definite date by giving at least 10 days notice to the other party stating that time is of the essence. The notice cannot be given before the estimated date.

Payment of Liens

5. A lien is the claim of another against real estate for (a) the payment of money owed or (b) the performance of an obligation. Examples of liens are real estate taxes, court judgments, and mortgages. The Seller shall pay all liens against the Property in full before or at the closing. Provided that the proceed of sale exceed the liens, the Seller or the Buyer shall have the right to direct that any liens be paid and satisfied from the proceeds of the sale at the closing. If necessary for this purpose, all or a portion of the proceeds of the

6.36   Real Estate Contract (continued)

sale may be deposited in the trust account of the Buyer's attorney and dis-
bursed accordingly.

Condition of Property at Time of Contract

6. The Buyer has inspected the Property or has had the Property inspected by
others. Except for any rights of inspection reserved in this Contract, the Buyer
accepts the Property "as is." The Seller makes no statement or promise about
the condition or value of the Property.

Condition of Property at Closing

7. The Seller shall transfer the Property to the Buyer in its present condition
except for normal wear caused by reasonable use between now and the closing. The grounds shall be maintained. They shall be in broom-clean condition.
All debris and the Seller's personal property not included in the sale shall be
removed. The walks and driveway shall be free of snow and ice. The Buyer may
inspect the Property within 7 days before the closing on reasonable notice to
the Seller.

Casualty Damage

8. The Seller is responsible for any damage to the Property except for normal
usage until the closing. If the Property is damaged by fire, vandalism, storm,
flood, or any other casualty between now and the closing, the parties shall
obtain an estimate, from an established contractor of their choice, of the cost
of repairing the damage. If the estimated cost is less than 5% of the purchase
price, the Seller shall (a) repair the damage before the closing at the Seller's
expense or (b) deduct the estimated cost from the purchase price. If the estimated cost is more than 5% of the purchase price, the Buyer may (a) cancel
this Contract, (b) require the Seller to repair the damage before the closing, or
(c) proceed with the purchase, in which case the estimated cost of repair shall
be deducted from the purchase price.

Assessments for Municipal Improvements

9. Municipalities may make local improvements such as the installation of sewer
systems. The cost is charged against the real estate receiving the benefit of the
improvement. This charge, known as an assessment, is in addition to real estate
taxes. If a municipal improvement to the Property has been completed before the
date of this Contract, the Seller shall pay the assessment at or before the closing.

If a municipal improvement to the Property has not been completed before
the date of this Contract, the Buyer shall pay the assessment as it becomes due.

Compliance with Laws

10. (a) The Seller shall obtain at the Seller's expense before the closing any
certificate of occupancy or other permit if it is required by the municipality.
The Seller shall make any repairs required for the issuance of the certificate.

6.36   Real Estate Contract (continued)

(b) If the Property has 3 or more units of living space, the Seller shall give to the Buyer before the closing proof of compliance with the New Jersey Hotel and Multiple Dwelling Act.

Statements of Seller

11. The Seller states that to the best of the Seller's knowledge:

(a) The Property is legally zoned for a   family house.

(b) The Seller has not received notice that any building or improvement is in violation of any housing, building, safety, health, environmental, or fire law, ordinance, or regulation.

(c) The Property is not in a Federal or State flood hazard area.

(d) All buildings, driveways, and other improvements are inside the boundary lines of the Property. There are no improvements on adjoining lands which extend onto the Property.

The Buyer may learn before the closing that any of these statements is not accurate and the Buyer may decide not to accept the Property under such circumstances. In that case, the Buyer's only remedy is to cancel this Contract. However, before canceling this Contract because a survey of the Property shows that statement (d) above is not accurate, the Buyer shall give the Seller at least 10 days to correct any defects.

Transfer of Ownership

12. The Seller shall transfer ownership of the Property to the Buyer at the closing, free of all claims and rights of others, except the following:

Utility Company Easements

(a) The rights of telephone, electric and gas, water, and sewer utility companies to maintain poles, wires, pipes, mains and cables over, along, and under the street next to the Property, the part of the Property next to the street, or any such utility services running to any improvement on the Property.

Restrictive Covenants

(b) Limitations on the use of the Property known as restrictive covenants, provided that they (1) are not now violated, (2) do not provide that the Property would be forfeited if they were violated, and (3) do not materially restrict the normal use and enjoyment of the Property.

Tenancies

(c) The rights of any tenants described in the following section 13.

Other Exceptions

(d)

6.36   Real Estate Contract (continued)

In addition, the Buyer must be able to obtain title insurance on the Property from a title insurance company authorized to do business in New Jersey, subject only to the exceptions set forth in this section 12 and in the following section 13.

The Buyer shall accept the transfer of ownership of the Property as it is described in this section 12. However, the Seller may not be able to transfer the quality of ownership described in this section 12 because of another exception (not the result of the Seller's willful default) which the Buyer learns of before the closing and will not accept. In the case the Buyer's only remedy is to cancel the Contract after giving the Seller at least 10 days to remove such exception.

Transfer of Possession

13. The Seller shall transfer possession and keys of the Property to the Buyer at the closing, free of all rights of tenants, except the following:

Tenancies

Name of Tenant	Area Rented	Lease or Month-to-Month
Monthly Rent	Security Deposit	

Attach copy of leases

The tenancies are not in violation of any laws, rules, or ordinances. No tenant has any rights in the Property by way of option to buy, right of first refusal, pre-paid rental, or otherwise. At the closing the Seller shall give the Buyer any security deposits and interest earned as required by law.

Deed, Affidavit of Title, Realty Transfer Fee, Corporate Resolution

14. At the closing, the Seller shall transfer ownership of the Property to the Buyer by a Deed of Bargain and Sale with Covenant as to Grantor's Acts. This Deed contains a covenant, defined by law, that the Seller has not encumbered the Property. The Deed shall be in proper form for recording. The Seller shall also give to the Buyer a sworn statement known as an Affidavit of Title. This Affidavit shall contain information about the Seller reasonably necessary to clarify the Seller's ownership of the Property, such as (a) the Seller's marital history, (b) rights of tenants, and (c) claims on record of persons having the same or similar name as the Seller. The Seller shall pay the Realty Transfer Fee required by law. If the Seller is a corporation, it shall deliver to the Buyer at the closing a resolution of its Board of Directors approving this sale and authorizing the signing and delivery of this Contract, Deed, Affidavit of Title, and other closing documents by specified officers. It shall deliver proof of any necessary shareholder approval.

Adjustment of Property Expenses

15. The parties shall apportion the following expenses relating to the Property as of the closing date according to the period of their ownership: (a) municipal real estate taxes, (b) water and sewer charges, (c) rents as and when collected, (d) interest and tax and insurance escrow on existing mortgage if assumed by

6.36   Real Estate Contract (continued)

the Buyer, (e) premiums on insurance policies is assumed by the Buyer, and (f) fuel oil in the tank at the price paid by the Seller. The parties shall not apportion the homestead rebate.

Broker

16. The Seller and the Buyer recognize   as the Broker who brought about this sale. The Seller shall pay to the Broker a commission of   when title closes and the Buyer pays the balance of the purchase price to the Seller.

Cancellation of Contract

17. In this Contract, the parties have the right to cancel this Contract under certain circumstances. In order to cancel, a party must give written notice to the other. If this Contract is so cancelled, the deposit shall be promptly returned to the Buyer. The Seller and the Buyer shall then be released from all further liability to each other. However, if this contract is cancelled by the Buyer because of the inability of the Seller to transfer the quality of ownership described in Section 12, the Seller shall in addition pay the Buyer for reasonable costs of search and survey. It is expressly agreed that upon the event of any default or failure on the part of the Buyer to comply with the terms and conditions of this Contract, the said deposit shall, at the Seller's option, be paid to the seller as liquidated damages. Upon default by the Seller, if the Buyer elects to rescind this Contract, they shall be repaid all sums paid hereunder and in addition shall be reimbursed by the Seller for their reasonable expenses incurred, not to exceed $_____.

Notices

18. All notices given under this Contract must be in writing. They may be given by: (a) personal delivery to the other party or to that party's attorney, or (b) certified mail, return receipt requested, addressed to the other party at the address written at the beginning of this Contract or to that party's attorney. Each party must accept and claim the notices given by the other.

No Assignment

19. The Buyer may not transfer the Buyer's rights under this Contract to another without the written consent of the Seller.

Certification of Non-Foreign Status

20. The Seller shall provide the Buyer at or before the closing with a Certification of Non-Foreign Status under IRC–1445

Full Agreement

21. This Contract is the full agreement of the Buyer and the Seller. Neither party has made any other agreement or promise that is not included in this Contract.

6.36   Real Estate Contract (continued)

Changes in Contract

22. The parties may not change this Contract unless the change is in writing and is signed by both parties. The parties authorized their attorneys to agree in writing to any changes in dates and time periods provided for in this Contract.

Contract Binding on Successors

23. This Contract is binding on the Seller and the Buyer and all those who lawfully succeed to their rights or take their places.

> *Insert termite and building inspection clauses if desired here or on a rider*

Signatures

The Seller and the Buyer agree to the terms of this Contract by signing below and that this document constitutes the entire agreement between the parties. If a party is a

Corporation, this Contract is signed by its proper corporate officers and its seal is affixed.

Witnessed or attested by:

| _____ | _____ Seller |
| As to Seller | _____ Seller |

| _____ | _____ Buyer |
| As to Buyer | _____ Buyer |

Managing Finance

Although financial management is a crucial component of a remodeling company's systems, it is often neglected. A sound financial management system provides the tools and structure to track revenue, cost of goods sold, and operating expenses, so you can calculate profit accurately. It also provides controls at every level.

As with every other system in your company, financial management should be efficient. An efficient system for financial data collection, reporting, and analysis will allow you to generate multiple reports but enter key numbers just once. Rather than building a financial platform from scratch, it is more practical to choose a basic computerized system you will be comfortable using. It should be simple to operate and should produce standard, easily understood accounting reports like the ones referenced in this chapter. Above all, your system must produce accurate, up-to-date reports that you can review and act upon to heighten efficiencies.

The Budget: Your Roadmap

When you prepared your business plan to accomplish the goals for your business, you established revenue and profit targets that would provide business security as well as owner's compensation. A financial management system provides the records, monitoring, and analysis necessary to progress toward meeting those goals.

The Annual Budget (7.1) is your financial roadmap for the year. It should be a realistic plan based on your company's past experience and shaped by an assessment of current costs, market conditions, and company innovations. As you travel through the year, occasionally "pull off" the road to review your progress compared with your annual budget. Are labor costs exceeding projections? Is vehicle maintenance or fuel more costly than anticipated? Are you selling fewer jobs, or smaller jobs, than your company is structured to handle? Repairing or changing these flat tires gives you the opportunity to make smoother progress on your annual business journey. The Gross Margin by Project form (7.2) will allow you to track each job and determine how much each type of project contributes to your profit goals.

Monitoring Progress

The following forms will help you collect, monitor, and analyze specific, measurable financial data:

- Company Balance Sheet (7.3), helps you calculate net worth, or company assets minus liabilities.
- Weekly Summary of Financial Status (7.4) shows cash flow (or payables and receivables).
- Company Profit and Loss Report (7.5) provides a snapshot of your business's financial health at a given time. The costs of goods sold are subtracted from the income produced.

Controls and Job Cost Records

Your financial management system should include procedures for tracking, recording, and substantiating all expenditures. *The Paper Trail* includes a Check Request Form (7.6), Expense Reimbursement Request (7.7) and a Mileage Sheet (7.8) for employees' use. The production superintendent or lead carpenter should verify that the expenses are appropriate and posted correctly to a job. Then, the company should reimburse employees promptly.

Estimate-Expense Form (7.9) helps your company maintain job cost records. You can use these to verify whether the company's database of costs used for estimating is current and accurate.

Compliance Records

Insurance companies, state workers' compensation officials, and perhaps the Internal Revenue Service periodically will want to review your records. With a sound, computer-supported system in place, providing the needed records will be much easier.

The following reports allocate payroll by construction activity and are help-ful in audits to determine the insurance rates your company should pay based on type of work performed:

- Insurance Audit Report by Activity (7.10)
- Insurance Audit Review (7.11)

Maintaining data often produces savings. For example, a payroll system that codes employees' activities may yield lower workers' compensation insurance rates because supervision, sales, drywall, and wallpapering activities are billed at a much lower rate than carpentry and roofing.

Understand Cash Flow

In addition to reviewing estimates against actual job costs, small remodeling companies should consider generating weekly cash flow reports. Calculated on an accrual basis, these reports show how much you spend as a percentage of the job as work proceeds. If you are halfway through a $5,000 project, for example, you should have completed about $2,500 worth of work. Even if the company has not received payment, reviewing expenditures against work completed will provide a quick, current snapshot of the company's finances. Moreover, a system that monitors and aligns payment schedules with expenses protects your com-pany from negative cash flow and financing costs.

Bank Draws

Compare the Bank Draw Schedule (7.12) with your requested draws. The draw schedule is a tool for projecting cash flow and for keeping track of when payments are due. Clients must understand and adhere to your payment schedule, whether they are using bank loans or paying for work with their savings. It is imprudent to work for a client who does not understand your cash needs during a project. Payment Schedule–Final Bill (7.13) is a dual-use report that tracks payments for administrative purposes and can be issued to the clients as a final invoice.

Protect Job Profits

For diversified remodeling companies, maintaining a Profit and Loss Report by Job (7.14) provides valuable information about where you earn most of your money. Although you may love remodeling bathrooms with luxurious options, your profit-and-loss reports will tell you whether those jobs are money down the drain. Window replacements may turn out to be your most profitable niche.

Keep track of each job's costs compared to what was budgeted using the Project Income and Expense Summary (7.15). This postmortem financial report identifies areas where the job did or did not meet budgetary expectations. Use it in post-job analysis and in fine-tuning your estimating assumptions.

With a click or two, you can integrate these and other reports into off-the-shelf software programs for conducting standard financial analyses. Routinely review these reports to spot trends and react to changes in the marketplace.

As company owner or senior manager, you are responsible for helping the company accomplish its long term goals. Profit and Loss: Year-to-Year Comparison (7.16) can help you spot trends that can be leveraged or repaired. The ultimate goal of company ownership is generating assets and minimizing liabilities. Reviewing a balance sheet and tracking changes in it over time can show you whether or not you are continuing to build wealth.

Numbers do not lie. Collect them, analyze them, and use them to make smart business decisions.

Chapter 7 Forms

Planning

7.1   Annual Budget (Excel)
7.2   Gross Margin by Project (Excel)

Monitoring

7.3   Company Balance Sheet (Excel)
7.4   Weekly Summary of Financial Status (Excel)
7.5   Company Profit and Loss Report (Excel)

Controls and Job Cost Records

7.6   Check Request Form (Word)
7.7   Expense Reimbursement Request (Excel)
7.8   Mileage Sheet (Excel)
7.9   Estimate-Expense Form (Excel)

Compliance Records

7.10 Insurance Audit Report by Activity (Excel)
7.11 Insurance Audit Review (Excel)

Income Management

7.1   Annual Budget

Company Name
Company Logo
Company Affiliations

	Jan 01	Feb 01	Mar 01	Apr 01	May 01
Ordinary Income/Expense					
Income					
4000 · Gross Sales	62,000.00	62,000.00	62,000.00	62,000.00	62,000.00
Total Income	62,000.00	62,000.00	62,000.00	62,000.00	62,000.00
Cost of Goods Sold					
5000 · Job Related Costs					
5100 · Materials	26,500.00	26,500.00	26,500.00	26,500.00	26,500.00
5125 · Plans, Permits, Approvals, etc.	1,815.00	1,815.00	1,815.00	1,815.00	1,815.00
5150 · Subs	9,300.00	9,300.00	9,300.00	9,300.00	9,300.00
5200 · Job Related Labor Costs					
5210 · Job Labor (Gross Wages)	6,700.00	6,700.00	6,700.00	6,700.00	6,700.00
5230 · Employer Payroll Tax Costs	850.00	850.00	850.00	850.00	850.00
Total 5200 · Job Related Labor Costs	7,550.00	7,550.00	7,550.00	7,550.00	7,550.00
Total 5000 · Job Related Costs	45,165.00	45,165.00	45,165.00	45,165.00	45,165.00
Total COGS	45,165.00	45,165.00	45,165.00	45,165.00	45,165.00
Gross Profit	16,835.00	16,835.00	16,835.00	16,835.00	16,835.00
Expense					
6000 · Overhead Costs					
6010 · Advertising	273.48	273.48	273.48	273.48	273.48
6040 · Dues/Journals/Seminars	253.44	253.44	253.44	253.44	253.44
6045 · Donations	20.00	20.00	20.00	20.00	20.00
6050 · Entertainment-Food	250.00	250.00	250.00	250.00	250.00
6070 · Insurance					
6071 · Specialty Contractors Package	500.00	500.00	500.00	500.00	500.00
6072 · Worker's Comp	600.00	600.00	600.00	600.00	600.00
6073 · Other Auto	27.37	27.37	27.37	27.37	27.37
6074 · Fire Insurance- liability	77.59	77.59	77.59	77.59	77.59
6075 · Health	1,000.00	1,000.00	1,000.00	1,000.00	1,000.00
Total 6070 · Insurance	2,204.96	2,204.96	2,204.96	2,204.96	2,204.96

	Jun 01	Jul 01	Aug 01	Sep 01	Oct 01	Nov 01	Dec 01	TOTAL Jan-Dec 01
	62,000.00	62,000.00	62,000.00	62,000.00	62,000.00	62,000.00	62,000.00	744,000.00
	62,000.00	62,000.00	62,000.00	62,000.00	62,000.00	62,000.00	62,000.00	744,000.00
	26,500.00	26,500.00	26,500.00	26,500.00	26,500.00	26,500.00	26,500.00	318,000.00
	1,815.00	1,815.00	1,815.00	1,815.00	1,815.00	1,815.00	1,815.00	21,780.00
	9,300.00	9,300.00	9,300.00	9,300.00	9,300.00	9,300.00	9,300.00	111,600.00
	6,700.00	6,700.00	6,700.00	6,700.00	6,700.00	6,700.00	6,700.00	80,400.00
	850.00	850.00	850.00	850.00	850.00	850.00	850.00	10,200.00
	7,550.00	7,550.00	7,550.00	7,550.00	7,550.00	7,550.00	7,550.00	90,600.00
	45,165.00	45,165.00	45,165.00	45,165.00	45,165.00	45,165.00	45,165.00	541,980.00
	45,165.00	45,165.00	45,165.00	45,165.00	45,165.00	45,165.00	45,165.00	541,980.00
	16,835.00	16,835.00	16,835.00	16,835.00	16,835.00	16,835.00	16,835.00	202,020.00
	273.48	273.48	273.48	273.48	273.48	273.48	273.48	3,281.76
	253.44	253.44	253.44	253.44	253.44	253.44	253.44	3,041.28
	20.00	20.00	20.00	20.00	20.00	20.00	20.00	240.00
	250.00	250.00	250.00	250.00	250.00	250.00	250.00	3,000.00
	500.00	500.00	500.00	500.00	500.00	500.00	500.00	6,000.00
	600.00	600.00	600.00	600.00	600.00	600.00	600.00	7,200.00
	27.37	27.37	27.37	27.37	27.37	27.37	27.37	328.44
	77.59	77.59	77.59	77.59	77.59	77.59	77.59	931.08
	1,000.00	1,000.00	1,000.00	1,000.00	1,000.00	1,000.00	1,000.00	12,000.00
	2,204.96	2,204.96	2,204.96	2,204.96	2,204.96	2,204.96	2,204.96	26,459.52

7.1   Annual Budget (continued)

Company Name
Company Logo
Company Affiliations

	Jan 01	Feb 01	Mar 01	Apr 01	May 01
6100 · Office Supplies	100.00	100.00	100.00	100.00	100.00
6120 · Office Salaries	1,700.00	1,700.00	1,700.00	1,700.00	1,700.00
6130 · Professional Fees					
6131 · Accounting	215.00	215.00	215.00	215.00	215.00
6132 · Legal Fees	500.00	500.00	500.00	500.00	500.00
Total 6130 · Professional Fees	715.00	715.00	715.00	715.00	715.00
6150 · Repairs & Maintenance	100.00	100.00	100.00	100.00	100.00
6160 · Service Charges	0.00	0.00	0.00	0.00	0.00
6185 · State Annual Report Fee	4.17	4.17	4.17	4.17	4.17
6190 · Telephone	776.00	776.00	776.00	776.00	776.00
6200 · Tools	100.00	100.00	100.00	100.00	100.00
6210 · Travel/Lodging	100.00	100.00	100.00	100.00	100.00
6220 · Utilities	266.89	266.89	266.89	266.89	266.89
6240 · Vehicle Expenses					
6241 · Gas & Oil	475.00	475.00	475.00	475.00	475.00
6242 · Repairs & Maintenance	350.00	350.00	350.00	350.00	350.00
6243 · Registration & License	70.00	70.00	70.00	70.00	70.00
Total 6240 · Vehicle Expenses	895.00	895.00	895.00	895.00	895.00
Total 6000 · Overhead Costs	7,758.94	7,758.94	7,758.94	7,758.94	7,758.94
Total Expense	7,758.94	7,758.94	7,758.94	7,758.94	7,758.94
Net Ordinary Income	9,076.06	9,076.06	9,076.06	9,076.06	9,076.06
Net Income	9,076.06	9,076.06	9,076.06	9,076.06	9,076.06

Company Address
Phone
Fax
E-mail
Web site

	Jun 01	Jul 01	Aug 01	Sep 01	Oct 01	Nov 01	Dec 01	TOTAL Jan-Dec 01
	100.00	100.00	100.00	100.00	100.00	100.00	100.00	1,200.00
	1,700.00	1,700.00	1,700.00	1,700.00	1,700.00	1,700.00	1,700.00	20,400.00
	215.00	215.00	215.00	215.00	215.00	215.00	215.00	2,580.00
	500.00	500.00	500.00	500.00	500.00	500.00	500.00	6,000.00
	715.00	715.00	715.00	715.00	715.00	715.00	715.00	8,580.00
	100.00	100.00	100.00	100.00	100.00	100.00	100.00	1,200.00
	0.00	0.00	0.00	0.00	0.00	0.00	0.00	0.00
	4.17	4.17	4.17	4.17	4.17	4.17	4.17	50.04
	776.00	776.00	776.00	776.00	776.00	776.00	776.00	9,312.00
	100.00	100.00	100.00	100.00	100.00	100.00	100.00	1,200.00
	100.00	100.00	100.00	100.00	100.00	100.00	100.00	1,200.00
	266.89	266.89	266.89	266.89	266.89	266.89	266.89	3,202.68
	475.00	475.00	475.00	475.00	475.00	475.00	475.00	5,700.00
	350.00	350.00	350.00	350.00	350.00	350.00	350.00	4,200.00
	70.00	70.00	70.00	70.00	70.00	70.00	70.00	840.00
	895.00	895.00	895.00	895.00	895.00	895.00	895.00	10,740.00
	7,758.94	7,758.94	7,758.94	7,758.94	7,758.94	7,758.94	7,758.94	93,107.28
	7,758.94	7,758.94	7,758.94	7,758.94	7,758.94	7,758.94	7,758.94	93,107.28
	9,076.06	9,076.06	9,076.06	9,076.06	9,076.06	9,076.06	9,076.06	108,912.72
	9,076.06	**9,076.06**	**9,076.06**	**9,076.06**	**9,076.06**	**9,076.06**	**9,076.06**	**108,912.72**

7.2 Gross Margin by Project

Name	Year	Type	Revenue	Target GM%	Actual GM%	GM% Variance	Target Profit	Actual Profit	Profit Variance	Comments
over $150K										
McLane	2008	Addition	$ 234,848	35.0%	26.8%	−8.2%	$ 82,191	$ 62,883	($19,308)	
Luyckx	2008	Whole House	$ 380,411	30.8%	21.7%	−9.0%	$ 116,981	$ 82,661	($34,320)	
Koerner	2008	New Home (shell)	$ 192,057	16.8%	24.3%	7.5%	$ 32,338	$ 46,722	$14,384	
Dukes	2008	Addition	$ 159,367	36.3%	34.9%	−1.3%	$ 57,804	$ 55,666	($2,138)	
			$ 966,683	29.9%	25.6%	−4.3%	$ 289,314	$ 247,931	($41,383)	
$75-150K										
Rowley	2008	Kitchen & Powder Bath	$ 133,847	38.4%	36.8%	−1.6%	$ 51,355	$ 49,247	($2,108)	
Neuman	2008	Addition	$ 90,620	33.6%	39.6%	6.0%	$ 30,457	$ 35,878	$5,419	
Finke	2008	Addition/Outdoor Kitch	$ 97,969	33.1%	29.5%	−3.6%	$ 32,473	$ 28,944	($3,529)	
Allison	2008	Pool Room	$ 105,600	30.9%	29.7%	−1.2%	$ 32,598	$ 31,364	($1,234)	
			$ 428,036	34.3%	34.0%	−0.3%	$ 146,882	$ 145,433	($1,452)	

$25-50K

Taylor	2008	Master Bath	$ 39,500	37.1%	30.5%	–6.6%	$ 15,405	$ 12,067	($2,600)
Miller	2008	Door Replacement	$ 44,500	48.5%	48.5%	–0.1%	$ 21,604	$ 21,572	($32)
Kilman	2008	Kitchen	$ 48,443	36.3%	26.2%	–10.2%	$ 18,056	$ 12,686	($4,920)
English	2008	Window Replacement	$ 31,344	22.7%	24.5%	1.8%	$ 7,113	$ 7,671	$558
Boise	2008	Addition/Patio Cover	$ 30,802	35.6%	33.0%	–2.6%	$ 10,955	$ 10,153	($802)
			$ 194,588	**37.6%**	**33.0%**	**–4.6%**	**$ 73,133**	**$ 64,148**	**($7,797)**

Under $10K

Thode	2008	Front Porch	$ 5,482	42.9%	29.1%	–13.8%	$ 2,295	$ 1,594	($756)
			$ 5,482	**41.9%**	**29.1%**	**–12.8%**	**$ 2,295**	**$ 1,594**	**($756)**

TOTAL									
TOTAL			**$ 1,594,789**	**32.08%**	**28.79%**	**–3.29%**	**$ 511,624**	**$ 459,105**	**($51,387)**

	# Jobs	% of GP	% Sales	GM%
>150	4	54.0%	60.6%	25.6%
75-150	3	31.7%	26.8%	34.0%
25-50	5	14.0%	12.2%	33.0%
<10K	1	0.3%	0.3%	29.1%

7.3   Company Balance Sheet

As of \<Insert Date\>

ASSETS

	9/30/08	8/31/08	Change
Current Assets			
Cash	$ 158,755	$ 29,261	$ 129,494
Accounts Receivable	33,533	55,687	(22,154)
Costs in Excess of Billings	48,992	13,470	35,522
Prepaid Expenses	6,467	12,250	(5,783)
Due from Stockholders	20,000	5,000	15,000
Other Current Assets	1,876	2,557	(681)
Total Current Assets	$ 269,623	$ 118,225	$ 151,398
Property and Equipment			
Furniture and Equipment	$ 15,478	$ 12,893	$ 2,585
Computer Hardware and Software	10,982	7,650	3,332
Motor Vehicles	65,877	43,295	22,582
Leasehold Improvements	5,422	-	5,422
	97,759	63,838	33,921
Less Accumulated Depreciation	52,720	50,720	2,000
	$ 45,039	$ 13,118	$ 31,921
Total Assets	$ 314,662	$ 131,343	$ 183,319

ABC Remodeler Balance Sheet
As of September 30, 2008

Liabilities and Stockholders' Equity

	9/30/08	8/31/08	Change
Current Liabilities			
Accounts Payable	$ 84,626	$ 57,259	$ 27,367
Payroll Taxes Accrued & Withheld	8,578	1,722	6,856
Billings in Excess of Costs	147,982	35,457	112,525
Current Portion–Long Term Debt	14,530	7,544	6,986
Other Current Liabilities	542	485	57
Total Current Liabilities	$ 256,258	$ 102,467	$ 153,791
Long Term Liabilities	48,460	28,930	19,530
	$ 304,718	$ 131,397	$ 173,321
Stockholders' Equity			
Common Stock	$ 200	$ 200	$ -
Retained Earnings	9,744	(254)	9,998
Total Stockholders' Equity	$ 9,944	$ (54)	$ 9,998
Total Liabilities and Stockerholders' Equity	$ 314,662	$ 131,343	$ 183,319

7.4 Weekly Summary of Financial Status

Prepared by _____ As Of _____

Checkbook Balance	
Savings Account #1	
Savings Account #2	
Accounts Receivable	
Accounts Payable	
Bank Loan Balance	
Summary Balance	
Available Line of Credit	

Accounts Receivable–Aging Summary

Total				
Current	30+ Days	60+ Days	90+ Days	

(see detailed A/R trial balance attached)

Sales Volume Invoiced

Week Ending:				
MTD Ending:				
YTD Ending:				

Work Quoted & Sold

work quoted

Week Ending:				
MTD Ending:				
YTD Ending:				

work sold

Week Ending:				
MTD Ending:				
YTD Ending:				

# Hours charged directly to jobs on payroll–Production Only–current week	
year to date	
# Hours charged directly to jobs on payroll–Design Only–current week	
year to date	
% of Direct Labor Hours vs. Total Hours Paid-Production Only-current week	
year to date	
% of Direct Labor Hours vs. Total Hours Paid–Design Only–current week	
year to date	

Company Address
Phone
Fax
E-mail
Web site

7.5   Company Profit and Loss Report

Jan–Dec 20xx

Ordinary Income/Expense			
Income			
4000 · Gross Sales			740,954.35
4900 · Purchase Discounts			4,019.00
Total Income			744,973.35
Cost of Goods Sold			
5000 · Job Related Costs			
5100 · Materials		216,000.00	
5125 · Plans, Permits, Approvals, etc.		21,790.34	
5150 · Subs		72,000.00	
5200 · Job-Related Labor Costs			
5210 · Job Labor (Gross Wages)	96,000.00		
5230 · Employer Payroll Tax Costs	10,018.88		
Total 5200 · Job-Related Labor Costs		106,018.88	
5300 · Tools		4,978.63	
5400 · Equipment Rental		2,394.60	
Total 5000 · Job-Related Costs			423,182.45
Total Cost of Goods Sold			423,182.45
Gross Profit			321,790.90
Expense			
6000 · Overhead Costs			
6010 · Advertising		3,281.77	
6040 · Dues/Journals/Seminars		1,200.00	
6045 · Donations		208.00	
6050 · Entertainment-Food		3,006.43	
6070 · Insurance			
6071 · Specialty Contractors Package	2,400.00		
6072 · Workers' Compensation	8,786.00		
6073 · Other Auto	328.38		
6074 · Fire Insurance-Liability	931.06		
6075 · Health	9,005.75		
Total 6070 · Insurance		21,451.19	

Company Address
Phone
Fax
E-mail
Web site

7.5   Company Profit and Loss Report (continued)

6100 · Office Supplies		
6101 · Computer Supplies & Expenses	1,554.07	
6100 · Office Supplies—Other	4,310.81	
Total 6100 · Office Supplies		5,864.88
6120 · Office Salaries		56,196.00
6130 · Professional Fees		
6131 · Accounting	2,575.00	
6132 · Legal Fees	6,000.00	
Total 6130 · Professional Fees		8,575.00
6150 · Repairs & Maintenance		110.17
6160 · Service Charges		109.48
6185 · NJ Annual Report Fee		50.00
6190 · Telephone		9,313.56
6200 · Tools		175.00
6210 · Travel/Lodging		15,099.87
6220 · Utilities		3,202.69
6230 · Uncategorized Expenses		0.00
6240 · Vehicle Expenses		
6241 · Gas & Oil	5,659.47	
6242 · Repairs & Maintenance	4,199.79	
6243 · Registration & License	834.17	
Total 6240 · Vehicle Expenses	10,693.43	

Total 6000 · Overhead Costs	138,537.47
Total Expense	138,537.47
Net Ordinary Income	183,253.43
Other Income/Expense	
Other Income	
6500 · SALE OF EQUIPMENT	12,000.00
Total Other Income	12,000.00
Net Other Income	12,000.00
	195,253.43

Company Address
Phone
Fax
E-mail
Web site

7.6   Check Request Form

Company Name
_____

Check Request Form

Date _____

Job Name _____

Check Made Out To _____
_____
_____

Amount _____   Date Needed _____

Reason/Purpose _____
_____
_____

Requested By _____   Approved By _____

Special Instructions _____
_____
_____

7.7   Expense Reimbursement Request

Company Name

_____

Page _____ of _____

Expense Reimbursement Request

Employee Name: _____   Date Prepared: _____

Amount Requested: _____   Job Name: _____

Date	Type of Expense & Location	Reason For Expense	Receipt attached Y or N	Amount
Total Due				

Employee Signature   Date   Superintendent Signature   Date

7.8   Mileage Sheet

Company Name
Company Logo
Company Affiliations

Mileage reimbursement rate:

Name: _____   Start Date: _____   End Date: _____

DATE	JOB NAME	MILES START	MILES END	TOTAL MILES	JOB NUMBER

Date   Name (please print)   MILES START   MILES STOP   TOTAL MILES

           Employee Signature   Total Miles for Page

                                                Total Miles for Week

           APPROVED (Supervisor, please initial.)   Page _____ of _____

Company Address
Phone/Fax
E-mail
Web site

7.9   Estimate-Expense Form

Company Name
Company Logo
Company Affiliations

Job Estimates vs. Actuals Detail for XYZ Job

All Transactions

	Est. Cost	Act. Cost	($) Diff.
Service			
01 Plan-Perm	5,915.00	4,372.00	(1,543.00)
03 Site Work	34,110.00	28,496.00	(5,614.00)
04 Excavation	3,000.00	4,029.17	1,029.17
05 Concrete	4,603.00	6,695.42	2,092.42
06 Masonry	15,958.00	12,667.80	(3,290.20)
07 Framing	45,659.00	37,566.01	(8,092.99)
08 Roof-Flash	5,650.00	9,201.09	3,551.09
09 Ext Trim	13,460.00	10,920.00	(2,540.00)
10 Dr/Wnd/Trm	22,650.00	21,641.13	(1,008.87)
11 Siding	15,223.00	16,500.00	1,277.00
12 Plumbing	10,500.00	10,156.00	(344.00)
13 HVAC	9,700.00	9,265.00	(435.00)
14 Elec-Light	9,500.00	13,879.00	4,379.00
15 Insulation	3,013.00	2,705.00	(308.00)
16 Drywall	19,143.00	7,756.00	(11,387.00)
17 Ceil-Cover	0.00	2,734.80	2,734.80
18 Mill-Trim	4,450.00	5,373.40	923.40
19 Cab-Vanity	8,000.00	9,859.33	1,859.33
20 Flr Cover	10,847.00	13,431.40	2,584.40
21 Paint	3,253.00	0.00	(3,253.00)
22 Cleanup	1,900.00	2,165.45	265.45
24 Misc. Work	667.00	635.82	(31.18)
25 Supervis	1,000.00	983.00	(17.00)
Total Service	248,201.00	231,032.82	(17,168.18)
Other Charges			
Change Order	0.00	0.00	0.00
Progress	0.00	0.00	0.00
Total Other Charges	0.00	0.00	0.00
Unclassified Items	0.00	1,239.91	1,239.91
TOTAL	248,201.00	232,272.73	(15,928.27)

Company Address
Phone
Fax
E-mail
Web site

7.10 Insurance Audit Report By Activity

Summary of 5/01/xxxx–5/1/xxxx Payroll by Item

Item	\<Empl #1\> laborer	\<Empl #2\> secretary	\<Empl #3\> carpenter	\<Empl #4\> laborer	\<Empl #5\> project mgr	\<Empl #6\> carpenter	\<Empl #7\> carpenter	\<Empl #8\> laborer	\<Empl #9\> carpenter	Total
avg hourly rate	$ 8.00		$ 12.25	$ 8.00		$ 16.00	$ 16.00	$ 11.00	$ 16.00	
demolition	$ 480.00			$ 108.00		$ 1,408.00	$ 832.00	$ 1,464.75	$ 320.00	$ 4,612.75
site work	$ 8.00									$ –
excavation			$ 67.38			$ 600.00	$ 328.00	$ 457.00		$ 1,460.38
concrete						$ 448.00	$ 128.00	$ 257.80		$ 833.80
masonry			$ 91.88	$ 112.50		$ 1,112.00	$ 608.00	$ 1,034.00		$ 2,958.38
framing			$ 196.00			$ 3,408.00	$ 1,256.00	$ 1,793.00	$ 456.00	$ 7,109.00
roof flashing/leaks						$ 36.00	$ 64.00			
exterior trim/deck-railings						$ 848.00	$ 464.00	$ 456.50		$ 1,768.50
doors & windows						$ 1,120.00	$ 400.00	$ 390.50	$ 64.00	$ 1,974.50

	1	2	3	4	5	6	7	8	9	Total
siding						$ 2,576.00	$ 288.00	$ 709.50	$ 24.00	$ 3,597.50
hvac							$ 176.00	$ 16.50		$ 192.50
drywall				$ 153.13	$ 9.00	$ 3,600.00	$ 4,848.00	$ 1,028.50	$ 160.00	$ 9,798.63
ceiling-cover						$ 608.00	$ 704.00	$ 121.00	$ 576.00	$ 2,009.00
millwork/trim				$ 49.00		$ 1,072.00	$ 312.00	$ 55.00	$ 288.00	$ 1,776.00
cabinets/vanities						$ 668.00	$ 456.00	$ 33.00		$ 1,157.00
floor covering						$ 352.00		$ 132.00	$ 56.00	$ 540.00
paint	$ 56.00			$ 686.00	$ 108.00	$ 400.00	$ 3,064.00	$ 858.00		$ 5,172.00
cleanup	$ 1,312.00			$ 85.75	$ 112.50	$ 960.00	$ 648.00	$ 1,666.50		$ 4,784.75
landscaping-paving	$ 244.00			$ 98.00	$ 171.00	$ 1,384.00	$ 488.00	$ 2,134.00		$ 4,519.00
misc work-punch list	$ 316.00				$ 175.50	$ 2,088.00	$ 944.00	$ 1,551.00	$ 10,992.00	$ 16,066.50
supervision/material pick up	$ 12.25					$ 1,012.16	$ 32.00	$ 363.00	$ 352.00	$ 1,771.41
vacation/holiday					$ 602.25	$ 1,060.31		$ 276.00	$ 150.00	$ 2,088.56
clerical		$ 21,287.00								$ 21,287.00
project manager			$ 21,287.00		$ 38,356.75					$ 38,356.75
					$ 38,959.00					
Total	$ 2,416.00	$ 21,287.00	$ 21,287.00	$ 1,439.38	$ 796.50	$ 24,760.47	$ 16,040.00	$ 14,797.55	$ 13,438.00	$ 133,933.89

7.11 Insurance Audit Review

Payroll Period 1/1/xxxx to 12/31/xxxx

Code #	Description	Payroll Amt
5645	Carpentry–Exterior	$ 7,750.96
6039	Grading–Land	$ 2,512.75
5200	Cement Work	$ 134.98
5022	Masonry	$ 1,007.27
5437	Carpentry–Interior	$ 5,192.65
5183	Plumbing	$ 182.34
5445	Drywall	$ 5,196.19
5409	Ceilings–Suspended	$ 2,232.81
5474	Painting	$ 3,792.63
5606	Proj Manager	$39,928.79
8810	Clerical	$22,959.50
		$90,890.87

See 2nd worksheet also

7.12   Bank Draw Schedule

Draw Overview: _____

Property: _____

Beginning Date: _____

Revised Date: _____

	BUDGET	% of work	Budget	Previously Drawn	This Request
1	Land				
2	Contingency				
	HARD COSTS				
3	Excavation				
4	Footings & Foundation				
5	Backfill				
6	Framing				
7	Rough Flooring				
8	Sheathing				
9	Roof				
10	Windows & Doors				
11	Garage & Basement Floor				
12	Stairs				
13	Fireplace & Chimney				
14	Siding				
15	Rough Plumbing				
16	Rough HVAC				
17	Rough Electric				
18	Insulation				
19	Drywall				
20	Trim				
21	Painting				
22	Cabinets				
23	Porches & Decks				
24	Tile				
25	Finished Floor				
26	Finished HVAC				
27	Finished Electric				
28	Finished Plumbing				
29	Exterior Complete				

Address
Phone-Fax
E-mail-Website

7.12　Bank Draw Schedule (continued)

	BUDGET	% of work	Budget	Previously Drawn	This Request
30	Appliances				
31	Sewer Hookup				
32	Driveways/Landscaping				
33	Contingency				
	TOTAL HARD COSTS				
	GRAND TOTAL				

7.13   Payment Schedule-Final Bill

Company Name
Company Logo
Company Affiliations

Statement

	Date
Client	Phone
Address	Work phone
City	Work fax

Work Description: Addition

Total Base Contract Price $79,700.19 $80,000.00

On Signing	$ 8,000.00	
Payment 6/01/01–Thank You		$ 8,000.00
Foundation Complete	$16,000.00	
Payment 7/01/01–Thank You		$16,000.00
Roof Framed	$16,000.00	
Payment 8/01/01–Thank You		$16,000.00
Windows Set	$ 8,000.00	
Rough Wiring	$ 8,000.00	
CO #1–Electrical Panel Upgrade	$ 650.00	
CO #2–Relocate A/C Condenser	$ 650.00	
Rough Plumbing	$ 8,000.00	
Payment 9/01/01–Thank You		$16,000.00
Drywall Installed	$ 8,000.00	
Payment 10/01/01–Thank You		$16,000.00
Storm Door Installation	$ 100.00	
Completion	$ 8,000.00	
Total Current Due (in bold)	$ 9,400.00	

Thank You

Address
Phone–Fax
E-mail–Web site

7.14 Profit and Loss Report By Job

Customer	Customer Name #1	Customer Name #2	Customer Name #3	Name #4	Name #5	Name #6	Total
Ordinary Income/Expense							
Income							
4000 · Gross Sales							
4100 · Uncatergorized Income	0.00	0.00	0.00	0.00	0.00	0.00	0.00
4000 · Gross Sales–Other	8,263.80	2,815.00	4,766.38	12,963.29	1,991.00	292,653.76	323,453.23
Total 4000 · Gross Sales	8,263.80	2,815.00	4,766.38	13,963.29	1,991.00	292,653.76	323,453.23
4900 · Purchase Discounts	0.00	0.00	0.00	0.00	0.00	0.00	0.00
Total Income	8,263.80	2,815.00	4,766.38	12,963.29	1,991.00	292,653.76	323,453.23
Cost of Goods Sold							
5000 · Job Related Costs							
5100 · Materials	1,556.96	760.14	2,931.73	1,290.03	444.44	170,835.54	177,818.84
5125 · Plans, Permits, Approvals, etc.	88.00	0.00	0.00	0.00	0.00	6,380.36	6,468.36
5150 · Subs	0.00	0.00	0.00	3,849.79	0.00	71,872.63	75,722.42

5200 · Job Related Labor Costs							
5210 · Job Labor (Gross Wages)	2,001.92	36.50	51.00	2,017.64	160.00	7,659.58	11,926.64
5230 · Employer Payroll Tax Costs	210.18	4.04	5.25	221.08	12.24	696.39	1149.18
Total 5200 · Job Related Labor Costs	2,212.10	40.54	56.25	2,238.72	172.24	8,355.97	13,075.82
5300 · Tools	0.00	0.00	0.00	0.00	0.00	0.00	0.00
5400 · Equipment Rental	0.00	0.00	0.00	0.00	0.00	975.39	975.39
5000 · Job Related Costs–Other	0.00	0.00	0.00	0.00	0.00	0.00	0.00
Total 5000 · Job Related Costs	3,857.06	300.68	2,987.98	7,378.54	616.68	258,419.89	274,060.83
Total COGS	3,857.06	300.68	2,987.98	7,378.54	616.68	258,419.89	274,060.83
Gross Profit	4,406.74	2,014.32	1,778.40	5,584.75	1,374.32	34,233.87	49,392.40

Company Address
Phone–Fax
E-mail–Web site

7.14 Profit and Loss Report By Job (continued)

	Customer Name #1	Customer Name #2	Customer Name #3	Customer Name #4	Customer Name #5	Customer Name #6	Total
Expense							
6000 · Overhead Costs							
6010 · Advertising	0.00	0.00	0.00	0.00	0.00	0.00	0.00
6040 · Dues/Journals/Seminars	0.00	0.00	0.00	0.00	0.00	0.00	0.00
6080 · Miscellaneous	0.00	0.00	0.00	0.00	0.00	0.00	0.00
6100 · Office Supplies	0.00	0.00	0.00	0.00	0.00	0.00	0.00
6130 · Professional Fees							
6132 · Legal Fees	0.00	0.00	0.00	0.00	0.00	211.56	211.56
Total 6130 · Professional Fees	0.00	0.00	0.00	0.00	0.00	211.56	211.56

6200 · Tools	0.00	0.00	0.00	0.00	0.00	0.00	0.00
6210 · Travel/Lodging	0.00	0.00	0.00	0.00	0.00	0.00	0.00
6240 · Vehicle Expenses							
6242 · Repairs & Maintenance	0.00	0.00	0.00	0.00	0.00	0.00	0.00
Total 6240 · Vehicle Expenses	0.00	0.00	0.00	0.00	0.00	0.00	0.00
Total 6000 · Overhead Costs	211.56	211.56	0.00	0.00	0.00	0.00	0.00
Total Expense	211.56	211.56	0.00	0.00	0.00	0.00	0.00
Net Ordinary Income	49,180.84	34,022.31	1,374.32	5,584.75	1,778.40	2,014.32	4,406.74
Net Income	49,180.84	34,022.31	1,374.32	5,584.75	1,778.40	2,014.32	4,406.74
% of Profit/Loss	15%	12%	69%	43%	37%	72%	53%

7.15   Project Income and Expense Summary

Company Name
Company Logo
Company Affiliations

Project Income and Expense Summary

Job # _____

Client   _____
Address   _____
Home Phone _____ Work Phone_____
Description: _____
Salesperson _____

Financial Summary

Contract Price: $ 100.00   **Payments:**

Ck#	Date	Amount
		100
		20
		0
		0
		0
		0
		0
total received		120

Change Order   1 $ 20.00
Change Order   2   _____
Change Order   3   _____
Change Order   4   _____
Change Order   5   _____
Change Order   6   _____
Total Project $ 120.00

Cost of Goods   **Job Totals as %**

Materials $ 40.00   33%
Subs $ 30.00   25%
Labor $ 20.00   17%

Total Costs $ 90.00

Gross Profit $ 30.00   25%
(Less Overhead)= $ 15.00   13%
Net Profit= $ 15.00   13%

Date Closed Out: ___/___/___

Manual entries needed are highlighted, the balance of the form is formulas

Company Address
Phone
Fax
E-mail
Web site

7.16   Profit and Loss: Year-to-Year Comparison

	Jan 1-Dec 31, 20xx	Jan 1-Dec 31, xx	$ Change	% Change
Ordinary Income/Expense				
Income				
4000 • Gross Sales				
4100 • Uncatergorized Income	3,050.70	136.62	2,914.08	2,132.98%
4000 • Gross Sales–Other	574,704.61	541,399.97	33,304.64	6.15%
Total 4000 • Gross Sales	577,755.31	541,536.59	36,218.72	6.69%
4900 • Purchase Discounts	1,579.89	1,863.79	-283.90	-15.23%
Total Income	579,335.20	543,400.38	35,934.82	6.61%
Cost of Goods Sold				
5000 • Job Related Costs				
5100 • Materials	180,705.88	158,715.22	21,990.66	13.86%
5125 • Plans, Permits, Approvals, etc.	7,986.46	18,222.34	-10,235.88	-56.17%
5150 • Subs	62,916.21	46,272.38	16,643.83	35.97%
5200 • Job Related Labor Costs				
5210 • Job Labor (Gross Wages)	76,369.31	68,408.34	7,960.97	11.64%
5230 • Employer Payroll Tax Costs	9,385.74	8,652.90	732.84	8.47%
Total 5200 • Job Related Labor Costs	85,755.05	77,061.24	8,693.81	11.28%

7.16 Profit and Loss: Year-to-Year Comparison (continued)

	Jan 1–Dec 31, 20xx	Jan 1–Dec 31, xx	$ Change	% Change
5300 · Tools	1,632.57	1,211.09	421.48	34.8%
5400 · Equipment Rental	1,596.94	1,994.60	-397.66	-19.94%
5000 · Job Related Costs–Other	355.19	0.00	355.19	100.0%
Total 5000 · Job Related Costs	340,948.30	303,476.87	37,471.43	12.35%
Total COGS	340,948.30	303,476.87	37,471.43	12.35%
Gross Profit	238,386.90	239,923.51	-1,536.61	-0.64%
Expense				
6000 · Overhead Costs				
6010 · Advertising	1,827.62	2,675.15	-847.53	-31.68%
6040 · Dues/Journals/Seminars	1,029.56	2,676.28	-1,646.72	-61.53%
6045 · Donations	338.00	208.00	130.00	62.5%
6050 · Entertainment-Food	2,452.01	2,291.79	160.22	6.99%
6070 · Insurance				
6071 · Specialty Contractors Package	11,430.58	5,522.98	5,907.60	106.96%
6072 · Worker's Comp	286.00	8,786.00	-8,500.00	-96.75%
6073 · Other Auto	196.02	0.00	196.02	100.0%

6074 · Fire Insurance- liability	301.24	541.06	-239.82	-44.32%
6075 · Health	8,236.76	6,610.61	1,626.15	24.6%
Total 6070 · Insurance	20,450.60	21,460.65	-1,010.05	-4.71%
6080 · Miscellaneous	351.01	0.00	351.01	100.0%
6100 · Office Supplies				
6101 · Computer Supplies & Expenses	1,423.54	1,382.56	40.98	2.96%
6100 · Office Supplies–Other	2,447.24	2,647.75	-200.51	-7.57%
Total 6100 · Office Supplies	3,870.78	4,030.31	-159.53	-3.96%
6120 · Office Salaries	19,727.75	15,319.00	4,408.75	28.78%
6130 · Professional Fees				
6131 · Accounting	2,650.00	0.00	2,650.00	100.0%
6132 · Legal Fees	19,667.11	22,776.07	-3,108.96	-13.65%
Total 6130 · Professional Fees	22,317.11	22,776.07	-458.96	-2.02%
6150 · Repairs & Maintenance	142.89	110.17	32.72	29.7%
6160 · Service Charges	114.91	109.48	5.43	4.96%
6185 · State Annual Report Fee	0.00	50.00	-50.00	-100.0%
6190 · Telephone	5,698.41	7,435.89	-1,737.48	-23.37%
6200 · Tools	0.00	175.00	-175.00	-100.0%
6210 · Travel/Lodging	5,195.12	14,243.76	-9,048.64	-63.53%
6220 · Utilities	2,375.89	2,506.36	-130.47	-5.21%
6230 · Uncategorized Expenses	210.09	0.00	210.09	100.0%

7.16   Profit and Loss: Year-to-Year Comparison (continued)

	Jan 1–Dec 31, 20xx	Jan 1–Dec 31, xx	$ Change	% Change
6240 • Vehicle Expenses				
6241 • Gas & Oil	5,555.82	4,235.08	1,320.74	31.19%
6242 • Repairs & Maintenance	4,484.29	2,800.84	1,683.45	60.11%
6243 • Registration & License	602.00	749.17	–147.17	–19.64%
Total 6240 • Vehicle Expenses	10,642.11	7,785.09	2,857.02	36.7%
Total 6000 • Overhead Costs	96,743.86	103,853.00	–7,109.14	–6.85%
Total Expense	96,743.86	103,853.00	–7,109.14	–6.85%
Net Ordinary Income	141,643.04	136,070.51	5,572.53	4.1%
Other Income/Expense				
Other Income				
6800 • Speaker Fees	0.00	2,618.50	–2,618.50	–100.0%
Total Other Income	0.00	2,618.50	–2,618.50	–100.0%
Net Other Income	0.00	2,618.50	–2,618.50	–100.0%
Net Income	141,643.04	138,689.01	2,954.03	2.13%

Epilogue

This book and CD will enable you to design systems, formulate job descriptions, and create checklists and forms to gird your company where it needs more strength, expertise, discipline, and guidance.

Even though they will include the basic organizational components as described in this book, your systems will be one of a kind—designed to fit your needs and those of your company. Getting to systems thinking is a quantum leap from being excellent in a trade or even from being a competent manager. How can you tell if your system is helping you operate your business at peak performance? Your business system is performing well for your company if it

- standardizes procedures and tasks, minimizing errors and omissions
- collects and disseminates timely information
- eliminates duplication and unnecessary steps
- minimizes dependence on individuals so the company runs smoothly even when a key employee is unavailable
- is clear, practical, and easy to use
- generates historical records
- enables the company to achieve profit and performance goals
- allows the company owner to use his or her time most productively
- ensures that the owner knows where his or her company stands at all times
- provides information for smart decision making
- enables the owner to reach personal income and lifestyle goals

As your company grows and gains experience, proactively update your systems and forms. Make changes that will keep your company efficient, informed, and on track. You will know you have "arrived" when you are fulfilling your stated goals. You may be able to set more ambitious goals, including philanthropic goals, and share your success with others. If your goals are not yet attained after due time, then rework your plan. Under his name on his business card, renowned remodeler Finley Perry of F. H. Perry Builder, Hopkinton, Mass., displays the words "Vision Accomplished." With his systematized, well-run company in good hands, Perry joins the rare ranks of those who can be proud that their vision has become reality.

Resources

Web Sites

Download safety checklists from Texas A&M University from Engineering SafetyNet at http://tees.tamu.edu/index.jsp?page=trc_checklists.

A lead paint disclosure letter and other public documents are available on the U.S. Environmental Protection Agency's Web site at http://www.epa.gov/lead/.

Business planning documents are available from the U.S. Small Business Administration at www.sba.gov and SCORE www.score.org.

Tax forms and publications for businesses and individuals are available from the Internal Revenue Service at www.irs.gov.

Construction safety bulletins and other safety materials are available from the Occupational Safety and Health Administration at www.osha.gov.

Information on home energy and home improvement lending is available from the U.S. Department of Housing and Urban Development at www.hud.gov.

Books

Abrashoff, Michael. *It's Your Ship: Management Techniques from the Best Damn Ship in the Navy* New York: Warner Books, 2002.

Walker, Frank R. *Walker's Building Estimator's Reference Book*, Lisle, Illinois: Frank R. Walker Company, 2006.

The following resources are available from BuilderBooks.com.

Business Management

Managing Your Employees by NAHB Business Management Department. Washington: BuilderBooks, 2003.

Construction Management

Residential Construction Performance Guidelines, Third Edition, compiled by NAHB Business Management and Information Technology Committee and the NAHB Remodelers. Washington: BuilderBooks.com, 2005.

Home Builders' Jobsite Codes: A Pocket Guide to the 2006 International Residential Code, compiled by NAHB and the International Codes Council. Washington: BuilderBooks.com: 2007.

Storm Water Permitting: A Guide for Builders and Developers, compiled by NAHB Regulatory Policy Department. Washington: BuilderBooks.com, 2006.

Shepard, Kent. *Jobsite Phrasebook, English–Spanish.* Washington: Builder Books.com, 2002.

Customer Service

Jaffe, David S., David Crump and Felicia Watson. *Warranties for Builders and Remodelers, Second Edition.* Washington: BuilderBooks.com, 2007.

Nicholle-Nelson, Tara. *Trillion Dollar Women: Use Your Power to Make Buying and Remodeling Decisions.* Washington: BuilderBooks.com, 2008.

Estimating

Asdal, William. *Defensive Estimating: Protecting Your Profits.* Washington: BuilderBooks.com, 2006.

Christofferson, Jay P. *Estimating With Microsoft Excel®, Second Edition.* Washington: BuilderBooks.com, 2003.

Financial Management

Shinn, Emma. *Accounting and Financial Management for Residential Construction, Fifth Edition.* Washington: BuilderBooks.com, 2008.

Green Building

Belcher, Matt. *Build Green and Save: Protecting the Earth and Your Bottom Line.* Washington: BuilderBooks.com, 2009.

The National Green Building Standard, compiled by the International Code Council and NAHB. Washington: BuilderBooks.com, 2009.

Safety

Home Builders' Safety Program, compiled by NAHB Labor, Safety, and Health Services. Washington: BuilderBooks.com, 2007.

NAHB-OSHA Fall Protection Handbook by NAHB Labor, Safety, and Health Services. Washington: BuilderBooks.com, 2007.

NAHB-OSHA Jobsite Safety Handbook: English-Spanish Edition, compiled by NAHB/OSHA. Washington: BuilderBooks.com, 2006.

NAHB-OSHA Trenching and Excavation Safety Handbook by NAHB Labor, Safety, and Health Services. Washington: BuilderBooks.com, 2009.

Scaffold Safety Handbook by NAHB Labor, Safety, and Health Services. Washington: BuilderBooks.com, 2004.

Toolbox Safety Talks, English-Spanish, by NAHB Labor, Safety, and Health Services. Washington: BuilderBooks.com, 2002.

Sales and Marketing

Gullo, Gina and Angela Rinaldi. *Option Selling for Profit: The Builder's Guide to Generating Design Center Revenue and Profit.* Washington: BuilderBooks.com, 2008.

Software

Christofferson, Jay P. EstimatorPRO™ 5.1. Washington: BuilderBooks.com, 2005.

Index of Forms by Subject

Selected Forms by Type

Legal Documents